Reassembling Democracy

Also Available from Bloomsbury

Secular Bodies, Affects and Emotions, edited by Monique Scheer, Nadia Fadil, and Birgitte Schepelern Johansen

French Populism and Discourses on Secularism, Per-Erik Nilsson

Edward Burnett Tylor, Religion and Culture, edited by Paul Francois-Tremlett, Liam T. Sutherland and Graham Harvey

Reassembling Democracy

Ritual as Cultural Resource

Edited by Graham Harvey, Michael Houseman,
Sarah M. Pike and Jone Salomonsen

BLOOMSBURY ACADEMIC
LONDON • NEW YORK • OXFORD • NEW DELHI • SYDNEY

BLOOMSBURY ACADEMIC
Bloomsbury Publishing Plc
50 Bedford Square, London, WC1B 3DP, UK
1385 Broadway, New York, NY 10018, USA

BLOOMSBURY, BLOOMSBURY ACADEMIC and the Diana logo
are trademarks of Bloomsbury Publishing Plc

First published in Great Britain 2021

For legal purposes the Acknowledgements on pp. ix–x constitute
an extension of this copyright page.

A catalogue record for this book is available from the British Library.

A catalog record for this book is available from the Library of Congress.

ISBN: HB: 978-1-3501-2301-4
ePDF: 978-1-3501-2302-1
eBook: 978-1-3501-2303-8

Typeset by Integra Software Services Pvt. Ltd.

To find out more about our authors and books visit www.bloomsbury.com
and sign up for our newsletters

Contents

List of Figures

Contributors

Agnes Czajka, Senior Lecturer in Politics, The Open University, UK
Gregory Delaplace, Associate Professor, Anthropology Department, Paris Nanterre University, France
Ken Derry, Associate Professor, History of Religions, University of Toronto Mississauga, Canada
Anna Fedele, Senior Researcher (Investigadora FCT), Instituto Universitário de Lisboa (ISCTE-IUL), Centro em Rede de Investigação em Antropologia (CRIA), Lisboa, Portugal
Ronald L. Grimes, Professor Emeritus, Department of Religion and Culture, Wilfrid Laurier University, Canada/Adjunct Faculty, Mythological Studies, Pacifica Graduate Institute, USA
Graham Harvey, Professor of Religious Studies, The Open University, UK
Ida Marie Høeg, Professor of Sociology of Religion, Department of Religion, Philosophy and History, University of Agder, Norway
Michael Houseman, Professor, Religious Studies Section, Ecole Pratique des Hautes Etudes, PSL University, Paris, France
Jens Kreinath, Associate Professor of Cultural Anthropology, Wichita State University, Kansas, USA
Marika Moisseeff, Senior Researcher, Laboratoire d'anthropologie sociale, National Centre for Scientific Research, PSL University, France
Sarah M. Pike, Professor of Comparative Religion and Humanities, California State University, Chico, USA
Jone Salomonsen, Professor of Theology, Faculty of Theology, University of Oslo, Norway

Permissions

Chapter 1, 'Improvising Ritual', has been reproduced by permission. Originally published in Ronald L. Grimes, *Endings in Ritual Studies* (Waterloo, Canada: Ritual Studies International, 2020).

Acknowledgements

This book is one outcome of the 'Reassembling Democracy: Ritual as Cultural Resource' project funded by the Norwegian Research Council (NFR 2013–2017, project number 220715) through the SAMKUL programme 'Cultural Conditions Underlying Social Change'. We are immensely grateful for NFR support.

The core research team members of the project – who participated from beginning to end – were Cora Alexa Døving, Gitte Buch-Hansen, Donna Seamone, Graham Harvey, Grzegorz Brzozowski, Ida Marie Høeg, Jens Kreinath, Jone Salomonsen, Kjetil Hafstad, Marion Grau, Michael Houseman, Morny Joy, Paul-François Tremlett, Samuel Etikpah, Sarah Pike and Tony Balcomb. In addition we are grateful for the invaluable contributions to the project by Sidsel Roaldkvam, Lotte Danielsen, Mari Lilleslåtten and Birte Nordahl, and to Anne Kjersti Bjørn, Audun Bratlie, Audun Engh, Birgitte P. Haanshuus, Frederica Miller, Kristin von Hirsch, the student assistants from the Faculty of Theology and the Faculty of Social Sciences, University of Oslo, and to Sigurd Ohrem and the 2015–2016 students at Skiringssal Folk Highschool.

We are also grateful for the participation of invited speakers and respondents at REDO research workshops and related events: Aage Borchgrevink, Adrian Ivakhiv, Agnes Czajka, Andrew S. Mathews, Anna Fedele, Anne-Christine Taylor, Åsne Seierstad, Atle Sommerfeldt, Aud Valborg Tønnessen, Benedikte Lindskog, Bernt Hagtvedt, Bron Taylor, Bruno Latour, Candace Slater, Carl Petter Opsahl, Catherine Keller, Chantal Mouffe, Dale Wallace, David Soares, Devin Zuber, Einar Braathen, Elisabeth Thorsen, Elisabeth Tveito Johnsen, Emma Gobin, Emmanuel Thibault, Eskil Pedersen, Gerald West, Greg Delaplace, Guri Hjeltnes, Henrik Syse, Inga Bostad, Ingeborg Hjorth, Ingrid Vik, Ingvild Folkvord, Inus Daneel, James E. Young, Jan Kjetil Simonsen, Janet Trisk, Jon Reitan, Jonathan Sheehan, Jonas Gahr Støre, Jørgen Frydnes, Karen Lykke Syse, Ken Derry, Kirsi Stjerna, Kjetil Fosshagen, Kjetil Wiedsvang, Knut Christian Myhre, Kyrre Kverndokk, Lars Laird Iversen, Lilian Siwila, Linda Noor, Line Gjermhusengen, Liv Tørres, Marianne Lien, Marie Gillespie, Marie Mazzella di Bosco, Marika Moisseeff, Marlene Ringgaard Lorensen, Martin G. Reynolds, Michael Noah Weiss, Nefise Ozkal Lorentzen, Nina Hoel, Peter Skov

Jakobsen, Raviro Mutonga, Rita Sherma, Robyn Henderson-Espinoza, Roger Griffin, Ronald L. Grimes, Rune Flikke, Samuel Robinson, Siobhán Garrigan, Sirin Eide, Sivert Angel, Stine Holte, Sturla Stålsett, Terje Emberland, Thorgeir Kolshus, Tonje Brenna, Tor Einar Fagerland, Trond Bakkevig, Yohana Junker and Zaki Nahaboo.

Introduction

Graham Harvey, Michael Houseman, Sarah M. Pike
and Jone Salomonsen

Diverse processes of democratic participation – and exclusion – are braided with or propelled onwards by ritual acts and complexes. This volume is the result of collaborations and conversations between international researchers who have focused on the employment and deployment of those cultural resources identifiable as 'ritual' as particular communities reassemble democracy. The juxtaposition of the key terms 'ritual' and 'democracy' enriches understanding of processes, performances and even polemics to which they might be attached.

The volume critically addresses democracy as concept, practice, model or vision in a time of climate crisis, nationalism, religious re-traditionalizing, fake news and aspirational fascism. It discusses ways in which ritual and ritualized practices give rise to modes of feeling, processes of representation and patterns of interaction in which democratic explorations, collective resistance and/or involvement with the larger-than-human world are engaged, energized or problematized. The big question integrating the volume concerns the ways in which the performative qualities of ritual resources achieve their potential as forms of political and personal (not necessarily individual) empowerment in our changing and challenging world. Chapters engage with these issues in relation to a diversity of case studies – for example, memorial gatherings, festivals, pilgrimages, worship services, dances, shamanic and interreligious ceremonies. They are the result of a four-year collaboration between international researchers who regularly gathered to discuss and debate emerging perspectives, analyses and conclusions. Before we introduce the chapters which form the three parts of this book, we outline the nature and processes of our shared project.

The REDO project

This book arises from a four-year (2013–2017) project funded by the Norwegian Research Council. Entitled *Reassembling Democracy: Ritual as Cultural Resource* (abbreviated as REDO), the project enabled a team of eighteen international scholars to pursue original research and to meet regularly for sustained face-to-face discussion of emerging themes and issues. In addition, other experts in the study of both ritual and democracy were invited to workshops which enhanced and (re-)shaped the team's thinking, approaches and emerging conclusions. Participants included anthropologists, philosophers, political scientists and scholars of religion and ritual.

The REDO project, prompted by the 2011 far-right terrorist killings in Norway, was based on the recognition that people and communities are currently faced with complex crises and changes in culture, environment, religion, language, media, economy and technology. It set out to test the thesis that in dealing with these transformations, people and communities mobilize cultural resources that may be drawn from varied and competing knowledge and experience bases. Interactions between persons, communities and environments, while potentially enriching democratic processes, may also bring about challenges to existing political and social structures. In cases of innovation and contestation, ritual practices habituated by previous cultural repertoires seem to be utilized – deliberately or casually, by explicit design or by responsive borrowing. In turn, these practices are disseminated and adapted in other contexts, shaping participants and communities as they too are shaped by varying circumstances, conditions and contexts. Cultural resources become visible in ritual acts, which in turn become new cultural resources, assembling and reassembling people and communities at once as actors and as acted-upon. The researchers involved in this project sought to understand this process and to better grasp the ways ritual gestures and modes of organization and expression can mediate how social assemblages develop and evolve. Drawing on descriptive material pertaining to a variety of social situations, they explored different models and theories in order to explain ritual resourcefulness and creativity.

Specifically, the research team sought to test the idea that ritual is not merely a mobilizer – constructed by particular groups and itself a precondition for the construction of social assemblages – but may usefully label processes and relations that themselves contribute to change. They identified communities and events which seemed likely to evidence creative responses to crises triggered by the dynamics of contemporary global transformation and in which culturally and religiously informed ritualized actions play interesting roles. They did not neglect ritualized practices that resist change or contest processes in which democratic participation and processes might widen and/or deepen. Indeed, much of the project's research engaged precisely with entanglements of expansion and resistance. Case studies included responses to the July 22 terrorist atrocities in Norway, drama in the Occupy movements in London and Hong Kong, communal tree planting in Zimbabwe, an interreligious choir in Turkey, radical environmentalists' protest rituals in the United States, collective New Age dancing of self-discovery, annual water festivals in Ghana, popular participation in a Catholic-founded festival in Poland and performance at cultural festivals like the Sámi organized Riddu Riđđu in Artic Norway.

During the course of the REDO project the researchers engaged with participants in these various activities, seeking to understand how – under what conditions and facing what barriers – they gave rise to new conditions for engagement and action, acquired and demonstrated novel competencies, and renegotiated social identities, thereby transforming diverse democratic processes. Project members studied selected rituals as performances that arise out of and inspire social and environmental activism and grassroots political change, helping to shape the future, create community and reassemble more democratic modes of participation in changing global contexts. They were particularly interested in new forms of participatory democracy, where respect for individual differences and the need for community are negotiated in new ways.

As a result, this book presents analyses of selected events and processes in which people address – successfully or unsuccessfully – their concerns about political breakdown, economic and social crises, environmental loss, change within and confrontations between cultural communities. It examines, for example, public memorials, acts of political protest and resistance, the performance of Indigenous identities, 'spiritual' experimentation and interreligious encounter. Chapter outlines (below) will provide further pointers to specific contexts, debates and issues.

Key terms

'Ritual', 'democracy', 'assembling' and 'resource' are the key terms of the REDO project. The central insight and provocative proposal of this book is that these terms are greatly enriched by their critical juxtaposition. Indeed, treating ritual without treating democracy or processes of assemblage and resourcing impoverishes understanding. Similarly, treating democracy in the absence of reflection on rituals and the resources they provide for processes and modes of assembling significantly curtails debate. Bringing these key terms together in diverse ways, as the chapters that follow demonstrate, opens up new avenues of inquiry and new perspectives on social relations.

Ritual is too easily associated with religion and thus demarcated from putatively secular, quotidian or worldly matters. But this has much to do with processes by which religion came to be defined in Europe as something separate from political and other public social pursuits. The recent and ongoing scholarly turn towards 'lived religion' and/or 'everyday religion' – regardless of the success or otherwise of assertions of a 'post-secularity' – contests this ghettoization of religion. Instead of being defined by privatized notions of transcendence (as it may be when thought of as 'belief in god(s)') and therefore, it is implied or asserted, irrelevant to politics, religion can inform, structure and mobilize all aspects of people's lives. At the same time, similar processes in the religious and secular history of Europe have insisted that religion is definitively hierarchical and its rituals supportive of undemocratic power structures and practices. While no one is likely to explicitly deny that political processes are highly ritualized – as exemplified in the opening ceremonies of legislatures, the costuming of public officials and the protocols marking meetings between heads of state – these are less often associated with ritual than otherwise similar religious events.

This book is not specifically focused on the narrowly political rituals of democracy. What is offered here is an examination of the roles of ritual as a resource when people – individually or gathered – seek to enhance participation in public processes. 'Assembling' and related terms (clearly and explicitly inspired by Bruno Latour's usage) direct attention towards processes and relations – especially, for this project, those between ritual and democracy – rather than to the kind of already fixed forms that 'society' implies. It is equally important that all our key terms are understood as dynamic, polyvalent, relational and contestable. Thus, for example, the rituals which people deploy as resources might be deemed more 'cultural' than 'religious' – even when we refuse to set 'religion' aside as a purely private concern. People might assert their presence and participation by wearing particular costumes or by carrying particularly freighted objects (e.g. flowers or flags). By sharing one another's musical traditions, mourning displays and therapeutic practices and other ritually informed acts, they might reject separations between groups – including those based on identity politics ('identities' often stressing in-group likenesses against their alterities).

Contributors to the volume are well aware that rituals may be deployed to limit, constrain or even oppose increased access to and participation in democracy. Indeed, much of the discussion that follows arises precisely from contests with those who oppose such opening up. A defining example of this is the 22 July 2011 assault on the Norwegian Labour Party youths associated (most strongly by their assailant) with multiculturalism – a form of expansive reassembling of the Norwegian polity. There is, then, no assumption that ritual *must* or *usually does* lead to increased harmony or other unalloyed 'goods'. Just as religions, in lived reality, evidence tensions between socially cohesive and socially divisive trends, and may function to disrupt or repair communal well-being, so rituals can be drawn on to support a wide range of ambitions. While rituals may effect social change – or energize efforts to enhance democracy – they may also reinforce existing norms, hierarchies and orders. Such frictions contribute to the debates that have enlivened our REDO project and shaped the discussions that have resulted in the chapters that follow.

Introducing Part One: Ritual and democracy

Part One of the book establishes provocative foundations for rethinking and reflecting on the key terms with which this book engages. It is made up of two chapters, by Ronald Grimes on 'ritual' and by Agnes Czajka on 'democracy'. Emphasizing the essential role of indeterminacy, they depart from prevailing approaches to frame these key concepts in exceptionally dynamic and somewhat counterintuitive ways that point to largely uncharted connexions between them.

Ronald Grimes goes against conventional wisdom by stressing the importance of improvisation not only in ceremonial practices that explicitly require inventive participation but even in the most well-established liturgical traditions. Drawing on academic works, detailed testimonies provided by ritual performers and ritual studies scholars, his own extensive video-based research on ritual creativity and the workings of improvisational skills in the performing arts, he provides overwhelming evidence to the effect that improvisation is not only an inevitable feature of ceremonial undertakings but also in many respects the mainspring of ritual effectiveness. On the one hand, improvisation, as 'making do with what you have', articulates creative initiative and recognizable structure in ways that allow participants to take into account the changing circumstances of their performance, thereby upholding the latter's ongoing relevance and persistence through time. At the same time, as 'composing while performing', it encourages interactive patterns in which mutual support, reciprocal attunement, critical self-awareness and sensitivity to context are given pride of place. Undermining in this way the established bipolar split between scripted and spontaneous performance, Grimes's argument is not only a welcomed contribution to ritual theory but also opens new perspectives on the role of ritual as a resource for democracy. Thus, towards the end of his chapter, Grimes raises the question 'What would a "democratic ritual" look like?', which he immediately rephrases as 'What ritual dynamic might facilitate assemblages that foster justice and the thriving of a multitude of species on the planet?' For 'the beginning of a provisional answer', he suggests looking to ceremonial performances having a sustained improvisational phase that facilitates self-critical reflexivity and stimulates attuned co-acting among human (and other-than-human) participants.

Agnes Czajka, in an equally unusual move, turns to Derrida's conception of democracy as a self-undermining and therefore inherently equivocal political process in order to explore what 'being democratic' in times of crisis may mean. Because the very principle of democracy is to recognize and accept even those opposed to its fundamental values, it is 'already always' in crisis. In this respect, Derrida argues, democracy is analogous to European identity whose definition, grounded in the ongoing incorporation of differences, is perpetually deferred, or to hospitality, plagued by unresolvable frictions between an ideal of absolute openness and the imbalance of power between host and guest that conditional welcome implies. A democratic community must define its membership and territory, but at the same time deal with members acting as inimical others. As such, it is perpetually at risk of setting off a self-destructive, 'autoimmune' response, as when the 1992 Algerian elections were suspended to avoid ushering in a government intent on destroying democracy. At the same time, however, democracy's inherent instability can also provide opportunities for negotiated choices that further democratic principles. Czajka argues that Derrida's approach, in allowing us to avoid unrealistic quests for a definite 'solution' to the conundrum of democratic practice, encourages us to take the measure of what being democratic might actually entail. In this spirit, as a conceptual guideline, notably with regard to present-day Europe, she proposes the notion of 'hospitable democracy' based on an openness to the other-than-democratic only to the point of not destroying itself. In keeping with its internal inconsistency (its 'aporetic' nature in Derrida's terms), hospitable democracy does not entail applying a general rule of 'law', but rather continually suspends possible resolutions to the problematic interplay between conditional and unconditional hospitality by favouring singular, negotiated, provisional 'acts of justice'. In short, hospitable democracy seeks to overcome its own crisis-producing limitations one concrete content-dependent case at a time. Czajka ends her chapter by suggesting that ritual may prove to be a fruitful resource for advancing this type of hospitable democracy. Indeed, ritual performances, by providing not definitive answers but new ways of asking the same questions of particular situations, seem especially well suited for upholding a political process whose self-contradictory general principles are destined to be left dangling.

Introducing Part Two: Reassembling communities

Part Two provides a series of case studies in which ritual and/or ritualized practices give rise to exceptional communities enlivened by democratic values and ideas, and typically composed of both human and other-than-human beings. Participants often assert that their highly memorable experiences of these democratically oriented assemblages – shamanic ceremonies, Indigenous festivals, spiritual dance meetups, walking pilgrimages, interreligious choirs – productively inform their everyday lives.

Local understandings of 'democracy' can have unexpected entailments. As Gregory Delaplace shows, in present-day Mongolia, democracy and the values of collective and personal freedom it conveys are closely linked to the possibility of reclaiming a connection with an illustrious past the communist regime is supposed to have suppressed. Access to this redemptive, collective heritage, animated by ancestral and other spirits, and epitomized by the figure of Chinggis Khan (Genghis Khan) and the harmonious Mongolian homeland he is said to have created, is achieved largely through shamanic practices that are flourishing anew. Delaplace, drawing on his field research from 2008 to 2019, documents this development by presenting two quite different, complementary ways in which shamanic rituals make it possible for individuals and collectivities to acquire an immediate experience of what they take to be their own history. In what Delaplace, in the light of cross-cultural comparisons, calls 'vertical' or 'liturgical' shamanism, officially acknowledged celebrants engage in what are presumed to be 'traditional' performances for the good of assembled polities. In what he calls 'horizontal' or 'inspired' shamanism, exceptional individuals incarnate powerful entities from bygone eras (ancestors, tutelary spirits, etc.) in order to protect their individual clients from harmful spiritual influences. In both cases, the past is brought to life through ritual performance. However, in the first case, this takes place through ceremonial iterations that consecrate the immemorial identities of local communities in whose name these ceremonies are undertaken, whereas in the second, it is accomplished through acts of extraordinary embodiment aiming to safeguard particular persons from unwanted interactions with ill-intentioned other-than-human beings. Although these two modes of shamanism, governed by radically divergent logics, are mutually exclusive, individual practitioners readily switch back and forth from one to the other in order to explore, in an eminently pragmatic fashion, the various avenues whereby ritually mediated performances of democracy can contribute to the refashioning of personal and public identities.

Graham Harvey's research at two cultural festivals which showcase Indigenous arts and performances results in a chapter which further examines notions of personhood and relations. Within the context of the annual Sámi organized Riddu Riđđu festival (in western Sápmi/Arctic Norway) and the London-based biennial ORIGINS Festival of First Nations, Indigenous actors, musicians, artists, film-makers, chefs, storytellers and other performers draw on the resources of customary ceremonies and protocols to present work to audiences. Inspired by critical studies of Indigenous literatures, Harvey considers movements between and among international Indigenous performers and their ideas, inspirations, expectations and aspirations. Specific moments in performances and conversations during the festivals are brought into dialogue with notions of personhood that could be summed up as 'dividualism' and 'new animism'. In the former, persons are not points or positions in a structure but inherently and necessarily relations. Beings become persons precisely by engaging and interacting with others. Rather than considering identities, dividual or relational personhood points to the definitive value of performance and interaction. The 'new animism' emphasizes that humans are in no way separate from other persons. They do not exist in a distinct environment but are made up of relations involving both human and other-than-human persons, all with needs and fears, some of which conflict with those of others. Indigenous performances draw on customary rites and knowledges which convey a pervasive (and definitively Indigenous) assumption of a larger-than-human community. Reassembling thoughts and practices related to 'democracy', in this perspective, necessitates consideration of relations with mountains, rivers, salmon, ancestors, masks and many others. Harvey argues that entertainment and education fuse within these festivals as Indigenous performers seek to inspire 'world-making' that is more inclusive and thus more democratic in a more-than-human world.

Michael Houseman explores the performative grounds of the special sociability that emerges in the course of weekly sessions of collective dancing explicitly aimed to promote 'authenticity', 'creativity' and 'connection with others': 5 Rhythms, Movement Medicine, Open Floor, Biodanza, Chakradance and the like. Taking Biodanza as his main example, he shows how these practices provide participants with memorable experiences of deliberate self-actualization in which they 'discover' their ability to become, however briefly, the spontaneous, open, sensitive persons they feel they are meant to be. They do so by drawing on facilitators' allusive directives, the bodily sensations and emotional expressions occasioned by moving to music, intense dance interactions with others and affecting words spoken during sharing/talking circles. These practices, however, are not oriented solely towards the ongoing production of participants' personal 'selves'. Thus, the latter are also induced to experience themselves members of a collectivity made up of such potentially self-determining individuals, in which continually negotiated, intimate interpersonal entanglements give way to looser, less problematic assemblages founded on relations of distanced intimacy. Indeed, the aim of these practices is not to encourage dancers to cultivate close relationships among themselves but to allow them to develop and demonstrate, through each other's intermediary, their aptitude for entering into close relationships with others at a further remove. The particular flavour of we-ness these dances put into effect – collective individualism or the state of being autonomous together – enacts a happy reconciliation between personal self-fulfillment ('an encounter with oneself … ') and collective interdependency (' … through others'). As such, it resonates both with certain 'democratic' values and with influential accounts of contemporary Western personhood and society. However, as a ritual performance, this exceptional sociality is to be understood not as a realistic model for everyday behaviour but as a compelling yet largely unfathomable conventional yardstick whereby participants can re-evaluate themselves, their everyday relationships and their place in the world.

Catholic Portuguese pilgrims express and confirm democratic forms when they walk together on sacred journeys. As Anna Fedele shows in her chapter, they do this through their bodies, moving together on the way to the shrine, embodying democratic social forms that suggest changes at the national level. Fedele's many years of fieldwork among Catholic Portuguese pilgrims walking to the Marian shrine of Fátima in Portugal involved collecting their life stories as well as walking and talking with them. During collective walking pilgrimages from their hometowns to the shrine of Fátima, participants experience patterns of support and solidarity that stand in stark contrast to the frictions and inequities characteristic of their everyday lives in a context of ongoing social and economic crises in Portugal. Moreover, these pilgrimages are enjoying increasing participation, while church attendance in Portugal is declining, making the pilgrimages important sites for understanding contemporary religiosity in southern Europe. Analysing the logistics Fátima pilgrimages entail (support cars, communal lodging, various organizations, media coverage, etc.), and drawing on the symbolism they bring into play, Fedele suggests that these sacred journeys be understood as 'strategies to reaffirm [the] grassroot forms of solidarity and democracy' so lacking in pilgrims' everyday lives. By foregrounding one woman's story, Fedele explores the various meanings of the *cajado*, a walking stick that many pilgrims use and that itself symbolizes the pilgrimage to Fátima. The *cajado* brings together past and present, family and national histories. Because it embodies a family lineage, carrying the *cajado* is one of the ways in which pilgrims never walk alone. Whether or not they travel in groups, they are intricately connected to relational networks. It has long been argued that pilgrims experience exceptional forms of solidarity during collective pilgrimages. The additional, innovative argument advanced here is that they relate these experiences to the possibility of a reconfigured national identity and a renewed mundane sociality, that is, to a 'different, thriving and "happy" Portugal'.

Drawing on ethnographic research about the Choir of Civilizations in Antakya (Antioch), Turkey, Jens Kreinath's chapter discusses the intricate relationship between ritual and democracy in the context of interreligious relations. The Choir was designed to represent the diversity of religious groups in the region (Hatay) – including the majority of Turkish Sunnis and Arab Alawites as well as smaller populations of Jews, Orthodox Christians, Armenian Christians and Catholics – in the form of a musical kaleidoscope of religious coexistence. The Choir began in the old town of Antakya with its already rich sonic environment or soundscape emerging from a complexity of religious buildings (especially the mosques and churches). The first members were familiar with each other and with the song and acoustic traditions of each other's religious and/or local and national folk cultures. As the stated ambition of the Choir was to represent the peaceful coexistence of people with different religious affiliations and commitments – some of which are entangled with conflict in some places – it would appear to be the perfect location to find that rituals provide excellent resources for the increase of democracy. In practice, the Choir's performances – for audiences of tourists, businesses, governmental and non-governmental organizations, and by any other group who invite them – set songs from the different traditions alongside each other. Rituals and/or liturgical elements are clearly drawn on as resources for these performances, but they are employed with the same intention and affect as the songs and music drawn from popular folk traditions. That is, the Choir presents existing diversity but does not pursue or achieve an ambition to enhance democracy or to change society. Indeed, perhaps it can be manipulated to portray an ideal of peaceful coexistence that masks interreligious tensions. In Kreinath's chapter, then, we have a powerful test of the thesis that rituals could provide democratizing resources and a clear counter to any naïve anticipation that they must always do so.

Introducing Part Three: Commemoration and resistance

The four chapters in Part Three are also about the reassembling of communities and the exploration of ritualizing as a contribution to democratization. They focus, however, on acts of commemoration and resistance. They are concerned with disruptive events and processes that put collective values to the test and highlight how different communities contest various ways in which democracy is diminished and assaulted.

When Anders Behring Breivik attacked Norwegian democracy by terrorizing Oslo and a social democratic youth camp at Utøya, the police closed off the streets and ordered people home. People obeyed and bewilderment and fear were a first response. The second response was protest. It started quietly as a condolence ritual in the square around Oslo Cathedral and quickly turned into a massive mobilization. For a limited time, it marked togetherness, solidarity and a different kind of 'love of country' than Breivik's nationalist feelings and extremist gestures. In subsequent years, memorials for the victims of Breivik's violence that have tried to capture this powerful non-violent gesture have been designed. In her chapter, Jone Salomonsen analyses Breivik's mission and the protest it aroused from 'the weak'. Ritual in the streets of Oslo and in two memorial events is analysed with a view to what they convey about ordinary people's ritual competence and sense of democracy. The political and democratic theories of Hannah Arendt and Chantal Mouffe are used to interpret the findings, and ritual is revealed to be both gate and fence between community and democracy. The chapter asks if the elusive forms of rituality that evolved post-2011 in Norway are integral to building a stronger democracy, or if ritual is, rather, a pre-political tool to secure the *precondition* of liberal democracy: that is an egalitarian community or polity which accepts others' humanity and rights.

The following chapter, by Ida Høeg, is also concerned with public reactions to Breivik's killing spree on 22 July 2011. It focuses on the central role played by flowers in the funeral/memorial services for three Muslim adolescents assassinated at the Labour Party youth camp on the island of Utøya. During these events that were significantly more inclusive, creative, participatory and anti-authoritarian than funeral celebrations generally, flowers were overwhelmingly present: ordered in advance or brought by those attending, they were held in mourners' hands, exhibited on the altar or stage, deposited on or around the victims' photograph, coffin and/or grave. Drawing on Bruno Latour's actor-network approach, Høeg argues that flowers intervened in these celebrations less as expressive representations (of personal sadness, national solidarity, religious commitment, etc.) than as ritual participants in their own right. By providing a readily accessible and evocative resource for mourners' joint participation in the performance of partially improvised liturgies (processions, memorial practices, etc.), flowers acted as mediators whose attendance encouraged and shaped interactions between mourners of different ages, backgrounds and religious traditions. By 'calling for action' in this way, flowers took on other-than-human agency in the creation and structuring of the consensual solidarity these celebrations were presumed to enact. Agency, however, whether human or not, cuts both ways. The unnegotiable presence of flowers prompted a majority of participants to perform certain actions together, giving rise to exceptional, inter-confessional assemblies. However, it also incited some mourners, ill at ease with what they perceived as an inflated manifestation of Norway's mainstream Christian celebratory tradition, to refuse to do so. Here again, we see that ritual performances of democratic pluralism are not exempt from the spontaneous drawing of culturally grounded boundaries.

Unexpected large-scale tragedies and catastrophes, such as the 22 July terrorist attacks in Norway, pose challenges to the typical ways death is ritualized (or more accurately, de-ritualized) in contemporary Western Europe. In her chapter, Marika Moisseeff explores how collective commemorations of the tragic deaths described in Salomonsen's and Høeg's chapters are similar to funeral rites in some non-Western cultures: emotions are expressed, and loss is shared in ways that articulate multiple points of view, in contrast to the internalization and privatization of grief more characteristic of Western cultures. By comparing contemporary Western deathways with those of Australian Aborigines and the Kaluli of Papua New Guinea, Moisseeff demonstrates that the externalization of grief in these latter cases is the opposite process of the more typical internalization of grief and the absence of the corpse in the West. Moisseeff proposes a comparative framework for a cross-cultural perspective on mourning, with which we might think through what is happening in the case of contemporary Western collective tragedies. The framework she outlines is composed of three parts: the material presence of a corpse, the emotional reactions of those directly affected by the death(s) and collective representations of death and loss. In the contemporary West, these three aspects are typically dealt with separately and emotional expressions of grief are constrained. By contrast, in many of the cultures studied by anthropologists such as Moisseeff herself, the three parts are treated all together in collective funerary rituals where the corpse is present and individual emotions are expressed and shared in communal settings. Marches and memorial services in response to collective public tragedies, such as terrorist attacks, involve the shared expression of emotions and ritualized position-taking for values that participants believe have come under siege, such as democracy, inclusivity and free speech. The disruptions, challenges to democratic structures and emotional trauma caused by a mass tragedy must be publicly acknowledged through shared representations of loss, even when there are no institutionalized forms – as there are for the Aboriginals and the Kaluli – for responding to them.

Ken Derry's chapter explores very different forms of resistance and agency in the context of three films by Indigenous film-makers. For Derry, the films *Maliglutit* (2016, directed by Inuk film-maker Zacharias Kunuk), *Mahana* (2016, directed by Māori film-maker Lee Tamahori) and *Goldstone* (2016, directed by Kamilaroi film-maker Ivan Sen) all suggest ways in which Indigenous people appropriate the tools of colonialism and put them to their own uses, indigenizing them, especially by reinventing rituals that blend and borrow from both traditional Indigenous and colonial practices. Through these varied processes of indigenization, reinvented rituals can function as medicine for the ills brought about by the long-lasting trauma of colonialism. Most importantly, these braided practices and reinventions enable healing from historical and ongoing colonial violence, including conflicts and violence within Indigenous communities, especially sexual violence. Using traditional tools as well as the tools of their oppressors, these three film-makers from three different Indigenous cultures (Canadian Arctic Inuit, New Zealand Māori and Australian Aboriginal), engage with and portray ritual practices from their cultures within the contexts of specific places as well as shared histories of colonialism, working with rather than against the environment. Through particular kinds of filmic narratives, a reconfiguring of traditional storytelling, these Indigenous film-makers have taken control of the process of representing their cultures. Interestingly, they do so in ways that incorporate and re-frame Hollywood genres such as westerns and film noir with Indigenous strategies as tools of resistance and empowerment. Moreover, Derry reminds us that 'democracy' is not everyone's ideal: Indigenous communities have their own forms and structures, but they do want to be given equal access to participate in the governing bodies colonial processes have burdened them with and to heal the damage done to their communities on individual as well as social and political levels.

Conclusion

The chapters that follow do far more than merely present the conclusions of a completed project. Our ambition as collaborative and interdisciplinary researchers and authors is to provoke and enrich further debate about the key themes of ritual and democracy. This book is intended to excite further attention to the ways in which democracy can be (re-)assembled (sometimes in conflicting ways) through processes that might be recognized and theorized as ritual. To do so requires that the key terms of the debate are themselves allowed to reassemble more dynamically, creatively and argumentatively than in some previous discussions. In the dangerous times in which we live and work, questions about what ritual actions reveal and mobilize in the ever-shifting assemblages of social, ecological, cultural, political, religious, national, ethnic and other relations have become crucial.

Finally, as a community of scholars who have enjoyed participating together in a collaboration replete with ritual and democratic experimentation, we are unashamed to assert our hope that rituals might not only reveal and mobilize contemporary cultural values and resources but also contribute to enhance democracy and change the world for the better.

Part One

Ritual and democracy

1

Improvising ritual

Ronald L. Grimes

Some hear the phrase 'improvising ritual' as a category mistake, like a 'green feeling'. They insist that creativity and improvisation have their proper home in the arts, not in ritual, especially religious ritual, or liturgy. I know of no definition of ritual that mentions improvisation. From the point of view of conventional theories, ritual tradition is passed on by authorities in oral teachings or written scripts, and these are imitated or reproduced by participants. Rituals are prescribed; there is a right and a wrong way to enact them. Ritual authorities control rituals to ensure that participants do not deviate, or if they do, not far. If rituals vary, they do so only under tightly controlled circumstances. Theorists conventionally link ritual to hierarchy, bureaucracy, prescription, repetition, stereotyping and tradition, all of which seem to preclude improvisation. From this perspective you might even define ritual as actions from which every trace of improvisation has been flushed.[1] Understood this way, ritual participants make the least number of choices, since they are neither authors of the script nor directors of the enactment. Traditional ritual is the least deviant, most predictable kind of human interaction.

The Second Vatican Council opened in 1962 and ended in 1965. Under the leadership of Pope John XXIII, it aspired to 'open the windows [of the Catholic Church] and let in some fresh air' (Sullivan 2002: 17). Liturgical revisions were afoot. But a heavy counter-reaction was set in motion by Joseph Ratzinger, a German theologian, whom you may know as the retired Pope Benedict XVI. From 2005 to 2013 he railed against creativity, improvisation and experimentation in Roman Catholic liturgy. Ritual change should consist of slow micro-adjustments in continuity with the past. He was severely critical of the liturgical reforms of Vatican II, especially as they were implemented in the United States. American post-Vatican II rituals, he believed, tossed out the baby (the Roman Missal and European classical music) with the bathwater.

Ratzinger declared, 'Wherever applause breaks out in the liturgy because of some human achievement, it is a sure sign that the essence of liturgy has totally disappeared and been replaced by a kind of religious entertainment' (2000: 198). In his view, creative, invented or improvised human rituals are expressions of arrogance. The result is idolatry, the prime example of which was the worship of the golden calf by the ancient Israelites. For Ratzinger, Roman Catholic liturgy is not merely a human attempt to communicate with God. Rather the liturgy *is* the divine presence in the form of a rite. The liturgy *is* Christ in a form apprehensible by participants. The implication is that people shouldn't tinker with Christian liturgy in the name of creativity; otherwise, the result is a bricolage or entertainment, not a liturgy. Liturgists shouldn't improvise on the mass, and they should not criticize it without being duly authorized. No ritual creativity, no ritual criticism.

Like it or not, ritual improvisation happens, sometimes by accident, sometimes as an act of resistance or renewal. A few Christian rituals have boundaries that are not so jealously guarded. In the video *A Footwashing Ritual for Maundy Thursday* (Grimes 2012a), the liturgy happens on the Green in New Haven, Connecticut, where American Episcopalians celebrate the feast outdoors and wash the feet of the poor (Grimes 2012a: 5:48–8:48). The date is 5 April 2012. A few hundred yards away, on the same city Green, is an improvised encampment, a sister camp to the Occupy Wall Street Movement in New York. Some Occupiers have joined the street people and the poor. As the film opens, viewers see a sign, 'All I need is an address.' The drummers are local, probably not Episcopalians. The leader is chewing a fat cigar stub. At his cue, the musicians improvise their beats. Some of the drummers are amateurs; you can hear musical mistakes. Many of the people who come for food, liturgy or music are homeless, a lifestyle that requires them to improvise where they sleep and how to get food. Ethically and theologically, these New Haven Episcopalians aspire to perform service for the poor; however, their liturgical demeanour is awkwardly suited to the outdoors, where the poor find themselves. Some Episcopalians, uncomfortable in liturgical garb, put it on and take it off. They are forced to yell sacred utterances to overcome the loud sirens that regularly cut through the soundscape.

In a scene near the end (8:34), a woman is getting her feet washed while eating. Everyone else has one foot washed at a time. She is having both feet washed simultaneously. I asked why she looked so happy. 'Honey', she says, 'eating while having my feet washed is as near to heaven as I will get, so, you bet, I'm enjoying it'.

This outdoor liturgy is roomy enough for her to make up a bit of heaven without feeling awkward or judged. Even though the Maundy Thursday celebration is liturgical and in some ways set, this one has open phases and open places, creating room for improvisation and sonic dissonance. Song lines are often in competition with one another. If people tire of the homily and liturgy, they can walk the improvised labyrinth. Walking in and out of formal worship on the Green was part of the ritual ethos.

The point of this illustration is not that improvisation makes a ritual good or bad, only that improvisation can be integrated with liturgy. Since improvisation happens, it should be not be excluded by definition from the conception of ritual.

Ritual as invariant

You might expect a pope to hold a rigid notion of liturgy, but there are anthropologists who hold similar views. Roy Rappaport studied pig sacrifices in Papua New Guinea. He defines liturgy (his term) as 'the performance of more or less invariant sequences of formal acts and utterances not entirely encoded by the performers' (1999: 24). The example Rappaport uses in his writings is, however, from his own Jewish background. It is the *shema*: 'Hear, O Israel, the Lord is our God, the Lord is One.' Traditionally, the *shema* is recited twice daily, when awakening and before going to sleep.

The *shema* is not as invariant as Rappaport would have us believe. Over the course of history, the *shema* has gone from having one part to having three; the three-part variant is now embedded in Jewish liturgy. There are other variants: eyes closed or open, standing or sitting and so on. The *shema* is a revered and ancient Jewish prayer. Jesus appropriates part of it, relabelling it 'the greatest commandment'. In modified form the *shema* morphs by entering into Christian discourse. Like the Catholic mass, the *shema* has a history of being borrowed, edited and reshaped. The *shema*'s forms and contexts, as well as the intentions of those who perform it, vary. And just so you know, Justin Bieber, said to be a devout Canadian Christian, recites the *shema* before his concerts. His manager is Jewish.

Ritualized perfection

Jonathan Z. Smith, a religious studies scholar, considers ritual a perfected and protected zone. Citing two brief parables, he explains why ritual precludes improvisation (Smith 1980: 112–27). The first is a parable from Franz Kafka, 'Leopards break into the temple and drink the sacrificial chalices dry; this occurs repeatedly, again and again; finally it can be reckoned upon beforehand and becomes part of the ceremony.' The second parable is from Plutarch, 'At Athens, Lysimaeho, the priestess of Athene Polias, when asked for a drink by the male drivers who had transported the sacred vessels, replied, "No, for I fear it will get into the ritual."' In the first case an accident makes its way into the ritual, so, repeated across time, the action becomes a change in the ritual. In the second, the priestess fears that some ordinary, mundane action will worm its way into the ritual, so a ritual change does not happen. Both are fictive rituals in parables, not actual rituals.

For Smith ritual is a 'focusing lens,' in which humans and the divine are transparent to each other, where things are perfected, thus incongruent with ordinary, imperfect life outside the ritual. So accidents or mistakes have to be incorporated as miracles or ruled out as blasphemies. Smith concludes: 'Ritual represents the creation of a controlled environment where the variables (i.e., the accidents) of ordinary life have been displaced *precisely* because they are felt to be so overwhelmingly present and powerful.' Then his famous definition: 'Ritual is a means of performing the ways things ought to be in conscious tension to the way things are in such a way that this ritualized perfection is recollected in the ordinary, uncontrolled, course of things' (Smith 1980: 63). Smith is a historian of religions, so he knows that rituals change, but his definition of ritual as a perfected, controlled environment emphasizes ritual's resistance to change.

The model that Ratzinger, Rappaport and Smith espouse is what I call a North Star theory. When everything is shifting and moving, survival depends on being oriented to something unchanging, or as Rappaport would put it, 'more or less' unchanging.[2] In North Star models a ritual, like Aristotle's God, is an Unmoved Mover, an anchor, a standard by which participants measure and judge ordinary, non-ritualistic life; accidents and innovations are actively suppressed or ignored. The North Star is useful for navigation, but Polaris (its real name) is not static; it has its own little orbit.

Scholars formulate North Star theories because they are important to practitioners. The beliefs of many religious practitioners are North Star theories. Could thousands of years of belief and practice be wrong? I am suggesting so. The problem with North Star theories is that they are based on a false premise: that an invariant or perfected model can orient practitioners in a flowing, changing universe.

Research with any historical depth or ethnographic breadth shows that rituals do, in fact, change. Occasionally rapid, dramatic shifts in ritual sensibilities happen: the Lutheran Reformation in sixteenth-century Germany and the ritual revolutions among nineteenth-century trust networks in Fujian province of south-eastern China and currently in Singapore:

> Singapore continues to act as a central node in evolving networks linking temples across Southeast Asia and Taiwan. These temples are currently caught in a cycle of mutual escalation of contacts and exchanges. These turbulent whirlwinds of interaction (the flow of ritual specialists, ritual change, new understandings of local traditions in globalized networks) create a new sense of space for the people participating in them … The situation begins to take on the complexity of contemporary models in physics of multiple coexisting parallel universes. (Dean 2015a: 287–8; 2015b)

As surely as the hour hand on a clock moves, rituals undergo editing, evolve or revolutionize. There is no such thing as stasis, not for clock hands, not for rocks and not for liturgies (even 'divine' ones). The premise of my counterargument, then, is that there is no unchanging ground either inside ritual or outside it. There are orienting patterns in movement but no fixed points. All is flow, all is flux; there are only differing rates of change. The tectonic plates of the earth move by subduction; they shift and float. Not only is the universe variant and imperfect, so are the rituals by which people negotiate and orient to it. Most theories and theologies account for the ways rituals persist but not how they emerge, change or die. An adequate theory must account for ritual creativity, ritual criticism, ritual revolutions and the deaths of rituals.

Improvisation in traditional rituals

It is tempting to set ritual creativity and improvisation on the one side and tradition on the other. Alfonso Ortiz, a Pueblo and anthropologist from San Juan Pueblo (*Ohkay Owingeh* is its traditional name) in New Mexico, once remarked to me that no one person knows the entire Pueblo ritual system, because ritual knowledge is held collectively. Mythically and ritually, he said, ritual knowledge originates not from a holy person but from the sacred mountains (Ortiz 1977). From there it is funnelled towards the village centre, where it is held and danced collectively. Pueblo ritual is both ecological and social. Ritual knowledge, in this natural-to-social dynamic is traditional but not static; it is continually reinvented. The innovation, play and critique in this ritual process lie not in individual experimentation but with collective adaptation. The Pueblo rituals of *Ohkay Owingeh* contain another improvised dynamic: ritual clowns (Ortiz 1977). They fix costumes and create scenes to refocus people's attention. Disrupting the ceremonial flow, they improvise, lurking on roofs, surprising and mocking people, cracking jokes and offering criticism. Their activity simultaneously supports and resists sacred ceremonial actions.

Improvisation can be woven into traditional settings. The Mohawk Condolence Ceremony is traditional and usually celebrated among Mohawks or other Iroquois people. In the video *A Mohawk Condolence Ceremony for Myriam* (Grimes 2014b: 12:25–15:45), this ritual is being enacted among Jews, Muslims, Christians and secular participants. This is a condolence for the friends and family of Myriam, a Muslim woman who converted to marry a Jew, had a child and died young. The ceremony is as improvisational as it is traditional. Francis Boots, who is enacting this condolence, is both following a tradition and improvising. He is enacting the ritual across the gaps separating several religious traditions and at the same time educating a mostly non-native group. He is consoling Myriam's family. He is speaking traditional ritual words in Mohawk and explaining them in English. He is editing the ceremony as he goes. He breaks the frame of seriousness by injecting it with humour. Each time he enacts the ceremony, it varies in response to the situation. It gets shorter; it gets longer. It is in Mohawk; it is in English. It is sombre; it is funny. It is traditional but not unchanging. It is adaptive.

Three scholars on ritual improvisation

The idea of improvisation in ritual is an anomaly among ritual theorists. Since improvisation in ritual is rarely written about, I asked three scholars to tell me informally in an email what comes to mind if asked about improvisation in the traditions they study. Ute Hüsken, who studies Hinduism, wrote:

> In Hindu ritual worlds one meets improvisation all the time and everywhere. When people enact ritual scripts, and these scripts are never exhaustive, the performers have to fill in. Improvisation is more pronounced if the performers cannot fall back on a performative tradition that they imitate.
>
> Improvisation is necessary in ritual actions that are only rarely performed, such as taking a wooden statue of the deity out of the temple tank every 40 years. There is hardly any performer who has seen this ritual twice. How do people fill in? In the Brahmanic temple tradition which prides itself on being very orthodox, people usually use staple acts borrowed from other, bigger rituals. Another example would be a ritual that is performed because of extreme circumstances (e.g., the 1000-water-pot ablution after a brutal murder in the temple).

> Historically, the Bhakti movements were trends towards individualization and improvisation, when access to the deity became defined through personal (often emotional) engagement with the god rather than through priests as mediators. The ritual expressions of Bhakti vary widely. This improvisation happened through all kinds of media such as poetry, dance, and songs. Bhakti movements also democratized access to the divine. Low castes and women were included. In fact, some of the gurus were women or low castes.
>
> Improvisation also takes place in ritual traditions without fixed scripts, where creativity, innovation, and efficacy are valued. Navaratri (the festival of the nine nights of the goddess) is one such example. In Tamil Nadu women set up the Kolu arrangement of deities in a miniature world, often using these arrangements as social critique or to mirror tastes and fashions. One sees much improvisation when the ritual of Kolu is adapted by low caste women, who then creatively make their own Kolu rituals.
>
> Similar things happen in small goddess temples. Every evening the priests decorate the temples and goddesses with different themes. The prototype of this kind of creativity is the Durga Puja in Kolkata, in which artists design the makeshift temples. In these temples one would generally find a small 'original' Durga, who receives traditional worship, so here improvisation and tradition go hand in hand.
>
> How are we to know what priests did before ritual scripts were committed to writing, standardized, and published? Judging from the different ways rituals are performed in different locations today, I assume this variation has a long tradition.
>
> I would also say that improvisation is to some degree a standard response to contingencies and unexpected situations that happen during longer and more complex rituals. In these the improvisational skills of a priest are a key to his success.
>
> Even ritual texts allow for improvisation: Sacrifice a goat! If you don't have a goat, sacrifice a chicken! If no chicken is around, sacrifice a rice ball! (Hüsken 2016)

Bert Groen, a specialist in Christian liturgy, wrote:

> During the first centuries of Christian liturgy, in some texts such as *Didache* and *Traditio Apostolica* there are remarks that a presider should 'pray like this,' or 'with other words' or 'with similar words'. The *Didache* explicitly says that the presider prays 'according to his ability,' which leaves ample room for improvisation. In the *Rule of St. Benedict*, one of the most influential documents in medieval Western Christianity, the author explains how the Psaltery must be prayed during the Liturgy of the Hours, and then says 'If someone has a better system, he should apply that.'

> Gradually, because of sacralization tendencies, these prayers became fixed; the texts themselves became holy. This change happens in both the East and West. The same applies to the readings. Initially there was a lot of freedom in selecting lessons, an important criterion being that they 'fit' the occasion, but gradually fixed lectionaries developed. Both in the East and West, directories were being written to specify how, when, and where the liturgy should be performed.
>
> The sixteenth-century Reformation, especially the Radical Reformation, offers more room for improvisation, but in these 'Free Churches' spontaneous prayer usually had fixed patterns.
>
> During and after the period of the Second Vatican Council, when the official liturgical books were being renewed, there was room for improvisation, but gradually the ropes were tightened again.
>
> Now there are many documents insisting that participants 'stick to the rules'. These rules are strict for the Eucharist and the other sacraments, less so for Word of God celebrations, and even less so for devotional practices. In Vatican II's *Constitution on the Liturgy* there is a warning that no priest should add, omit, or change anything of the liturgical texts and rites. In my experience, practice varies. I know Catholic priests who improvise all Mass prayers, including the Eucharistic one. Others never do so. Some omit this; others add that. In ecumenical celebrations such as the Thomas Celebrations, improvisation continues to be an essential part of the ritual.
>
> Although it seems that everything is fixed in the current Byzantine rite, the amount of texts, songs, and rituals is so large that one cannot abide by them all. Therefore, the *Typicon* (directory) makes all kinds of suggestions about what can be left out and what must be done. In practice, many priests decide for themselves what to do and what not to do. Conservative liturgists complain about the chaos they think this practice creates. (Groen 2016)

Larry Hoffman, who teaches Jewish liturgy, wrote:

> The question you ask is complex. Originally, all Jewish prayer was improvised. It was an age of orality and nothing was written down. Whereas former scholars sought out an ancient text for every old prayer, by the 1950s we had learned not to do that. There is no such solitary text to find. But eventually prayers were written down, and with printing, everything was recorded, black on white, as if coming direct from Sinai. In the traditionally Orthodox world, even today – as in the late medieval world before it – our liturgy was largely, if not wholly, set in stone. One simply consulted one's memory or a book, and said the right thing. I recall two examples, even in my own lifetime, that stand out as examples: one historical (from the Shoah) and one more recent, from my own family experience.

The first is a manuscript I came across of the Passover Seder, written by hand in a concentration camp near the end of the war. Of course the writer had no way to know the war was ending soon. He was simply a concentration camp inmate who had no Passover Haggadah with him, but who knew it by heart and who took it upon himself to write down the ritual for anyone who still wanted to (and could) celebrate it – without the traditional food, we may well surmise. I read through the handwritten manuscript expecting some reference to the horrid conditions that prevailed. This is the rite of redemption, after all, the occasion on which God took us out of Egypt by a mighty hand and outstretched arm. The ritual recalls other such occasions. It laments the fact that 'in every generation there rise up those who want to destroy us.' Surely, I thought, the author would say something about the camps, Hitler, the death of so many all around him. But he said nothing. He wrote the rite down from memory; that was all. He could have been in the sunny medieval Riviera, for all the reader could gather. Only at the end – after the rite was completely finished and he had prayed for 'Next year in Jerusalem,' he allowed himself the luxury of a single added line in Yiddish (not the sacred Hebrew, but the Yiddish that he and the others would know from home): 'May this be the last Haggadah written in exile!' he says. That's it.

The other story concerns my daughter's intractable epilepsy and one of many times she was in hospital. Although she rarely has grand mal seizures (she has a different kind), on this occasion I arrived at her room to see nurses and doctors huddled over her bed. She indeed had a grand mal seizure and the healing staff were gathered around her to make sure oxygen was plentiful and she regained her consciousness. I waited at the door, being careful not to get in their way. As I waited, the Orthodox Jewish chaplain arrived, by chance. I had been told that he existed, and I expected such a visit, but not then. As he began walking into the room, the nurse tried to stop him, pointing out the severity of the situation. But he insisted. 'I'll just be a minute,' he said. 'I'll just say a prayer.' With that he shouldered her aside, and I took over, explaining who I was, 'What's your daughter's Hebrew name?' he inquired, and then he added (not knowing I was a rabbi), 'I am just going to say the prayer for the sick. It won't be long.' With that, he launched into a rote recitation of the standard prayer for the sick, inserting my daughter's name in the right place. He made up not one word. The Orthodox rabbi added nothing, because in his world there was nothing to add. He said the right prayer and hoped God would send healing.

To be sure, these two examples represent traditionalism, not modernity, and nowadays, it is commonplace to find rabbis making up healing prayers, adding to the one they have, and otherwise inserting creative meditations of all sorts. One of the most moving such prayers I know of is something I found in a Cantor's handbook from New York of 1840. The cantor had penned in a prayer for the well-being of England and France, the two countries that had intervened with the Ottoman Empire in a famous case known as the Damascus Incident. Jews had been rounded up in Damascus, charged with the Blood Accusation, and tortured. England and France objected and the *Times of London* even printed a full-page copy of the Passover Haggadah on its front page to indicate that Jews do not use children's blood on Passover. No doubt, the governmental intervention was all part of the political conflict with the Ottomans, but the cantor in New York didn't know that. He served in a Sefardi congregation that hailed from the Middle East; these were his and his congregant's countrymen being held and tortured. Hearing the unbelievable news that two modern nations intervened on the Jews' behalf, he took it upon himself to compose a prayer for them. He wrote it down; so we do not know how improvised it was. It follows a standard form of prayer for the welfare of communities. But perhaps he made it up the first time and then repeated it: or perhaps he didn't trust his ability to make things up, so he wrote it down that day before services, making sure to use traditional models. I suspect that is the case; a sign of the way tradition (he was Orthodox) had trouble with improvisation, but also how improvisation occurred anyway.

Nowadays improvisation happens more frequently, at least in modern circles, not just Reform but Orthodox and Conservative and others. New Age Jews (Renewal Judaism) probably do it most. I expect it happens frequently also among Reconstructionists and in the Boston seminary (Hebrew College) where Art Green is a major influence. We still teach little about it [ritual improvisation] at our Reform seminary. I insist that my students learn how to make up prayers: benedictions, at least, other things too. But in most established seminaries it is still little practiced, except by a few. At Hebrew Union College, it is somehow becoming commonplace to add improvised blessings during the Grace After Meals. I do not know where the students got the idea, but it happens frequently at a communal lunch that we have weekly.

I have improvised my own rituals – I regularly pass around a cup that I call 'the cup of hope and blessing' at our family seder, and ask people to speak aloud their hopes and dreams of blessing, then to pour wine from their cup into the one being passed to them. I conclude with a prayer that cites the 23rd psalm, 'My cup runneth over.' I also have guests at a wedding improvise blessings for the bride and groom. I have taught these practices all over the continent by now.

Sorry I cannot say more. By its very nature, improvisation is hard to track after it happens, because it is oral, improvised, and ended – usually without a trace of its happening. (Hoffman 2016)

One conclusion from these informal email exchanges is that improvisation is not noticed, even by those who engage in it, so it disappears. Another conclusion is that improvisation can be quick or slow, almost imperceptible. So we cannot conclude that improvisation is absent from ritual, only that its presence is not noticed or not remarkable. I study ritual by using video. When I edit, sometimes frame-by-frame, I notice improvisations that one would have missed while reading a ritual script or even watching a live performance.

Improvisation research

Surmising that ritual and improvisation are not mere opposites, I decided in 2011 to take a detour through the arts, where improvisation is more at home, to understand its dynamics. My research for the ritual-improvisation project tacks back and forth between rituals, the performing arts and interviews. One result is a Vimeo Showcase called *Ritual Creativity, Improvisation, and the Arts* (Grimes 2012e) consisting of seventy-three videos. The capstone video is *Rite to Play* (Grimes 2012d); the other result is this chapter.

Contemporary interdisciplinary research on improvisation is exploding. The publication of the scholarly journal *Critical Studies in Improvisation* began at the University of Guelph in 2004. Much of the research culminates in 2016 with the publication of *The Oxford Handbook of Critical Improvisation Studies* (Lewis and Piekut 2016). The two, six-hundred-page volumes include not only studies of improvisation in music, dance and the performing arts but also scientific studies in interspecies improvisation, digital improvisation in interactive game-playing, psychological studies of the effect of improvisation on empathy, contact improvisation, the use of improvisation in farm-land burning, improvisation in business management, hypergestural improvisation in politics and many other surprising topics.

In the West, jazz, blues and flamenco are known for featuring improvisation, but historically and cross-culturally it appears in many other arts and practices: in classical Greek rhapsody, Italian popular comedy, French liturgical organ, stand-up comedy, modern dance, music therapy, freestyle rap, storytelling, performance art and even European classical music. Classical Indian music is constructed around ragas, a set of rules, or musical qualities, that frame improvisation. Korean Pansori, a musical storytelling genre, is also improvisation-based.

Classical musicians of the West and East were trained in improvisational skills. Bach, Beethoven, Chopin, Handel, Mozart, Liszt, Mendelssohn and Verdi were skilled improvisers (Grimes 2012c). The divide between composed and improvised music became rigid only during the rise of symphony culture in the twentieth century. Christopher Small studied the musical, ethnic and ritualistic dimensions of symphonies and jazz. He concludes that in African and African American music the dualism between composed and improvised music never occurred (1998).

Orchestral sheet music sits on a music stand, but that is not *the* music – the primary, sensory stuff that enters the ears and arouses emotions. Violinists activate page-music by using micro-improvisations, small stylistic adjustments and ornamentations, throughout the performance (Grimes 2011c). For singers, micro-improvisations in timbre, tone and vibrato contribute to a vocalist's distinctive style. They go on all the time in the performing arts, and a performer can either dampen them or play them up.

Definitions of improvisation

Musicians can get away with declaring improvisation a mystery. The violinist Stéphane Grappelli says, 'You can write a book about [improvisation], but by the end no one still knows what it is. When I improvise and I'm in good form, I'm like somebody half sleeping. I even forget that there are people in front of me. Great improvisers are like priests, they are thinking only of their god' (quoted in Nachmanovitch 1990: 4). Stephen Nachmanovitch (1990: 41) says, 'Improvisation is intuition in action.' Derek Bailey (1992: 142) says, 'Improvisation can be considered as the celebration of the moment.'

As with the term 'ritual,' there are competing definitions of 'improvisation'. Frederic Rzewski tells this story: 'I ran into Steve Lacy on the street in Rome. I took out my pocket tape recorder and asked him to describe in fifteen seconds the difference between composition and improvisation. He answered, "In fifteen seconds the difference between composition and improvisation is that in composition you have all the time you want to decide what to say in fifteen seconds, while in improvisation you have fifteen seconds"' (Bailey 1992: 141). The parable implies a definition of improvisation: 'composing as you perform', as distinct from '*first* composing, *then* performing'.

'Composing while performing' seems to make improvisation a cult of genius; most of us could not imagine doing it. However, when two people converse, they are simultaneously composing and performing. We improvise during conversations because we know the vocabulary and understand the grammar. So a second definition is implied: 'adapting your knowledge to changing circumstances'. Improvisation can also mean 'making do with what you have' or 're-purposing available or discarded materials': building a Trinidadian steel drum from discarded oil drums, slapping two spoons back-to-back as a rhythm instrument or creating art by gluing found objects together into a bricolage.

Improvisation is not mere spontaneity, anarchy or doing what you please. It is a practised skill enabling you to respond in an environment that is changing, sometimes rapidly, sometimes unpredictably.[3] Beginning or unskilled improvising musicians repeat musical patterns more often than skilled ones; they fail to innovate (Lehmann and Kopiez n.d.). Improvisation tends to occur in situations where resources are limited or restricted, on frontiers where experimentation or resistance is required for survival or among people wanting to distinguish themselves from the mainstream.

If musicians East and West were trained to improvise, and if ordinary people improvise all the time in conversations, it would be odd if there were no evidence of improvisation in ritual. In the video *The Day the Clock Stopped* (Grimes 2015: 5:47–8:36), residents of Oslo witness rituals springing up in the cracks created by disasters (Post and others 2003). On 22 July 2011, Oslo's streets were flooded with large-scale, public examples of improvised ritual activity: being silent, processing, carrying roses, burning candles, singing hymns and folk songs.[4] At the island of Utøya commemorative shrines were improvised by parents and friends of murdered youth. In the city funeral ceremonies were modified or changed. Many of the actions were improvised, so were the spaces. The 22nd July Centre in Oslo and the island of Utøya were reclaimed, redefined, rebuilt. As a visitor arriving for the first time at the ring in Utøya or at the Centre, you have to improvise or imitate what others were doing. So we would do a disservice to ritual by imaging it only as an immovable structure, a rock sitting still through the eons.

The dynamics of improvisation

One of the most widely known forms of improvisation is stand-up comedy. Tina Fey, best known as a performer on *Saturday Night Live* and *30 Rock*, offers one of the most often-quoted summaries of the rules of improvisation:

> The first rule of improvisation is AGREE. Always agree and SAY YES. … If we're improvising and I say, 'Freeze, I have a gun,' and you say, 'That's not a gun. It's your finger …', our improvised scene has ground to a halt. But if I say, 'Freeze, I have a gun!' and you say, 'The gun I gave you for Christmas … ' then we have started a scene because we have AGREED that my finger is in fact a Christmas gun.

> The second rule of improvisation is say yes … AND. You are supposed to agree and then add something of your own. If I start a scene with 'I can't believe it's so hot in here,' and you just say, 'Yeah … ' we're kind of at a standstill. But if I say, 'I can't believe it's so hot in here,' and you say, 'What did you expect? We're in hell … ' It's your responsibility to contribute.
>
> The next rule is MAKE STATEMENTS. This is a positive way of saying 'Don't ask questions all the time.' If we're in a scene and I say, 'Who are you? Where are we? What are we doing here? What's in that box?' I'm putting pressure on you to come up with all the answers. In other words: Whatever the problem, be part of the solution. Don't just sit around raising questions and pointing out obstacles …
>
> MAKE STATEMENTS also applies to us women: Speak in statements instead of apologetic questions. No one wants to go to a doctor who says, 'I'm going to be your surgeon? I'm here to talk to you about your procedure? I was first in my class at Johns Hopkins, so?'
>
> The best rule: THERE ARE NO MISTAKES, only opportunities. If I start a scene as what I think is very clearly a cop riding a bicycle, but you think I am a hamster in a hamster wheel, guess what? Now I'm a hamster in a hamster wheel. I'm not going to stop everything to explain that it was really supposed to be a bike. Who knows? Maybe I'll end up being a police hamster who's been put on 'hamster wheel' duty because I'm 'too much of a loose cannon' in the field. In improv there are no mistakes, only beautiful happy accidents. (Fey 2011)

Improvisation begins with a diffuse receptivity to what is transpiring in the moment. By joining the flow of action rather than blocking it, you become vulnerable to others and the environment. If the emergent actions or sounds seem 'out of tune' or 'off-key', you, as a respondent, can include them in a larger frame of actions or sounds, making them part of an emerging interaction. You have the opportunity to transform off-key sounds into music rather than noise. As a result of this kind of interaction, a conversation, joke, story, dance, ritual or some other example of collective creativity can emerge. When the flow flows, participants become attuned to one another by entering a collaboration to which they jointly contribute. What emerges is a cycle of mutual support.

To prepare for this oceanic rhythm, participants have to practice and to practice is to make mistakes – together, in concert. After the interaction, participants need reflexivity, self-critical examination, to identify blocks and other mistakes so they can continue to improve their improvisational skills.

This prose summary, synthesized from several sources, can be idealized.[5] Few who practice or write about improvisation say much about *dissenting* from an opening gesture (saying 'no' to an invitation), but power dynamics are displayed in improvisation as much as in scripted performance. So learning how and when to say no is as crucial as saying 'yes'.

Improvisation can create a space for ritual change. Just as musicians distinguish between jazz, a jam session and an improv soiree, so we scholars who study ritual need to work out a continuum of ritual change. 'Ritualizing' is the term I use for deliberately creating rituals. There are many kinds of ritualizing: from slow, traditional, anonymous 'editing' and micro-improvisations, through design-and-execution models, to composing as you perform.

Imagine that the top end of the continuum is heavily structured; here we would locate ritual that is both scripted and read (with micro-improvisations in the performance). At the bottom, 'ritualists' (people who enact rituals) compose as they perform, making up the ritual as they go.[6] In the middle of the continuum are other possibilities: rituals with an improvisational phase[7] or improvisation used as a way to compose rituals.

- scripted and read
- scripted and memorized
- scripted but the script is ignored or laced with spontaneous talk or actions
- seeded improv: you are given a few notes or a theme and expected to expand on it
- selected ritual options: there is too much, or there are multiple suggestions, so ritualists pick and choose – this, but not that
- incomplete directions: the script assumes ritualists already knows what to do
- adaption: doing what fits the situation
- invited improvisation: you are asked to say or do something that was not previously planned
- improvisation before the performance, improvisation as means of composing rituals
- improvised during performance using practised formulas or patterns
- covertly cued ritual: you may improvise but only when signalled to do so
- scenario-driven improvisation: the narrative structure is given and you may improvise within it
- invented rituals: exceptional, rare or new circumstances for which there are no rituals, so you or a group invents one
- composing while performing: making up actions or words on the spot

The list is not exhaustive; there are other possibilities. The point is to disrupt the easy bipolar split: scripted versus spontaneous performance.

Where might we look – not for models, because I doubt there are any – but for actual instances of ritual improvisation, bits of inspiration to seed our imaginations? Scholars should focus on rituals that emphasize flow and performance rather than liturgical structure (Humphrey and Laidlaw 1994: 8), examining rituals that include improvisational phases: Haitian Vodoun, Pentecostalism, Quakerism. Ritual improvisation and innovation have been prolific among several groups: First Nations and intertribal gatherings, the LGBT community, interreligious meetings and interritualistic events, immigrant groups, protest movements. We should study traditional religions that include clowning, play and open critique and look at situations for which new rituals had to be invented because there was no existing ritual: the reburial of human remains among First Nations people or ash-scattering after cremations in the Netherlands. We should study rituals that run inside or alongside regular rituals. Wild Fasnacht in Switzerland was a counter-ritual that ran within the Basel's official Fasnacht. In the Czech Republic Vaclav Klaus, much disliked as a president, was 'deinaugurated' by the citizens of Prague. He was made into a straw man and thrown off the Charles Bridge. The Women's March of 2017 ran outside the precincts of official power to counter Donald Trump's inauguration. The march included 4 million participants in the United States and 300,000 more participants around the world.[8] Collectively, these sister protests constituted the largest one-day protest in US history. Counter-rituals require advance planning, but once they hit the streets, much can be improvised to great effect. And, of course, mistakes happen. In New York City some of the streets were so jammed that people could not walk.

Ritual, improvisation, democracy

It is common to associate ritual with top-down, male-dominated hierarchy, so readers would not expect a discussion of ritual to end with reflections on democracy. The top-down view of ritual is a stereotype. If not, associating ritual with democracy is either wishful thinking or the aspiration of a minority.

As early as 1987 the music educator Christopher Small (1987) was arguing that improvisation in jazz and other kinds of African-based music underwrites a socially responsive form of community-building different from the well-heeled society engendered by composed, conducted orchestra music. George Lewis, a trombonist and music educator at Columbia University, considers improvisation a symbol of democracy itself (Lewis and Piekut 2016: 19). Improvisation, he says, has the capacity to cultivate empathy and generosity, so it is a key to negotiation, because it provides participants with the courage and freedom to be transformed by others (Lewis 2011). Daniel Belgrad argues that improvisation nurtures a democratic sensibility and fosters egalitarian community (2016). David Lawes and John Forester show that improvisation functions effectively to enhance street-level democratic behaviour in the Netherlands (2015). Improvisation, then, is not just an art process but also a practice that can help people live and thrive (Madson 2005).

Reassembling Democracy (also called REDO), a Norwegian research project on ritual, raises the question whether there is, or could be, a link between democracy and ritual.[9] In my view there is no *necessary* connection; the one doesn't imply the other. Every ritual has its own internal politics implied in the way the ritual was created, how it is enacted, how it is maintained and how it interfaces with its ambient society and environment. So I would ask more precise questions: Which rituals? Which democracies?

A democratic ritual could be one whose words espouse a democratic ideology, but what people say about their politics or rituals has to be measured against what they actually do. Haudenosaunee (Iroquois Confederation) people say, 'We are all the same height.'[10] Americans, borrowing from the Haudenosaunee, say, 'All men are created equal.' These ideologies articulate ritually inflected aspirations, but the politics of a ritual are more deeply reflected in what people *do* than what they *say*. Some of the US Constitution-makers owned slaves, and women did not have the right to vote. Ideologies, myths and theologies, whether political or religious, do not necessarily reflect actual practice, and actual ritual practice does not necessarily predict actions outside the ritual context.

Since *Reassembling Democracy* started, I have tried to imagine: What would a 'democratic ritual' look like or sound like? Would it be one in which participants had a vote on what participants do? Would they vote for *every* change in the ritual? Would they vote for the leader? For a party? Would they vote before, during or after the ritual? How often? Every four years? After a non-confidence vote? Which models for democracy should we assume?

After the election of Donald Trump many have been re-reading Alexis de Tocqueville's classic critique of early American democracy (Tocqueville 2000 [1835]).[11] Tocqueville writes eloquently about 'the tyranny of the majority', reminding readers that democracies are not immune to fascism. In fact, some forms of democracy may actually cultivate it.

Like all key terms 'ritual' and 'democracy' accumulate baggage. Sometimes it is more effective to redefine or dump them altogether. I have already suggested ways of redefining 'ritual' (Grimes 2014a: 185 ff.), so I conclude with brief reflections on 'democracy'. There are many variants of democracy, so it is worth experimenting with 'assemblage'. Among ecologists the term 'assemblage' refers to the gatherings of multiple species in a geographical setting. Interactions in an assemblage happen by juxtaposition rather than by intentional or hierarchical coordination. Assemblages are designed from within, not from above (Stroud and others 2015). So my preferred version of the ritual/democracy question is: What ritual dynamics might facilitate assemblages that foster justice and the thriving of a multitude of species on the planet?[12] The beginning of a provisional answer is something like: rituals that include, or are preceded by, at least one sustained improvisational phase that stimulates attuned co-acting among the species and that facilitates self-critical reflexivity. Whether we call this an ecological or democratic view of ritual hardly matters. What matters is whether we have the courage to imagine and try it.

Survival value

Charles Darwin is reputed to have said, 'In the long history of humankind (and animalkind, too) those who learned to collaborate and improvise most effectively have prevailed.'[13] Probably he was thinking about ordinary social life in the environment: how to form groups for protection, how to get medicine from trees, how to stay warm in the winter. But ritual too was among the tools by which people oriented themselves to others and the earth. Ritual had survival value, and to invent rituals people had to improvise.

Rituals might have survival value today if they taught us to improvise and collaborate, act in concert, resist injustice, practice responsivity and adapt to an ever-changing universe. A ritual with survival value would have to be designed for teaching participants to respond to pervasive flux and change, so the ritual would have to be open, flexible, creative, critical – not a North Star. Circumstances change, sometimes unpredictably: the GPS fails; the map is out of date; the North Star cannot be seen from the southern hemisphere. New rituals should be laced with improvisational capabilities.

This is a tall order. We need a model that accepts uncertainty and unpredictability. Sarah Pike's *For the Wild: Ritual and Commitment in Radical Eco-Activism* studies planned and improvised rituals of resistance. She also considers indigenous and non-indigenous cooperation and conflict in ritualized protest (Pike 2017: 170–6).[14] Merrilyn Emery's *Participative Design for Participative*

Democracy (1993), based on an open-systems epistemology, embraces many of the same values as certain indigenous worldviews. An assemblage hatched at this convergence point – indigenous/open system – could brood practices capable of transforming its participants, if not the world.[15]

Several big questions haunt this aspiration for rituals with survival value:

1. Since *sustaining* an improvisation creates a tradition, can improvised rituals take root and last across generations?
2. Can ritualists overcome the self-consciousness that plagues self-created rituals?[16] How can self-consciousness be transformed into self-awareness?
3. Can these rituals be just: fair to indigenous people, kind to the planet, accessible by the poor, equally open to all kinds of people?

To enact rituals in an open, improvisational way is to make errors. Human DNA is a replicating machine. Of the billions of times that DNA replicates, there are sometimes 'misprints;' an error occurs.[17] On the one hand, this deviation can be read as a mistake. On the other hand, it may be the first step in a genetic mutation, an environmental improvisation.[18] Nature moves forward by both: replicating and making mistakes. If ritual-makers identify ritual with perfection, sameness, hierarchy and repetition, mistakes look like the enemy. But if participants understand that ritual is *not* the performance of perfection but rather the enactment of collective aspirations cobbled together provisionally in a fluctuating universe, a different outcome is possible (although not predictable). If a widely shared aspiration is to live together justly, among a multitude of species on the planet, and if all evolution, including that of human life, thrives on prolific experimentation, a mistake-tolerant ritual would have survival value. So sin bravely, make ritual mistakes.

2

Hospitable democracy: Democracy and hospitality in times of crisis

Agnes Czajka

For at least the past three decades social, political and cultural theorists have been diagnosing multiple crises in European societies. The cultural and political crises generated by the reunification and eastward expansion of Europe (and gradually also the European Union); the financial crisis; the refugee crisis; the rise of populism and the extreme right; and now the fracturing of the European Union have all been invoked and scrutinized as illustrative of a crisis-ridden twenty-first century or, indeed, a single, polytypic crisis (Czajka and Isyar 2013). This is not to say that twenty-first-century Europe is especially crisis ridden. With the destruction sown by the wars and famines of the nineteenth and twentieth centuries, the twenty-first century seems relatively stable and prosperous, at least in Europe. It is to say that crisis is back on the European agenda and might seem (at least to us contemporaries, who have not lived through the previous crises) to be of existential proportions.

To the sundry of aforementioned crises many have added the crisis of democracy – either as a cause, consequence or both. The chapter focuses on this crisis, the contribution that the work of Jacques Derrida can make to its analysis and the possibilities such analysis opens up for thinking and acting democratically in times of crisis. A considerable number of philosophers, theorists, politicians and policymakers have been diagnosing the hollowing out of democracy or the 'democratic deficit', offering an assortment of solutions (see Ercan and Gagnon 2014; Chou 2015). Others, perhaps less optimistically, have identified a post-democratic or even post-political condition (Crouch 2004). Derrida did none of these, at least not straightforwardly. So why focus on Derrida?

Derrida was not a theorist of democratic crisis, at least not in a way one might expect. His work on democracy has also remained peripheral to the fields of democratic theory and democracy studies, at least in part because he has paid relatively little attention to the rituals traditionally associated with democracy, including constitutions, elections and party politics. Yet democracy and crisis were among Derrida's fundamental concerns, and if he did not say much about a twenty-first-century crisis of democracy it is because, for Derrida, democracy is always and intrinsically in crisis. What is more, it is in crisis not because it is under attack from forces external or foreign to itself, but because it is inherently aporetic and autoimmune and thus prone to immanent crises and self-destruction. For Derrida, then, the crisis of democracy is fundamentally unresolvable, if by resolvability one means the permanent eradication of crisis.

Yet if this is the case, what are we to do? And is Derrida's contribution all that useful if one considers democracy worth salvaging? Can Derrida's work tell us anything about how to be democratic in times of (permanent) crisis? The aim of this chapter is to suggest that it can and to illustrate how. Since its point of departure is the crisis of democracy in Europe, the chapter will first attend to Derrida's understanding of Europe, drawing links between his conceptions of Europe, democracy and crisis. The chapter will then offer a more systematic account of Derrida's understanding of democracy, focusing on its aporetic and autoimmune properties. It will conclude by suggesting that the intersection between Derrida's conceptualizations of democracy and hospitality – both replete with rituals – can serve as a resource for thinking and acting through crisis, reflecting specifically on the potential of 'hospitable democracy'.

Europe, democracy, crisis

The chapter takes as its point of departure the crisis of democracy in Europe. This is not meant to suggest an intrinsic relationship between Europe and democracy or Europe and crisis, even though Derrida and some of his interlocutors do imply that at times. It is also not to suggest that the crisis of democracy is more acute in Europe than it is elsewhere. It is, however, the context with which I am most familiar, by which I am most directly affected and, thus, which seems to me most urgent at this moment. It is not one that directly preoccupied Derrida, though he did have some to say about Europe and crisis. Over a quarter of a century ago and occasioned by the 'reunification' or eastward 'expansion' of Europe, Derrida discerned a fundamental crisis in Europe (1992). Perhaps not unexpectedly, he diagnosed the crisis as a crisis of European identity. His understanding of what caused and characterized the crisis, however, was rather more unexpected.

Counterintuitively, Derrida suggested that the crisis was not occasioned by the dilution or absence of a fixed, unified and unifying European identity but precisely by the search for one. For Derrida, the search for a European 'self' – distinct from and set against or in relation to a non-European other or others – was the source of the problem and not its solution. Europe and European identity, Derrida argued, were structured through interminable encounters with others. The interminability of these encounters produced an inherently unfixed and volatile identity or, perhaps more appropriately, a non-identity for Europe. What is more, and perhaps more importantly, Europe did not exist as an object separate from, and standing in relation to the others through and in opposition to whom it was continually reinventing itself. The 'others' were always already within it. It was 'non-identity to itself, or … the difference within itself' that constituted Europe, perpetually unhinging and reinventing it, and it was this non-identity that Europe had to embrace (Derrida 1992: 9).

For Derrida, Europe's identity, or non-identity, is thus not constituted dialectically or relationally. It is not constituted through a synthesis of antithetical elements into a unified whole nor in relation to or against external others. Europe (as occident) is not, for instance, simply constituted against or in relation to its oriental 'other'. Like most of Derrida's other concepts or structures, Europe perpetually (re)constitutes itself through itself – with the 'self' in 'itself' always already and interminably an other; a culture of itself as a culture of the other; 'a culture of the double genitive', of difference to itself (Derrida 1992: 10). Derrida's Europe is thus characterized by precarious non-identity: if we continue with the occident–orient example, by the immanent presence of the oriental 'other' in its occidental 'self'. Its unity and identity are thus perpetually deferred through interminable becoming (of something other than 'itself'), through the difference-to-itself that is the constitutive element of this non-identity. '*What is proper to a culture*', writes Derrida of Europe, '*is not to be identical to itself*. Not to not have an identity, but not to be able to identify itself, to be able to say "me" or "we"', at least not with any sense of finality or conviction (Derrida 1992: 9)

While he does not explicitly reference Derrida's treatment of Europe, philosopher Mathias Fritsch points out that 'the conclusions Derrida reaches in his treatment of diverse moral and political concepts turn out to be rather similar to one another: The concepts are said to be aporetic, that is, beset by inherent, conceptual contradictions' (2011: 440). Derrida's treatment of law and justice, and the rituals of gift-giving, friendship, democracy, sovereignty, forgiveness and hospitality, involves the revealing of the 'aproetic structure besetting the concept in question' (Fritch 2011: 441). As Fritsch points out in relation to democracy, and as I explore more systematically elsewhere (Czajka 2017), 'to maintain its sovereignty, a democratic state must define (that is, circumscribe and limit) its membership and territory, but it must also claim hospitality to singular others, including the members who are declared enemies of democracy' (2011: 442).

A homologous aporia structures both hospitality and its attendant rituals, which Derrida explicitly addresses through the concept of hostipitality (2000). Fritsch summarizes the aporia of hospitality as the demand for an unconditional openness to alterity that is inherently and irresolvably in conflict 'with the need of the host to place conditions on the stranger in order to remain master of the premises and sovereign with regard to its borders, without which there would be no host and hence no hospitality' (2011: 441). Europe, democracy and, indeed, hospitality are thus perpetually and irrevocably in crisis precisely because of their aporetic structure, because of their inherent incongruity with themselves.

Democracy in crisis

Yet if this is indeed the case, if Europe, democracy and hospitality are inherently aporetic, necessarily and intrinsically embodying their undemocratic and inhospitable 'others', how are we to conceive of, let alone salvage European democracy (or hospitality) in times of crisis? Aren't democracy, hospitality and Europe themselves just ciphers for crisis? What are the implications of this for the concept of hospitable democracy, to which I alluded to in the Introduction and posited as a way through this overdetermined crisis? In characteristic Derrida fashion, but also for good philosophical reasons, Derrida's work does not offer unequivocal answers or straightforward solutions. But it can, I think, be inherited in ways that offer a resource for thinking and acting in and through crisis, democratically and hospitably, without sacrificing democracy and hospitality to their immanent, non-democratic or inhospitable 'others'.

An inheritance is never given; it is always a task. It is a task because it requires work: the work of selection, assemblage, exegesis and interpretation. 'If the readability of a legacy were given', argues Derrida, 'if it were natural, transparent, univocal, if it did not call for and at the same time defy interpretation, we would never have anything to inherit from it' (1994: 16). In this and the subsequent section of the chapter, I attempt to inherit Derrida's work on democracy in a way that enables us to posit and explore the concept of hospitable democracy as a way of thinking and acting through the contemporary crisis of democracy in Europe. My primary concern is to experiment with what Derrida has to offer or what he can be made to offer to thinking democracy in (times of) crisis. In doing so, I hope to lay some of the conceptual groundwork for successive chapters, which explore the role of ritual in enacting what I would like to conceive of as a hospitable democracy.

Derrida explores democracy most directly in *The Politics of Friendship* (1997) and *Rogues* (2005a), working from the assumption that democracy is marked by indeterminacy. Democracy, Derrida suggests, has always lacked a 'proper, stable, and unequivocal' meaning (2005a: 9). This lack of 'proper meaning, the very meaning of the selfsame' (Derrida 2005a: 37), has meant that democracy, more so than any other conceptual construct, marks an 'essence without essence … a concept without concept' (32). That almost every government can call itself a democracy, suggests Derrida, is not just hypocrisy but a consequence of the structure of democracy itself – 'it has no one model, no one form, for it makes possible many' (Derrida in Haddad 2013: 53). By definition and in 'essence', democracy cannot 'gather itself around the presence of an axial and univocal meaning' (Derrida 2005a: 39).

Democracy is thus grounded in or, more appropriately, unmoored by *différance*: by the inherent and permanent difference and deferral of meaning – and so not determined and delineated at all, but rather indeterminable and uncircumscribable (Czajka 2017: 21).[1] Thus, like most of Derrida's other concepts, democracy is riven with irreparable spatial and temporal difference: it has no essential meaning, its meaning indefinitely deferred. Yet it is also distinct: more noticeably aporetic and volatile, with a fundamental proclivity for autoimmunity, a process Derrida first alludes to in 'Faith and Knowledge: The Two Sources of "Religion" at the Limit of Reason Alone' (2002a: 80) and later revisits in *Rogues* (2005a: 81).

The distinctiveness of democracy derives from the fact that 'democracy is the only system in which, in principle, one has or assumes the right to criticize everything publicly, including the idea of democracy, its concept, its history, and its name' (Derrida 2005a: 86–7); it is 'the only one that welcomes the possibility of being contested, of contesting itself, of criticizing and indefinitely improving itself' (Derrida in Borradori 2003: 121). It thus demands, more than any other political system or comportment, 'the exposure to an open-ended future' (Fritsch 2002: 577). It is this that makes democracy a cipher for crisis, a 'form of society in which men consent to live under the stress of uncertainty', dependent as it is on perpetual self-transgression (Bensaïd 2011: 32).

As Derrida's engagement with democracy suggests, and as Selen Ercan and Jean-Paul Gagnon (2014) write in their introduction to a special issue of

Democratic Theory, 'there is nothing terribly new about the democratic crisis diagnosis' (Ercan and Gagnon in Chou 2015: 49). In a review of recent work on democratic crisis, which includes that of Ercan and Gagnon, Mark Chou submits that 'democracy is in a state of crisis' but 'that is neither a new nor a bad thing' (Chou 2015: 50). Democracy is a product of unfinished struggles, 'continually renewed, redefined and reinvented' (Chou 2015: 49) or, as Derrida had put it, inherently unstable and indeterminable. Hence, it is always already in crisis. But crisis is not synonymous with failure and democracies should not necessarily be considered 'in trouble' when they are met with or, perhaps more appropriately, 'produce crisis' (Chou 2015: 48). While crises have the potential to hamper or destroy democracies, they also possess the capacity to reinvigorate them (Chou 2015: 48). As Michael Naas, one of Derrida's most important interlocutors has observed, crisis is simultaneously a threat and a chance for democracy (2006).

It could probably be said that much, if not all, of Derrida's work is grounded in the exploration of crisis and the conclusion that it is simultaneously a threat and a chance. Fritch's (2011) previously cited work suggesting that autoimmunity functions as infrastructure in Derrida's oeuvre seems a version of this argument. Derrida demonstrates the coexistence of threat and chance through a variety of concepts, autoimmunity and *phármakon* (the Greek word that can imply both poison and cure) among them. As previously mentioned, Derrida first develops the notion of autoimmunity in the essay 'Faith and Knowledge', where he uses the concept to analyse the relationship between religion and science. There, in a footnote to the analysis, Derrida offers a concise definition of the process of autoimmunity: 'The general logic of auto-immunization consists for a living organism, as is well known and in short, of protecting itself against its self-protection by destroying its own immune system' (2002a: 80, fn. 27). Thus, as I have written elsewhere,

> the logic of autoimmunization outlines a process whereby an immune system, which protects a 'body' from what is foreign, alien and potentially fatal to it (or, in the case of some of the examples offered by Derrida, safeguards the integrity of the 'self' against potential incursions from the world outside), is actually compromised by the body, in a seemingly misguided and counterintuitive attempt to protect itself against its own protection. In an effort to preserve its immunity, it actually compromises it. In an effort to immunize it(self) against that which is alien and other to it, it actually breaches its defences, and allows it in.
>
> (Czajka 2017: 35)

In exploring the process of autoimmunization, Derrida points to both the threat and the potential it generates. While referring to it as 'terrifying' and 'fatal', he also points to the 'positive virtues of immune-depressants destined to limit the mechanisms of rejection and to facilitate the tolerance of certain organ transplants' (2002a: 80). Thus, while an autoimmune response can be threatening, self-destructive and, indeed, suicidal (Derrida 2005a: 45), it can also constitute a chance for a body, community, or in our case, democracy, to 'open itself up to and accept something that is not properly its own, to the transplanted organ, the graft, something it might otherwise reject, but which is crucial to its survival' (Naas 2006: 25).

In the case of democracy, autoimmunization can lead to its expansion, to more democracy for more people. As Samir Haddad argues, the exclusion of different groups – women, slaves, non-propertied classes, racialized minorities – from the right to vote was an immunizing move designed to insulate and protect democratic society from those constituted as irrational and dangerous (2013: 60). A struggle for and eventual expansion of the franchise would thus be an iteration of the autoimmune logic of democracy that involves a threat to democracy and a chance for its expansion and enrichment. It is thus crucial to remember that autoimmunity is not only a threat but also a chance for democracy. Chance, Derrida argues, is always given as an autoimmune threat, but it is also a 'chance for the incommensurable; it is what gives access to it' (Derrida 2005a: 35).

Indeed, if it is democracy that is in question, such openness, as previously suggested, is constitutive of its (non-essential) essence. It is what makes democracy more aporetic, more autoimmune, more prone to crisis than other political systems. In a further iteration of autoimmunization Derrida notes that it

> consists not only in harming or ruining oneself, indeed in destroying one's own protections, and in doing so oneself, committing suicide or threatening to do so, but, more seriously still, and through this, in threatening the I [*moi*] or the self [*soi*], the ego or the autos, ipseity itself, compromising the immunity of the autos itself: it consists not only in compromising oneself [*s'auto-entamer*] but in compromising the self, the autos – and thus ipseity. It consists not only in committing suicide but in compromising sui- or self-referentiality, the self or sui- of suicide itself. Autoimmunity is more or less suicidal, but, more seriously still, it threatens always to rob suicide itself of its meaning and supposed integrity. (2005a: 45)

Thus, what is of greatest consequence in the autoimmune process is that it compromises the 'I' – the autos, ipseity, self-sameness, self-referentiality, immunity of the self. It is a suicide, or murder of the self (Czajka 2017: 38), which actually reveals the impossibility of self-identity being 'proper to itself'. This, as I alluded to at the beginning of the chapter in relation to Europe, is not necessarily a problem or concern for Derrida. Rather, attempts at immunization, at fixing, gathering, unifying and stabilizing – in short, attempts to conceal that the self is always already adulterated, compromised, *différant* – are what constitute the more serious threat.

Hospitable democracy

It would be foolish, not to mention rather un-Derridean, to say that openness is the 'chance' and closure the 'threat'. The nature of *phármakon* is that it is both one and the other. As Michael Naas puts it, 'the opportunity is the threat, and the threat the chance' (2006: 28). Derrida illustrates as much in one of the most commented on examples of autoimmunity he offers: the suspension of the Algerian elections in 1992. As Derrida describes it, and as I explored in greater detail elsewhere (Czajka 2017: 39–40), the 1992 election would have most certainly given power to a majority that described itself as 'essentially Islamic and Islamist' and to whom '[was] attributed the intention, no doubt with good reason, of wanting to change the constitution and abolish the normal functioning of democracy or the very democratization assumed to be in progress' (Derrida 2005a: 31). Thus, through perfectly democratic means, Algeria risked ushering in a government intent on destroying democracy. Put differently, democratic elections, one of the quintessential rituals through which democracy attempts to immunize itself against its non-democratic other(s) – monarchy, oligarchy, totalitarianism and so on – would have actually facilitated the others' arrival. In an attempt to protect itself from this other (that was actually already within 'itself'), democracy turned on itself, weakening its own immune system by suspending one of its core rituals, thus achieving precisely what it had feared, if by self-inflicted means.

Derrida describes the processes and outcome as follows:

> The suspension of the electoral process in Algeria would be, from almost every perspective, typical of all the assaults on democracy in the name of democracy. The Algerian government and a large part, although not a majority, of the Algerian people (as well as people outside Algeria) thought that the electoral process under way would lead democratically to the end of democracy. They thus preferred to put an end to it themselves. They decided in a sovereign

> fashion to suspend, at least provisionally, democracy for its own good, so as to take care of it, so as to immunize it against a much worse and very likely assault. By definition, the value of this strategy can never be either confirmed or confuted. (2005a: 33)

In an attempt to immunize itself against its non-democratic 'other', Algerian democracy cast aside one of its fundamental and constitutive rituals. In doing so, and in an attempt to stave off its murder, it fell on its sword (Czajka 2017: 41).

Even if we have faithfully followed the twists and turns of Derrida's arguments until now, the above might be a bit difficult to swallow. For many, including Derrida, while 'voting is not indeed the whole of democracy … without it and without this form and this accounting of voices, there is no democracy' (Derrida 2002b: 305–6). This means that the ritual of voting must thus be protected, its results sacrosanct. Yet, as Derrida also argued, and many would likewise acknowledge, we must simultaneously

> take a stand against whoever would not respect … democratic life, a legal state … free speech, the rights of the minority, of political transition, of the plurality of languages, mores and beliefs, etc. We are resolutely opposed – it is a stand we take clearly, with all of its consequences – to whoever would pretend to profit from democratic processes without respecting democracy.
>
> (Derrida 2002b: 305–6).

Thus, with the Algerian election – as with other elections and referenda of the more recent past – we are nowhere if not in the eye of the storm, at the centre of the aporia of democracy, witnessing autoimmunity at work. Acknowledging this, however, does not bring us any closer to knowing how we might act in times of democratic crisis. Killing democracy (to save it) or letting it kill itself (to save it) both seem like bad options if salvaging democracy is what we are after. Suggesting, as Derrida does in *Rogues*, that the value of the strategy adopted in Algeria 'can never be either confirmed or confuted' (2005a: 33) is likewise of limited use, if what we are after are resources for thinking and acting through such aporias.

Derrida's work, one might argue, is not the best place to look for such resources. Derrida's work cannot provide us with a programme or even guidance on what decisions and judgements one should make in times of democratic crisis. Aporias are, by definition, unresolvable. What is more, Derrida's oeuvre is premised on the assumption that for a decision to be made, for it to be a decision at all, it must be a product of a moment of undecidability. In that moment everything must remain possible, including 'for the decision to have been otherwise' (Hill 2007: 61). A decision is only possible 'when it is not possible to know what must be done, when knowledge is not and cannot be determining' (Derrida 1992: 149). Otherwise, the 'decision' is not, in fact, a decision at all; it is, rather, a mechanical application of a rule, a perfunctory observance of law, a deferral to a programme – 'one knows what has to be done, it's clear, there is no more decision possible; what one has is … an application, a programming' (Derrida 1992: 148).

What I would like to propose, however, is that while Derrida's work cannot provide us with a blueprint for how to salvage democracy in times of crisis – nor should we want one, as that itself would sound the death knell of democracy – his work can still provide us with some resources for thinking and acting in times of crisis. Particularly useful, I think, is the intersection between Derrida's work on democracy and hospitality. As I have previously noted, hospitality is among Derrida's aporetic concepts, beset by inherent and unresolvable contradictions. The contradiction at the heart of hospitality is that between its conditional (or limited) and unconditional (or absolute) variety. Derrida's reflections on hospitality are largely grounded in Greco-Roman, Judeo-Christian and Western philosophical traditions, which produce a particular instantiation of the aporia.

Conditional hospitality, as Derrida's concept of hospitality implies, is always already tinged with a kind of hostility, an imbalance of power between a host and a guest. The host admits the guest into *his* home, where he is, 'master of the household, master of the city, master of the nation, the language or the state' and from where he permits the guest to cross its threshold (Derrida 2000: 6). Opening a door and stepping aside so as to *allow* the guest to enter is always already an illustration of power. Power impregnates all rituals of welcome and gestures of hospitality as they are all liable to withdrawal.

Derrida likenes unconditional hospitality to the religious concept of visitation. 'Visitation', suggests Derrida, 'implies the arrival of someone who is not expected, who can show up at any time … if I am unconditionally hospitable, I should welcome the visitation … I must be unprepared, or prepared to be unprepared, for the unexpected arrival of any other' (Derrida 1998: 70). 'If there is pure hospitality', Derrida continues, it should consist of an opening 'without horizon or expectation, an opening to the newcomer whoever that may be', an opening that might indeed be difficult or even 'terrible', because the 'newcomer may be a good person, or may be the devil' (Derrida 1998: 70). Unconditional or absolute hospitality might thus also be tinged with hostility, though of a different kind. As political theorist Dan Bulley suggests, unconditional hospitality might generate an 'even more extreme' hostility, demanding, as it does, that we allow our selves, homes and, indeed, democracies to be 'persecuted, questioned and occupied' by an other (Bulley 2006: 660). 'How could we not', Bulley continues, 'feel hostility to, and from, that which has made … our "at-homes" tremble?' (Bulley 2006: 660).

Yet absolute hospitality is also an impossibility. Welcoming is conditional on the existence of a threshold across which to welcome. It is for this reason that Edward S. Casey insists that hospitality takes place at or on an edge (2011: 43). There would be no hospitality without 'the ingrediency of edges, their effective ingression into this act – whether these be edges of gates or doors, bodies or cultures' (Casey 2011: 45). Absolute hospitality, however, must nevertheless remain our ethical horizon. Hospitality, thus, requires a decision – which, as previously noted, is possible only if it emerges from a moment of undecidability, ceasing to exist if it is pre-scripted in advance – and a negotiation. If, as Derrida argues, 'the two meanings of hospitality remain mutually irreducible', then, 'it is always in the name of pure and hyperbolic hospitality that it is necessary, in order to render it as effective as possible, to invent the best arrangements [*dispositions*], the least bad conditions, the most just legislation' (2005b: 6). A negotiated hospitality must thus consist of 'doing everything to address the other, to accord him, even to ask him his name, while keeping this question from becoming a "condition", a police inquisition, a blacklist or a simple border control. This difference is at once subtle and fundamental' (Derrida 2005b: 7).

Yet what is also crucial is that a negotiated hospitality must remain open to the other, 'only to the point of not destroying [the] host … Once the host's generosity reaches a point where she stands to lose ownership over those premises that permitted her to serve as host in the first place, or otherwise surrender her ability to act as a moral agent, it would no longer be mandated by the idea of hospitality' (Fritsch 2011: 448). What is more, as negotiation is permanent – it means 'no thesis, no position, no theme, no station, no substance, no stability, a perpetual suspension, suspension without rest' (Derrida 2002c: 16) – singular decisions about the lengths and depths of hospitality will have to be made and remade at every instance, in response to every new arrival, every other guest.

It might not seem that all of this has brought us any closer to resolving the dilemma that killing democracy or letting it kill itself seem two equally bad options. But I think we have actually inched closer, not to a resolution but to a resource for thinking and acting through the permanent crisis of democracy, namely, the kind of negotiated hospitality that Derrida puts forth. Thinking and acting democratically in times of (permanent) crisis requires a (permanently) negotiated and renegotiated hospitality: we must, in every situation, strive for the horizon of unconditional hospitality while ensuring that we do not destroy our (non-ipseic) selves in the process.

Elsewhere, I have suggested that the concept of a 'just democracy' might capture the (everlasting) negotiations and (provisional) decisions that underpin openness to unforeseen others – and thus make us democratic – without sacrificing democracy to non-democratic others (Czajka 2017). I had suggested it because, for Derrida, like absolute hospitality, justice is the (impossible) ethical horizon towards which we must nevertheless orient ourselves. Like hospitality, justice obliges us not only towards our 'fellows' or those who are most 'like us' but also towards those 'others', those who are least 'like us' – the furthest away and most unrecognizable (Czajka 2017: 110). Like hospitality, acts of justice must also be singular, in both their comportment and their content, 'must always concern singularity, individuals, irreplaceable groups and lives, unique situations' (Derrida 2002d: 245).

It is for these reasons that I have previously argued that the intersection of justice and democracy (or the construct of 'just democracy') offers a useful resource for working, thinking and acting through one of the fundamental aporias of democracy: the aporia occasioned by democracy's constitutive need for openness to its absolute others. But it might be that the conceptual construct of 'hospitable democracy' is better suited. Hospitality and justice are parasynonymous for Derrida, so in some ways, the distinction between just and hospitable democracy is semantic. But the reflections Derrida and his interlocutors offer on hospitality serve, I think, as clearer resources for acting democratically in times of crisis.

Hospitable democracy, on my reading, enables us to walk the tightrope of openness and closure precisely because it is inherently subject to negotiation. It enables us to acknowledge that among democracy's intrinsic features is its openness (and just comportment) to its others and to those who are least 'like us'. It compels us to ensure that such openness be preserved, even in times of crisis and even if such openness presents a threat. In Derrida's reflections on the Algerian election, such threat was palpable: the openness of democracy and of the democratic process to a non-democratic other is what threatened to destroy Algerian democracy. Yet to paraphrase what Fritsch and Derrida suggested in relation to hospitality and graft it onto the construct of hospitable democracy, hospitable democracy must remain hospitable to the other only to the point of not destroying itself (Fritsch 2011: 448). Thus, it need not be unbounded nor extended to those whose institutions and programmes fail, in turn, to be hospitable to, and preserve singularity, and instead presuppose its annihilation. Totalitarianism, fascism and authoritarianism – the non-democratic others – erase difference, fix meaning and, thus, annihilate singularity. As such, they cannot demand a hospitable response. Hospitable democracy must thus 'avoid the perverse effects' of an unlimited hospitality and democracy by 'calculat[ing] the risks … but without closing the door on the incalculable, that is, on the future and the foreigner' (Derrida 2005b: 6).

When thinking through the 'limits' of hospitable democracy, it might also be helpful to consider the ways in which hospitality is narrated in non-Abrahamic religious traditions. As Brian Treanor points out, 'Those of us tilling in the field of continental European philosophy, conditioned as we are by the Judeo-Christian-Islamic tradition, tend to see the conditioned laws of hospitality as a perversion of the unconditional law of hospitality' (2011: 59–60). On a reading of hospitality grounded in such tradition, which Treanor argues is also Derrida's reading, 'pure hospitality, generosity, forgiveness, and similar dispositions represent myriad ways that we fail to "be perfect as [our] Father in Heaven is perfect" (Matthew 5:48). We can never realise such lofty goals' (Treanor 2011: 60). Yet the aporia of hospitality has also been 'resolved' differently. In Hinduism, the call to unconditional hospitality exists in conjunction with narratives that suggest that 'the way in which we ought to exhibit hospitality … is dictated by our position and role in life' (Treanor 2011: 61). Thus, the hospitality of a mother of two young children is different from the hospitality of a single man, and, crucially, 'these differences are proper, and they *ought* to be so' (Treanor 2011: 61). Compared to the Abrahamic tradition in the context of which Derrida articulates his aporia of hospitality, the Hindu account of hospitality thus offers a much less 'tragic' account of the negotiation between conditional and unconditional hospitality (Treanor 2011: 62). As Treanor suggests, 'perhaps different people *should* respond to the same *unconditional* call differently' (2011: 61–2). In the context of this chapter, perhaps hospitable democracies should respond differently – with different kinds and degrees of hospitality – to different circumstances.

Conclusion

That we are living in times of crisis has been the adage of the twenty-first century. The chapter focused on the crisis of democracy and the contribution that Jacques Derrida's work on democracy and hospitality can make to thinking and acting democratically in times of crisis. The chapter took as its point of departure the crisis of democracy in Europe, exploring the relationship between democracy and crisis by attending to Derrida's work on the crisis of Europe. Working through some of Derrida's cardinal concepts – aporia, autoimmunity, non-identity and *différance* – the chapter proceeded to explore Derrida's conceptualizations of democracy and hospitality and what they might offer to an understanding of the contemporary crisis of democracy. It concluded by suggesting that a conceptual construct of hospitable democracy might offer a useful resource for imagining (and rescuing) democracy in times of crisis.

Given that ritual performances are especially well suited to disclosing and preserving the aporetic nature of existence, they might well be pivotal to advancing the kind of hospitable democracy I have imagined. To be sure, neither the construct of hospitable democracy nor ritual can offer a cure for democracy's aporetic or autoimmune tendencies, nor for its intrinsic propensity for crisis. They might, however, offer a way through the crisis, empowering us to think, judge and act from within it.

Part Two

Reassembling communities

3

Enchanting democracy: Facing the past in Mongolian shamanic rituals

Gregory Delaplace

Something is enchanted in the state of Mongolia. Surely, this enchantment has something to do with the fact that Mongolian government has officially allowed shamanism to flourish again alongside Buddhism, after a long period of repressive regimes.[1] And high-ranking politicians, indeed at times the president himself, have been keen since then to have religious specialists conduct official ceremonies on behalf of the government (e.g. Delaplace 2010; Merli 2010). But the enchantment of Mongolian politics in the post-socialist period runs even deeper. More profoundly indeed, the performance of democracy, the embracing of liberalism as an economic doctrine and the enactment of individual liberties have been surrounded with the aura of a certain mystique. This mystique has set what Caroline Humphrey (1992: 377) called the 'deep past' at the source of any kind of 'moral authority', construing it as a framework within which any decision concerning the collective future of Mongolian people should be made.

Firmly established at the core of this source of moral authority is the figure of Chinggis Khan, considered the founder of Mongolian polity and referenced as the creator of the very world Mongolian people have been bestowed (Shimamura 2014: 22–4, 303–5). Honouring Chinggis Khan's legacy is more or less explicitly regarded as the prerequisite to any policy or collective decision, at every level of the state. This legacy might take the form of the 'blood' (*tsus*) Mongolian people inherited from him,[2] or that of the '(home)land' (*nutag*) he secured and in which his spirit lives on, or even that of the customs he has established, in a more or less direct way, for Mongolian people to live in 'harmony' (*ev*). This general understanding of Mongolian people's responsibility towards their own past is likely to come up in many kinds of public matters. Most lately, for instance, politicians have been publicly accused of selling off Mongolian land and collective heritage through mining licences handed out to foreign companies, thus jeopardizing the perpetuation in the future of a vital link with the past: a link that is regarded as the main source of Mongolian – and indeed of the world's – vitality (Irvine 2018).

What 'democracy' (*ardchilal*) is therefore believed to have brought about in Mongolia is first and foremost the collective possibility to claim back and pursue this heritage, while the communist regime is still consistently accused to have acted to suppress it.[3] More concretely even, the re-emergence of shamans throughout the country has led more and more people to discover they themselves had shamanic ancestry, as those they consulted came in contact with the spirits of forefathers whose memory had been lost because of the genealogical disruption supposedly caused by communist-inspired materialism before the 1990s (Shimamura 2014). It has become rather commonplace, in post-socialist Mongolia, to blame spirits' anger for the crises met by the country since the IMF's 'shock-therapy' and throughout the liberalization process in the 1990s and the 2000s. Disgruntled to have been let down for such a long time, spirits manifest themselves through shamans and demand proper treatment at last, lest the country will revert to its post-socialist stagnation (Buyandelgeriyn 2013).

Thus, performing democracy in Mongolia could be seen as a matter of enabling people's collective and individual freedoms to achieve the yet unaccomplished potential contained in their illustrious and powerful history. According to Humphrey (1992), this has been done either by *mimicking* or by *embodying* the past; the way these two modalities play out *both* at an individual *and* at a collective level is the main concern of this chapter. While indeed state symbolism is imbued with archaistic references meant to call for the return of a time when Mongolian people seemed able to rule the whole world and while politicians *mimic* the deep past they wish to emulate, it remains difficult for them to tap into it in a more direct and authoritative manner, by *embodying* it rather than just representing it. They have had to rely for this on ambiguous and often unruly figures, such as Buddhic reincarnations and shamans.

This chapter focuses on a set of shamanic rituals taking place in Mongolia over a decade, from 2008 to 2019. It sets out to show how – that is through which relational configurations – these rituals work to connect Mongolian people both individually and collectively to a lived experience of their own past. Two main modalities are at play here, whereby the past is *either* mimicked in grand performances directed to a collective audience *or* embodied in the form of a spirit tending to an individual patient. Drawing on a brief review of the literature on shamanic ritual modalities across South America and Inner Asia, I will show that such a duality is far from being unheard of elsewhere, to the point that it could be considered characteristic of human-organized attempts to relate to the invisible. More specifically, however, the purpose of this chapter is to describe how the practice of democracy – how the enactment of a certain idea of individual and collective freedoms – might be achieved through an ever-transforming set of ritual apparatuses.

Dual shamanic regimes in Amazonia and Asia

It has not been uncommon for social anthropologists writing on shamanic rituals in North Asia and South America – the two main regions in the world where mediumistic rituals have traditionally been branded 'shamanic' – to emphasize their deeply heterogeneous nature. Even in the particular case of contemporary Mongolia, it would prove quite difficult to single out one specific form of ritual protocol as characteristic of what Mongolian people might recognize as 'shamanism' (*böö mörgöl*) in general. This is not only due to the fact that, as Mongolian shamans themselves like to emphasize, 'there are as many ways to shamanize as there are shamans' (*böö böögiin böölöh ondoo*, quoted in Buyandelgeriyn 1999) – and indeed, we shall see here that there *is* a singularly dynamic inventiveness at play in Mongolian shamanism nowadays. Yet, beyond the inherent multifarious character of shamanic practices, anthropologists working in North Asia and South America have often recognized a *dual nature* to these practices.

In a volume they co-edited in 1994, Caroline Humphrey and Nicholas Thomas stressed what they felt was a bias in cross-cultural studies of shamanism. Shamans, they argued, were consistently characterized through their role as inspirational healers and the 'ecstatic techniques' (*à la* Eliade 1964) they mobilized or even on the characterization of their supposed 'mode of consciousness'. As a rule, shamans tended to be considered as 'single ritual practitioners', rather than as political actors in their own right: the volume was thus an attempt to consider how shamanism as a ritual practice could be shaped by the state and how it may shape it in return. For many contributors to the volume, this implied distinguishing between different *kinds* of shamanism.

In his seminal contribution to the volume, Stephen Hugh-Jones (1994) thus identified two main ritual modalities across the North-western Amazonian societies of Arawakan and Tukanoan linguistic ensembles; he branded these two ideal types 'vertical shamanism' and 'horizontal shamanism':

> Though all forms of shamanism combine knowledge with inspiration, in [Vertical Shamanism] the predominant component is esoteric knowledge transmitted within a small elite, while in [Horizontal Shamanism] the emphasis is more democratic, depends less on 'saying' than on 'doing', and involves the more classic shamanistic features of trance and possession.
>
> (Hugh Jones 1994: 32–3)

This translated into a general opposition between two distinct ritual specialists with very different modes of operation. There were people known as *payé*, on the one hand, who made extensive use of hallucinogenic (*parica*) snuff in order to gain heightened perceptive capabilities. This enabled them to locate pathogenic components in a person's body and evacuate these through various physical operations such as 'water throwing' and suction. Besides these powerful and feared inspirational mediums, however, existed another kind of specialists, called *~kubu* in Tukanoan languages, who operated their mediation in a completely different fashion. Rather than possession and drug-induced visionary travels to different cosmic layers of the world, they performed a calm recitation of esoteric chants that described the fate of their patient's soul and the various stages of its curing.

In her own contribution to the same volume, Caroline Humphrey (1994) showed that in North Asia too, among nineteenth-century Manchu and Daur populations at least, there were two ritual modalities at play which could be called 'shamanic' – and they were *actually* called so in Manchu, a language related to Tungus, from which the term 'shaman' was indeed borrowed in the first place. She called the first one 'transformational': in this context, specialists were religious virtuosos able to let spirits speak through them, to make prophecies about the future and to cure ailments in the present. They were considered powerful, although a bit unpredictable, and they were supposed to have been chosen by spirits themselves. Another sort of shamans, however, showed more of a 'patriarchal' orientation, as their ritual activity mainly revolved around the reproduction of the patrilineage. They performed hierarchical rituals meant to revitalize the community through a proper propitiation of ancestral spirits, which were thought to reside in particular locations within the land.

Most recently, Charles Stépanoff (2019) has proposed another dual model to order the diversity of shamanic ritual apparatuses that can be found throughout the boreal regions of North Asia and North America. In a convincing demonstration spanning centuries of archival material and covering a trans-continental area linking up both sides of the Bering Strait, Stépanoff shows that shamanic practices differ in the way they envisage the particular issue of delegation. While some populations delegate the task of dealing with the invisible to particular people in virtue of their distinctive, innate and permanent ability to do so, others consider that virtually anybody within the community might be qualified to channel non-human presences. Thus, while some populations practice a definitely *hierarchical* form of shamanism, whereby the inequality in religious qualification is both institutionalized and irreversible, some others have kept a *heterarchical* approach to their mediumistic practices, allowing various people for various periods of time to occupy a central position in the administration of human/non-human relations. These modalities are predicated on very different kinds of rituals: hierarchical traditions favour visual and direct performances of the specialist's travel through a well-established cosmic geography, while heterarchical ones characteristically prefer apparatuses where the shaman's mediation disappears, in order to let communication between human members of the community and their non-human counterparts flow freely. The Mongolian cases discussed in this chapter clearly belong to the hierarchical modality in Stépanoff's model. However, in keeping with Steven Hugh-Jones and Caroline Humphrey's own case studies, I suggest there is more than one way to effect the hierarchical delegation characteristic of shamanic practices in these regions. These two modalities involve contrasted interactional apparatuses and a radically different sort of involvement of the specialist's own person within the ritual.

The 'renaissance' (*sergen mandal*) of Mongolian shamanism, its early rise 'from shadow to light' in the capital city Ulaanbaatar, has been well documented by Laetitia Merli (2010). Merli has also described the emergence of a particular brand of shamans, less concerned with individual problems than with the welfare of the Nation as a whole. These practitioners appeared as real public figures, giving interviews in the newspapers, writing books and creating 'shamanic centres' under the auspices of famous scholars and political traditionalist associations. These public shamans thus envisaged their ritual practice as a process of fundamental reconnection between Mongolian people and the invisible entities immanent to the land. Their aim, Merli reported, was not so much to cure individuals as to heal the Nation, or at least, the first was expected to derive from the second. The government itself was called to resume its association with 'state shamans' (*töriin zairan*), held to be able – as they did in the heydays of imperial glory – to lead the country on the path to greatness. Merli

(2010: 239) has described this process as a gradual 'recuperation' of shamans and shamanism by nationalist associations and particular individuals who sought to establish it as a state religion – a 'reinvented' and 'reconstructed' cosmology and ritual practice (2010: 309) that bore only formal superficial resemblance to the individual healing modality it seemed to emerge from. Merli, in other words, has tended to consider this politically oriented, priestly modality of shamanism as originating from people, institutions and strategies external to the shamanic practice itself.

In the remainder of this chapter, I propose to adopt another perspective on the duality of shamanic practices in contemporary Ulaanbaatar. Drawing on a brief description of a few rituals I have been attending since 2008, I will show that while they indeed instantiate two different modes of relating with the past, they can both be seen as political acts – ritual enactments of a perceived 'democratic' freedom to tap into the powerful resource of Mongolian history. Whether these rituals allowed ancestral spirits to emerge from Mongolian history to interact personally with an individual or staged a more generic representation of identity, emanating from the performance of certain 'traditions', they all enacted 'democracy' as an exercise in collectively facing the past. In each case, meanwhile, shamans seemed to follow a specific *modus operandi*. What they effected in both contexts is what I would like to call an apparatus of manifestation: a set of relational technologies, discourses and actions meant to allow something invisible to appear. Thus, while horizontal/inspirational shamans *embodied* spirits in order to keep people away from them, vertical/liturgical ones *mimicked* ancestors in order to connect Mongolian people to their own history.

Embodying spirits and healing people: Inspirational practitioners at work

When I first met Ariuka in 2008 she was just nineteen and yet considered a powerful shaman already. She was welcoming patients in the small space of an apartment on the outskirts of Ulaanbaatar, together with her adoptive mother Saraa who was also acting as her 'assistant' (*tüshee*) during rituals. Ariuka had completed her initiation the year before with an established shaman, who had diagnosed her as possessing a shamanic 'essence' (*udha*). It was understood that she had inherited it from her biological grandmother, herself also a powerful shaman in her time. There had been signs of her shamanic calling quite early in her life: Ariuka would consistently see things that other people could not or deliver predictions received through visions and dreams. Ariuka's adoptive mother Saraa, on the other hand, was not devoid of a shamanic essence herself either: she had been chronically ill in the years before Ariuka's initiation, to the point of fearing for her life, and no doctor seemed able to point a medical way out of her troubles. The same shaman who was supervising Ariuka's initiation actually revealed Saraa's grandfather was also a shaman himself, adding that Saraa's illness was the sure sign that her shamanic lineage needed to be perpetuated too. As Saraa was too weak and felt too old to accomplish this, it was agreed that Ariuka would take it upon herself to continue both lineages – her own and her adoptive mother's – thus killing two birds with one stone, as it were, through her shamanic initiation.

As a consequence of this particular situation, the configuration of Ariuka's shamanic performances was fundamentally dual: she was conducting two different types of rituals which revolved around the summoning of her two tutelary spirits. During the afternoons, she would call to 'Grandmother' (*Emee*) and 'let [her] descend' (*buulga-*) in her body in order to address matters related to love and romantic relationships. When a woman – patients were mostly women in this case – wanted to 'call a companion' (*han' duuda-*) in order to find a partner, when she wanted to know whether the boyfriend she had found would make a good husband, or else, most importantly, if a wife wanted her husband to stop drinking and/or cheating, she would take her request to 'Grandmother'. Ariuka would put on a white and light blue costume, and she would use a pentagonal drum to conduct the ritual.

After nightfall, on the other hand, she would summon the spirit of 'Grandfather' (*Övöö*), her adoptive mother's ancestor shaman, and she would address darker and heavier issues such as 'responding to curses' (*haarald hariula-*) or more generally curing illnesses caused by envy, gossip and bad-mouthing (*hel am*), which are held to be the plague of Mongolian modern city life (Delaplace and Humphrey 2013; Højer 2019). To this end, she would don a dark blue costume and use a nine-sided drum, which during the day was exhibited in her living room next to the TV set. This and a small altar to 'divinities' (*burhan*) were the only items signalling the ritual vocation of the place in-between séances.[4]

Both ritual modalities, meanwhile, roughly followed the same procedure. Whether she was calling Grandmother or Grandfather, Ariuka started by lighting candles and juniper powder in front of her altar, beating the corresponding drum and reading invocations meant to have it 'come down' (*buuj ire-*). When she would feel the time was right, Ariuka would get up and put her costume on, aided by her mother. Slowly, as if she were already not quite herself – and yet not anybody else either – she would wear a hat with fringes covering her face and she would slip her hand through the wrist-straps of a whip and a drumstick. In the middle of the room now filled with juniper smoke, she would sit on a stool and beat her drum energetically until the resounding sound became almost palpable to the patients, who were anxiously observing the scene while standing along the walls of the living room. All of a sudden, Ariuka would get up from her stool and spin until she lost her balance and almost fell in her mother's arms. When she would find her footing again, she would look different. Bent in half and barely able to walk, she showed difficulties to breathe. Heavy, hesitant and wheezy, she would be driven by the assistant to a square cushion on which she would sit cross-legged, providing the bemused patients with the vivid impression that a very old person had just entered the room. As soon as she had sat, the assistant would offer tea and hand a pipe to her, in the bowl of which a cigarette had been fitted and lit. As would be expected with any visitor in a yurt, the assistant would then ask her whether she had a good trip, addressing the shaman as if she were an elder. The shaman, with a shrill voice, out of breath – a voice beyond the grave, really – would answer yes, and small talk would ensue.

The patients were then instructed to come one after the other to sit in front of the shaman, in order to converse with what at that time appeared to be a spirit. 'Appear' is probably the wrong term for what was happening at that moment, however, as it was really through everything else than sight that the presence of the spirit could be felt. The shaman's costume, concealing the body and most of all the face of the practitioner, would encourage the patients to mentally distance themselves from the visual image they kept of the person they were sitting in front of and to open themselves to other signs that were somehow blurring her actual identity. When I myself was called up to take a seat in between the shaman and her assistant, I felt something like a doubt as to whom exactly I was interacting with. Surely, this was the shaman, this was still the same individual I had interviewed a few hours before; obviously she had not disappeared. And yet there was something about her, something that felt just a little bit more complicated than this. The wheezing of her breath, the texture of her voice and, most importantly, the sheer heaviness of her clumsy hand on my neck at some point during the ritual let me in disbelief as to whether this was actually a fresh and joyful nineteen-year-old girl who still was in front of me. The powerful sense of presence conveyed in this ritual rested not so much on the fact that the shaman would *look like* a grandmother or a grandfather (apart from the different costume, actually, I failed to see any difference in the way they would each manifest themselves) than on the extent to which she did not quite look like herself anymore. Doubts were raised, to say the least, as to her exact 'position' as an enunciator (see Severi 2015: chap. 3). Interestingly, therefore, it is as much through a process of concealment and blurring (with the costume, the hat and to a lesser extent the juniper smoke and the heavy drumbeating), as through a technique of representation, that the spirit was made to appear in this context.[5]

Spirits, moreover, were not the only things that were made to appear in Ariuka's rituals: their purpose was actually to make the cause of the patients' troubles manifest to them, to find out which invisible affects had caused visible effects in their lives. This was achieved through the gradual translation and interpretation of the spirit's speech by the shaman's assistant, who led the patient into deducting from cryptic assertions a precise diagnosis on their situation. Both Grandmother and Grandfather expressed themselves in some sort of a coded language: as they were supposed to belong to a past era, they used archaic idioms to say such usual words as 'hello', 'goodbye' and 'thank you'. For the same reasons, they used naïve periphrases to describe items that supposedly did not exist in their time – planes were 'iron birds', cars were 'iron ants' and so on. Some of these idioms were straightforward, but others could be more challenging (a 'white thing', for example, happened to be an hospital), even for the assistant who at times needed to ask the spirit to explain what she meant with a particular expression. As a rule, patients were expected to be able to adjust and quickly learn or guess the code in order to exchange directly with the spirits. Often, however, the distorted voice of the shaman coupled with the opacity of some of the spirits' assertions made it difficult to get the meaning of what was said, and patients turned to the assistant for a 'translation'.

Moreover, the spirit's initial diagnosis was often quite vague ('you've been cursed by an envious person') and needed to be specified in order to make any sense. This was done by the assistant through the parallel questioning of the spirit ('when was that?' or 'what does the person look like?') and of the patients themselves ('have you recently had a promotion which could elicit envy?', 'have you noticed envy around you lately?', etc.). This triangular interaction thus gradually made an invisible cause appear to the patients: starting with the suspicion of a 'curse', they ended up with the conviction they had been affected by 'a curse from X caused by envy after the promotion received at that particular time'. The actual cure was often rather benign and unimpressive (a few gentle strokes on the back with the whip and a liquid preparation of some sort to be poured outside in a particular direction), which suggests that it was really the manifestation of the spirit and the production of the diagnosis that constituted the crux of the ritual.

The diagnosis produced by the spirits harnessed by these inspirational practitioners might be much more serious, however, and it might involve a completely different kind of invisible things. In another ritual I could attend in 2008, a family was made to learn from spirits speaking through a shaman that they were haunted by the wandering souls of dead convicts from a neighbouring jail (Delaplace with Sambalkhundev 2014). In this case like in others (see Swancutt 2008), the ritual apparatus brought about by the shamans was quite different from Ariuka's: instead of summoning two different spirits in two different rituals, they had a series of different spirits intervene successively during each ritual they performed. Some of these spirits were the shaman's tutelary spirits (*ongon*) and manifested themselves almost every time, while others belonged to the particular location where the ritual was held and could appear only once – sometimes even they were the ones responsible for the family's trouble. Beyond the differences each particular ritual configuration would show, these horizontal/inspirational shamans thus worked by making invisible spirits (and curses) appear in order to 'separate' (*salga-*) people from them (fig. 1).

Figure 3.1 Batmönh, a shaman of the inspirational type, 'lets spirits descend' for a family in Ulaanbaatar. (2008).

Mimicking the past and cajoling ancestors: Liturgical shamans at the nation's rescue

Byambadorj is certainly one of the most famous shamans in Mongolia. A prolific author and a media personality, he claims to hold the title of 'state shaman' (*töriin zairan*) and he has a certificate to prove it, issued by an association of Mongolian scholars. At the time I met him back in 2008, he had pictures of him performing shamanic ceremonies with a former president on a national holiday. The liturgy he had elaborated for his rituals was very stable and rather transparent. It revolved mainly around the declamation of invocations – often read out loud from his own books – celebrating Mongolian land, ancestors and imperial history. Absolutely pivotal in this liturgy was the worship of the 'Eternal Skies' (*Mönh Tenger*), generally held to be the overarching transcendent principle in Mongolian people's land and lives and often believed to have been at the very centre of Mongolian religious practice in medieval times. Byambadorj's declared purpose was indeed to re-establish shamanism as it used to be carried out at the time of Chinggis Khan, as a religion of the Eternal Skies that led the Empire to conquer the world, until the conversion to Buddhism estranged Mongolian people from their traditions and ancestors. He was not isolated in this endeavour; other shamans pursued the same goal with varying support from political parties and traditionalist associations, conferring both with spirits and with scholars to recreate the supposedly exact form of ancient Mongolian shamanic practice (see Merli 2010 for an overview).

In 2008 and 2009, Byambadorj received patients in his Shamanic Centre (*Böö Mörgöliin Töv*), where he also conducted rituals in association with several of his disciples. Set up on a small plot of land north of the city, the Centre was dominated by a large stone cairn covered in blue ceremonial scarves. Incoming patients were admitted in a yurt in the middle of the courtyard, flanked with a small cement house used as a shop and as a resting place for shamans in between rituals and consultations. The inside of the yurt seemed to take visitors to another era – mostly imaginary although vaguely reminiscent of movie representations of pre-revolutionary Mongolia. An archaic tripod replaced the metallic stove found at the centre of any yurt today, and the altar opposite the door was crowded with piles of ritual artefacts: spirit figurations of all kinds and depictions of wolves howling in the snow hanged next to costumes and ritual props such as wooden sprinkling spoons. Dominating this chaotic hodgepodge, a large portrait of Chinggis Khan seemed to be overseeing the pantheon of tutelary spirits, ancestors and animal figures laid out in this ritual space.

Sitting on the left side of this yurt, Byambadorj and his disciples received patients throughout the week; they came to consult them on all kinds of issues involving misfortune and/or sickness. Using divinatory means, the shamans would deliver a diagnosis, and most of the time, instruct them to come back on Sunday for what they called the 'reparation day' (*zasalt ödör*). On 'reparation day', all the patients' troubles were dealt with collectively through a weekly congregational ritual which could not but evoke some sort of a grand shamanic mass. In order to attend reparation day, each patient was told to bring a specific set of things: a bottle of vodka and a plate of biscuits and candies, and sometimes also a portrait of a particular spirit or deity. When I arrived at the Centre one Sunday shortly before eleven to attend the ritual myself, I found a good fifty people waiting on their own in the ritual yurt, sitting on benches lined up in the middle of the yurt and chatting among themselves about what they should expect. The whole space looked completely packed.

At eleven o'clock sharp, two of Byambadorj's disciples made their entry in the yurt and found their way between congregants to the empty space in front of the altar opposite the door. As an assistant was handing vodka bottles to the shamans, they kept emptying them by sprinkling great quantities of liquor on the altar over the spirit figurations. Chinggis Khan, in particular, seemed to receive a large part of these offerings, to the point of having vodka literally drip from the lower side of his portrait. The two shamans, calm and composed in their full costume, then proceeded to raise their arms, kneel and prostrate themselves before the altar, below Chinggis's and other ancestors' portraits. Then, still raising their arms to the sky, they recited one of the invocations to Mongolia's land, rivers, mountains and tutelary spirits contained in Byambadorj's book, interspacing these with repeated prostrations. Meanwhile, the public was sitting with their hands open and their palms upwards, as if to receive the invisible benefits of the practitioners' invocations (fig. 2). Each time the shamans would pronounce the fortune-calling formula *hurai hurai hurai*, well known to every Mongolian (and not specific to shamanic practice, see Chabros 1992), they were echoed by the whole of the congregation, which did not need to be told so to perform in unison the circular gesture customarily associated with this invocation. The purpose, in this ritual setting, seemed first and foremost to acquire individually a fortune bestowed collectively by ancestors after they were rightly cajoled by the shamans' well-established liturgy.

After new series of aspersions on the spirit figurations, the two shamans ostensibly seized their drums and started beating them in different rhythms while chanting unintelligible words. They acted with a growing excitement

Figure 3.2 Byambadorj's disciples during worship on 'Reparation Day' (2008)

and seemed to progressively lose control of their movements, doing more and more erratic gestures with their torso and their drums. Sometimes, however, *hurai hurai* could be still heard in their chanting (and it was still echoed by the public). Sometimes also place names could be made out from their otherwise incomprehensible chanting. Meanwhile, the assistant had resumed the aspersions and kept drowning the spirit figurations in litres and litres of vodka. After a final prostration before the altar, the second part of the ceremony started, in which each patient was personally seen by one of the shamans, who were now sitting on each side of the yurt. Sitting at a table in front of her patient, a shaman would play on her mouth-harp and ring her bell over the bottle of vodka they had brought, this without uttering a word of explanation about what she was doing. After a while, she would light a match and throw it in the bottle: depending on how it went out, the 'reparation' was judged successful or not, and the operation was stopped or resumed accordingly. In some cases, when the patients had been prescribed a 'body reparation' (*biyeiin zasal*), they were ushered behind a curtain: after instructing them to take off their top, a shaman would spit vodka all over their torso (Byambadorj usually did this part) and wield swords or whips around them with theatrical gestures. Before they left, patients would go and see the other shaman on the opposite side of the yurt, and they would be given a small parcel containing juniper powder and spring water potentialized with the sound of a mouth-harp. They were instructed to use it to wash their hands and face, facing a specific direction, and not to give away the biscuits and candies they had brought to people other than their own household members.

The difference between the liturgy of the 'reparation day' and the spirit-channelling practices of inspirational shamans is striking indeed. The purpose of Byambadorj's disciples' invocations and gesticulations in front of the altar seemed not really to have the spirits 'descend' in them. Throughout the ritual, as a matter of fact, offerings and prostrations were explicitly (even insistently) made *towards* the altar, suggesting the spirits were still to be reached through their figurations, rather than through the shamans. It is actually even doubtful that the purpose of the ritual was to have spirits appear at all. Their presence, mediated by the obscure pile of paintings and carvings which represented them on the altar, did not vary in intensity throughout the ritual. Most importantly, spirits did not express themselves through the shamans, whose performed trance and beating of drums was not meant to channel an invisible being supposed to deliver a message through their mouth. The impersonation of shamanic folklore and the performance of an imagined past through a fixed and precise liturgy, actually, seemed to be directed less to the audience than to the tutelary spirits themselves. In other words, the purpose of this 'reparation day' seemed not so much to allow spirits to deliver a message to ailing humans than to ensure that (ailing?) spirits would get the message that humans were sending to them. And the message to be delivered was rather clear: we Mongols, as a community, are united through our past and our relationship to our land. Pretty much in line with the model of 'vertical shamanism' described by Hugh-Jones (1994) in North-western Amazonia, these shamans healed individuals by ensuring first and foremost an ordered and long-lasting collective relation with the country's tutelary spirits and historical ancestors – rather than through the individual and punctual intervention of a spirit on a single patient through a possessed shaman.

Conclusion

When I went for a visit at Byambadorj's Shamanic Centre in Ulaanbaatar in the summer of 2019, I was in for quite a surprise. It was his daughter who was running things now, and it was her that shamans and assistants going about in the Centre called their 'teacher' (*bagsh*). Byambadorj was still around, people told me, but he did not come so much as before, and he preferred to stay in his country house where he would receive visits from time to time. His books were still for sale at the Centre – a couple more had come out since last time – and the Centre's activities seemed basically unchanged. A small placard on the yurt's door advertised the daily opening hours for consultations and the schedule of weekly rituals; it was Sunday, and I was planning to attend 'reparation day' as I had done a decade before. My hopes were up, it was almost eleven and several shamans seemed ready to take part; Byambadorj's daughter was not present herself – it was summer, the attendance was low and she was out on a trip – but another young shaman was here to fill up for her and head the ceremony. Another floor had been added to the concrete building and this is where collective ceremonies were held now. I sat on one of the benches, with a bit of a snug confidence in my ethnographic savvy. Nobody knew me, but I already knew what was going to happen. I was waiting for the prostrations, the heavy aspersions, the erratic movements and the invocations drawn from the latest among Byambadorj's books. Perhaps there would be a few changes, something to add in a footnote in future ethnographic accounts, but I knew the basic structure would remain unchanged. It had to, because this was one of the two possible modalities that I had identified time and again in the rituals I had attended since 2008.

And yet, it did not. 'Reparation day' had changed dramatically. After a few aspersions to the altar – still as furnished and eclectic as before, with Chinggis Khan still in the most honoured place – each shaman started beating their drum in one particular section of the room. Some mouth-harp could be heard emerging at particular moments. A particular sonic atmosphere started coming together, piece after piece, to which each performer contributed in an independent and yet coordinated way. Compared to the intentional cacophony I had witnessed back in 2008 and 2009, this sounded like an opposite effort of mutual adjustment. It is not until then that I noticed each shaman was flanked with one particular assistant, who had prepared the tea, vodka and food platter used to welcome incoming spirits during the therapeutic rituals of shamans of the inspirational type. And indeed, one after the other, in an independent yet coordinated way, they started letting in a spirit, transforming their attitude under the influence of the particular spirit they had summoned. Often it was that of an old person, characteristic in the voice, breath and broken posture, but I could also make out other demeanours, such as that of a young coquette. Some seemed to let in one spirit only, others a succession of different ones (fig. 3).

I was quite taken aback. What I had seen Ariuka and many other shamans do in individual rituals since 2008 was now performed collectively. The neat opposition I had held to be structural in Mongolian shamanic practice, between collective

Figure 3.3 'Reparation Day' in 2019

ceremonies directed by liturgical masters and inspirational rituals involving the actual manifestation of spirits, seemed to be blurring before my eyes. What I saw that day may be short-lived, or it might take very soon a wholly different shape; yet it is nothing if not a testimony to the labile character of shamanic practice in Mongolia and to the continuing ritual inventiveness through which Mongolian people cultivate a mystical relation to the deep past they put at the centre of their personal and collective lives. This new ritual configuration could also be taken as a hint and perhaps as an encouragement to look at the relational apparatus implemented during rituals as cosmopolitical device of far-reaching import. Watching these small relational nodes of interconnected individuals, collectively conversing with spirits in an autonomous yet coordinated way, I could not help seeing in this the enactment of a particular take on liberal democracy. Here was a situation of common adjustment where everybody tended collectively to one's own private business in the relative secrecy of mutual anonymity: within this ritual apparatus, facing the deep past became a responsibility that everybody bore collectively, and freely, for everyone else.

4

Indigenous rituals remake the larger-than-human community

Graham Harvey
The Open University, UK

What would democracy look like if it involved the larger-than-human community? What events would promote and structure such multispecies communal participation? How could moves be made away from globally dominant anthropocentric notions and practices of politics and society-making towards thoroughly pluralistic and truly inclusive alternatives? What barriers surround the status quo of human exceptionalism or separatism, maintaining and protecting it from challenging visions and possibilities? Conversely, what matters within current cultural imaginations and systems could nurture more expansive ways of forming communities and enhancing relationships? What current conversations among humans expand into more widespread dialogue and diplomacy among that larger-than-human community? Crucially: What kind of persons are implicated in the making of the diverse kinds of democracy evoked in or behind these questions?

In this chapter I consider ways in which some Indigenous[1] festivals and some performances within them emerge from ritual repertoires and contribute towards addressing some of the above questions. Research at the annual Sámi organized, Riddu Riđđu festival[2] and the biennial ORIGINS Festival of First Nations[3] in London provides the primary material from which my reflections emerge. Like other festivalgoers (locals and visitors), I have been both entertained and educated, enthused and provoked. 'Deep hanging out' (Geertz 1998) and casual conversations that turned out be freighted with great significance have been part of the process of my learning from, among and with Indigenous hosts and knowledge-holders. Some more formal interviews have largely been means of checking the adequacy of my understanding of what I think I have experienced or been told. My rootedness in the academic study of religions has predisposed me to attend to the more ritualized or ritually informed aspects of these and other festivals and performances. Experience, reading and discussion with colleagues (some included within this book) have deepened my appreciation of boundary-transgressing flows between ritual and theatre, education and entertainment and other apparent dichotomies. In particular, it is the sense that some performance pieces are potentially initiatory and transformative that alerts me to the possibility that festivals might create or enhance democracy for a larger polity.

Introducing Riddu Riđđu

Riddu Riđđu is an annual Indigenous cultural festival organized by a coastal Sámi community in an area simultaneously known as western Sápmi[4] and Arctic Norway. It is hosted in Olmmáivággi (Manndalen in Norwegian) in the arctic municipality of Kåfjord in July each year since 1991. The festival's name means 'small storm at the coast'. It was initiated in the wake of the Sámi cultural revival – or perhaps the revival of pride in being Sámi which preceded that cultural revival. The festival's website is updated each year, but it always includes a summary of the history of the festival. The current page (Riddu Riđđu 2019) usefully sets out the festival's evolution from youthful conversations at a barbeque in 1991 to a cultural event of considerable international significance (also see publications by Siv Ellen Kraft 2009 and Thomas Hilder 2014).

Riddu Riđđu's origins and ethos as a storm of controversy about what it means to be Sámi, how to express sovereignty and, for some, how to develop the resources of traditional culture have continued to generate a storm of cultural creativity. Alongside Sámi participants, the festival now attracts performers and artists from many Indigenous nations globally. For example, it can include Māori rock bands, Mayan theatre groups, Mongolian throat-singers, Andean rappers, Khoi jazz poets and Cree film directors. The majority of festivalgoers are probably Sámi from the nearby locality and from across Sápmi. However, buses from regional airports (Tromsø and Alta) enable significant attendance by broader national and international audiences, many of them Indigenous. For all the excitement of festivity and spectacle, Riddu Riđđu has never lost its vision of encouraging and enhancing participation in Sámi and other Indigenous communities and cultures, and of contesting Indigenous marginalization in cultural, political, economic and other arenas. The festival's demonstration of Indigenous creativity and global connectedness promotes self-determination and self-representation as vital aspects of Indigenous sovereignty. In these and other ways, Riddu Riđđu expands the possibilities for understanding democracy.

The main festival site is in a bend in a river flowing from the mountains to the nearby fjord. A permanent cultural centre (the Center for Northern People) houses the organizers' offices, a library, gallery and seminar rooms, a performance space, showers and other facilities useful both for the festival and for local people outside of festival times. The site has a main stage area and nearby spaces that become a marketplace for Indigenous goods and the location of bars for alcoholic and soft drinks. Several food outlets are set up during the festival. A permanent cedar-log longhouse (constructed in a style traditional among the Nisga'a First Nation from British Columbia, Canada) is the most prominent construction in an otherwise temporary cultural village in which an earth lodge, lavvus (Sámi tents), tipis, small marquees and other structures are used during the festival for various events and displays. The festival has two main camping areas, a 'party field' near the main site and one further away up a hill for families and those desiring a quieter environment. (During the continuous daylight of the arctic summer the sleep patterns of festivalgoers do not always coincide.) There is a youth camp in which local youths meet each year with others invited from another Indigenous nation (e.g. Ainu or Evenki) to learn and party together. The festival also has a parallel children's programme, including both educational and entertainment events. In addition to main stage concerts, the cultural centre and the cedar log-house host theatrical performances, talks and seminars, art exhibitions, book launches and other literary events and film shows.

Introducing ORIGINS

The ORIGINS Festival of First Nations has been hosted biennially in London, UK, since 2009. Organized by the Border Crossings Company, it brings Indigenous musicians, theatre-makers, visual artists, film-makers and cooks to exhibit and explain, to perform and inform, to debate and celebrate. Put more boldly, 'ORIGINS creates a unique opportunity to engage with Indigenous artists and activists at the cutting edge of cultural resistance, environmentalism and spiritual tradition' (Border Crossings 2019a). Venues across London host diverse events including (but not limited to) dances and musical recitals in the British Museum, films and gallery tours in the National Maritime Museum, comedy and talks at Rich Mix, theatre in Shakespeare's Globe, ritual/spectacle in West End Parks, art in the Baldwin Gallery and in embassy galleries, and walking tours to encounter sites of Imperial and Indigenous engagement. Some of the participants visit schools to provide special intercultural educational opportunities for various age groups. The festival audiences are predominantly Londoners or otherwise British. However, there are events in which performers and other contributors to the festival meet together and enrich their understandings of each others' cultural and artistic traditions. While audiences are expected to be entertained, they are also presented with educational and inspirational opportunities and challenges. The primary goal of the festival is to highlight Indigenous perspectives on contemporary issues including 'the environment, globalization, truth and reconciliation, and healing' and to provide a forum in which audiences and opinion-formers can engage directly with Indigenous representatives. A short film, 'Indigenous in London' (Open University 2016), accessible on YouTube not only introduces ORIGINS but also presents some of the festival performers addressing themes discussed in this chapter.

Trans-Indigeneity, custom and ritual

Riddu Riđđu and ORIGINS expand the possibilities of Chadwick Allen's term 'trans-Indigenous'. He coined this to advance critical consideration of literatures and other cultural productions in which works from different places, communities or cultures contribute to a global Indigenous movement. He argues that comparative conjunctions (e.g. 'American Indian *and* Maori') can encourage invidious assertions of likeness or difference, doing nothing to produce 'an enlarged view of evolving cultures or their (post)colonial histories, or a more precise analysis of self-representation' (2012: xiv). Conversely, the prefix *trans-* enables more productive scholarship by attending to processes of juxtaposition, crossing, unequal and/or uneven encounter, change and, most powerfully, transformation. At Riddu Riđđu and ORIGINS Indigenous performers, artists and culture teachers encounter each other and participate in the co-creation of transformative events and inspire further respect for Indigenous arts, cultures and lives. Indeed, they are the creation of global Indigeneity, rich with complex similarities, differences, diplomacy and conversation.

The festivals also provide rich examples of the resonance between Allen's 'trans-Indigenous' and the term 'trans-customary' which inspires him. As he writes,

> Māori artist and art scholar Robert Jahnke has developed a conceptual model for contemporary Māori visual art that imagines a continuum running between the pole 'customary' (art created by Māori that maintains 'a visual correspondence with historical models') and its opposite pole, 'non-customary' (art created by Māori in which 'visual correspondence and empathy with historical models [is] absent'). Much of contemporary Māori art is produced in the vast middle space between these poles, Jahnke argues, and it is neither 'hybrid' nor caught 'between' but 'trans-customary': art that establishes not a strict correspondence with customary forms but rather a 'visual empathy with customary practice' through the use of 'pattern, form, medium and technique'.
>
> (Allen 2012: 153, citing Jahnke 2006: 48–50)

In other words, ancestors handed on patterns or protocols that had served well as they adapted to situations in their time and established a 'customary pole' to which further generations could resort as necessary.

Such trans-customary resources are employed in evolving all sorts of performances, as illustrated in the following brief examples from Riddu Riđđu. A Tuvan zither (a *yat kha*) might be played to accompany not only the Tuvan *kanzat kargyraa* throat-singing style, but also Indigenized reggae, rock or country genres. ('Indigenized' alludes to the analytical continuum 'indigenization–extension' proposed by Paul C. Johnson 2005.) First Nation Canadian and Māori bands invite Sámi colleagues to meld yoik chants into their performances. Allen and Jahnke's 'vast middle space' is strongly evoked by frequent references to the authority of Nils-Aslak Valkepää, the late poet-laureate of Sápmi, whose revitalization of yoik as a contemporary art form with historical inspiration is widely celebrated. Similarly, in her several appearances at Riddu Riđđu festivals, Moana (lead singer of Moana and the Tribe) has opened her band's set by calling 'From our mountains to your mountains, from our rivers to your rivers'. This translates one element of traditional Māori greetings (particularly in guest-making *powhiri* ceremonies) to achieve various purposes including locating performers and audiences in relation to places of origin, honouring the local (Indigenous) land and its custodians, placing visitors and hosts in relation to Indigenous traditional knowledges and protocols and acknowledging that mountains and rivers actively participate in these relationships.

In these examples, the customary pole of the continuum in Jahnke's model is largely formed from rituals. These are adapted and improvised on to create performance acts of many kinds. Potentially, here as elsewhere, the juxtaposition of the terms 'ritual' and 'performance' is transformative. According to Jonathan Z. Smith's definition:

> Ritual is a means of performing the ways things ought to be in conscious tension to the way things are in such a way that this ritualized perfection is recollected in the ordinary, uncontrolled, course of things. (1982: 63)[5]

More recent scholarship (e.g. Grimes 2006, 2014a) focuses on what people actually do and what actually happens when people do rituals. It is less impressed by distinctions between ritual and theatre – because both require the collaboration of all those present during performances, because both can be life-changing to one degree or another and because the interplay of script and improvisation is shared between them. Inspired by Allen, Jahnke and Grimes's provocations, I propose that Smith's dictum might be shifted to make it both future facing and subjunctive, as follows:

> Ritual is a means of performing the ways things *might become* in *conversation with customary practice* in such a way that this ritualized *innovation might inform* the ordinary *and always emerging*, course of things.

The relationship between theatre and ritual is not usefully described by contrasts between, for example, fixity and innovation, performers and audiences, transformation and entertainment. These putative contrasts more often play out as creative flows. Such perspectives on ritual and performance inform the following discussion of what happens at Riddu Riđđu and ORIGINS when Indigenous performers draw on customary rituals to innovate performances that captivate and potentially educate others about relating with(in) the larger-than-human world.

Relationality, dividuals and rituals

To grasp some of what is at stake in the constitution of Indigenous communities, it is useful to consider the notion and performance of *dividual* relationality. The term 'dividual' originated with McKim Marriot's (1976) discussion of 'diversity without dualism' among Indian Hindus and with Marilyn Strathern's (1988) contrast between the ambitions of Melanesians and 'Westerners' to grow different kinds of person. Both Marriot and Strathern contrasted ideal types and recognized that in lived reality both conceptions of personhood and relationality are evident everywhere. In the specifics of real life, cultures emerge from continuous tensions between differences of valuation, emphasis and ambition to grow individuals or dividuals. Whatever the value of Bruno Latour's assertion that 'we have never been modern' (1993; also see Latour 2013), the project of Modernity has emphasized the interiority, separateness and singularity of individuals. For example, in the realm of politics and citizenship, Modern persons are expected to demonstrate loyalty as individual taxpayers and voters in Nation States, neither constrained nor compelled by other kinds of relationship. Citizens might also be cousins, chefs, drivers, pet-owners, club-members, bloggers and other kinds of relation. While such relationships are not negated by the requirements of citizenship, they are seen as different, other-than-political ways in which each putatively bounded and discrete self relates to other individuals. Principally, however, it was the curtailment of transnational loyalties (e.g. loyalties to Roman Catholic or Protestant princes) in the process of organizing Nation States according to Westphalian system principles (Cavanaugh 1995, 2009) that most forcefully shaped Modern citizenship.

In several conferences I have contrasted definitions of 'person' which privilege interiority with a relational and/or animistic understanding of the 'in-between-ness' of persons-as-relations. In attempting to evoke the integral and definitive dividual relationality of animists, I have portrayed personhood as something that happens *between* people as they engage with others. This requires more careful reflection, especially because, as Arnar Árnason points out, the Modern assumption is that 'social relations exist between points, or roles, in a structure, or at best *between* the people temporarily occupying these positions' (2012: 68, original emphasis).[6] Dividual personhood is conceived differently. Persons are not points or positions in a structure but assemblages of (plural and fluid) relations. It is precisely in engaging and interacting with others that personhood emerges. It is not a matter of identity but of performance or interaction. A person is the performance of relationality with and among others. Perhaps I really should follow Nurit Bird-David more closely as she insists that we should think and speak about 'relatives' rather than 'persons' (Bird-David 2018). My reluctance to abandon 'person' is only encouraged because it does seem to trouble more dominant notions about personhood. However, the crucial point here is that because some relations are closer than others, kinship and locality-rooted relations are often crucial to performances and interactions in Indigenous festivals. Encounters with persons with different kinship and locational relations provide opportunities for conversation and the enrichment of trans-Indigeneity.

These contrasts between Modernity and Indigeneity and between individuals and dividuals are all the more important here because they are braided or entangled with divergent valuations of ritual. The religious reformations of Early Modernity paralleled and fuelled developments in political, military and other cultural complexes by hardening and policing the boundaries between previously fluid transnational religious affiliations (again see Cavanaugh 1995, 2009). Certainly there had been previous objections to some ways of doing ritual – biblical and other ancient texts inveighed against ritual divorced from morality and they opposed 'mere show'. But Western European religious reforms privileged belief over action or forms of thought over performances – especially when the latter could mask questionable loyalties. A string of other effects logically followed. Mind and interiority were valued above the sensorium of bodies and matter. At extremes, theatre and dance were also made dangerously suspect unless they could be domesticated and cultivated to serve 'national interests' or 'religious virtues'.

Conversely, Indigenous knowledge systems continued to exalt ceremonies and dramatic storytelling. In periods and places where Indigenous ceremonies were banned, Indigenous knowledges were denigrated and their performers or sharers were persecuted, the subterfuge of 'entertainment' could be employed to aid what Gerald Vizenor calls 'survivance' and 'transmotion' (1999; 2019: 37–51). Powwows and other dances could sometimes not only maintain social connections but also mask the continuing practice of world-making and/or initiatory ceremonies. Such dance cultures continue to evolve to meet contemporary needs and challenges. The more recent flowering of Indigenous literature and film is also similarly resistant to the deadening or depressing imagination of 'disappearing natives' in the face of (claimed) white supremacy. Presence, resistance and creativity are themes of both Riddu Riđđu and ORIGINS, but it is the particular evocation of relations with and among the larger-than-human community which invites further reflection. Entertainment at festivals is part of the entrainment in which ethical imperatives and cultural expectations are presented. Stories encourage knowledge about how to become a *good* person (usually in a lifelong negotiation with local norms) while rituals are among the ways in which ideas or norms become enacted.

Festivals and the larger-than-human community

Festivals are hugely entertaining and enjoyable events. They are full of drama, excitement, novelty, creativity and emotion. Even when performers, films or discussions tackle genocide, colonialism, dislocation, language-loss and other difficult topics they are typically engaging and inspiring. In a chapter like this it is hard to avoid making festivals sound overly serious. While the festivity of these events should not be ignored in favour of elevating all the cultural and political ferment they involve, this chapter focuses on some ways in which festivals bring a larger-than-human community – or a more inclusive polity – into view and consideration. It is about what 'citizen' and 'citizenship' can mean when these are juxtaposed with kinship and other relational terms used in and/or about performances. These are necessary steps in reflecting on how ritually informed performances can broaden and deepen notions and practices of democracy.

It is important to note that the most obvious references to democracy at these festivals focus on relationships between Indigenous communities and the Nation States that dominate them. Treaties, sovereignty, Indigenous and tribal governance, land-rights, respect for subsistence practices and language-use are all more explicitly presented as political issues than relationships with animals, fish and other members of the larger-than-human community. Nonetheless, the latter are not treated as merely romantic additions to the pursuit of liberty and democracy. Indeed, as festivals devoted to contemporary Indigenous performance it is the strong sense that Indigenous arts and creativity are vital to the assertion of sovereignty that makes them valuable in considerations of democracy and its rituals. Within that arena, it is precisely because the notion of a larger-than-human polity cannot be taken-for-granted as a necessary contribution to understanding and improving democracy that it demands attention. The following discussion, therefore, largely pays attention to the performance of relationality to argue that Riddu Riđđu and ORIGINS share with other Indigenous activities an insistence that the project of democracy will remain incomplete until the larger-than-human polity is respected.

Understanding Indigenous polities and their (extensive) citizenry begins with introductions. At Riddu Riđđu and ORIGINS Indigenous performers commonly identify themselves in relation to specific places. This statement might seem banal. Many people introduce themselves as coming from particular nations, regions, cities or communities. Depending on the context they might name the place of their birth or refer to their current hometown or workplace. However, locations are more programmatic within Indigenous cultures. It is not so much the context of colonialism, removal or dislocation – or other aspects of victimry or betrayal (Vizenor 1999, 2019) – but, rather, the definitively Indigenous reference to belonging and kinship that is referenced. There is a shared sensibility among Indigenous participants in these festivals that makes statements about places resonant. Places are not just locations to come from and return to. People belong to places at least as much as places belong to people. Places are communities in which belonging brings responsibilities as well as rights. They emplace kinship and customs. As Keith Basso learnt from his Apache colleagues, 'wisdom sits in places' (1996) and 'sense of place' becomes 'a "mode of communion with a total way of living" … [and] may gather unto itself a potent religious force, especially if one considers the root of the word in *religare*, which is "to bind or fasten fast"' (Basso 1996: 145, citing Seamus Heaney 1980: 133).

Much of this is encapsulated in Moana's Riddu Riđđu greeting ('From our mountains to your mountains, from our rivers to your rivers'), cited earlier. She self-identities as Indigenous to a place and offers respect to the place she now stands in – the place-community of others' Indigeneity. This establishes and shares awareness of the ideological and physical common ground on which Indigenous people meet each other while paying respect to both homeland and the current host community. But Moana's innovation from customary Māori speech-making also makes her a diplomat. She deploys words from guest-making rituals (i.e. ceremonies that transform strangers into guests on Māori land and in Māori communities) to bring a message from distant mountains and rivers to the mountains and rivers surrounding the festival site. This is more than a reference to scenery and not only a merism – that is a rhetorical device in which 'mountains and rivers' refers to the entire place and community. Rather, it acknowledges mountains and rivers as full and active participants in larger-than-human communities. Although spoken in less than ten seconds, Moana's greetings achieved, enacted or performed much of what Riddu Riđđu is about.

Another aspect to Indigenous performers' introductions that might widen our view of the nature of community can be heard in the identification of clan and totemic relationships. Examples are included in the Open University (2016) film 'Indigenous in London'. These show that performers do not consider themselves to be virtuoso individuals but as authorized by their communities to share matters of importance. For those who name themselves in relation to clans and totemic groups it is not only human kin who are referenced but also members of other species. In their understanding, animals, plants, lands and waters are not only 'good to think' (Lévi-Strauss 1969: 89) or heraldic symbols but actual relations, kin within a wider community from which rights and responsibilities follow (also see Harvey 2013: 126–7).

In addition to naming the place- and clan-communities from which they come, Indigenous performers at Riddu Riđđu and ORIGINS typically acknowledge the priority, prestige and authority of their host communities. Moana's greeting does this in its acknowledgement of local mountains and rivers and those located in relation to them. Others use phrases like 'we honour the traditional owners or custodians of this land'. This is more than 'it's nice to be here' or 'thanks for having me'. Often it involves seeking permission from hosts to share knowledge or customs brought from elsewhere. At Riddu Riđđu this is as straightforward as it is in other Indigenous-led events, especially those on lands not ceded to colonial or settler Nation States. Nonetheless, precisely because it refers to ideas and practices that have evolved in distant communities, it can be challenging because of its difference from local customs. At its most positive, the honouring of hosts or local knowledges is a bright thread woven through the festival – well exemplified when visiting performers invite Sámi colleagues to join them on stage, perhaps to add yoik chants to their acts.

At ORIGINS things are more complex. The opening ceremony is conducted according to protocols that Indigenous people recognize as respectful ways to initiate events (Harvey 2018). Visiting performers and participants are greeted, speeches of welcome are offered and references are made to location and ancestry. The festival director, Michael Walling, does this in concert with Indigenous colleagues. They always include an Indigenous Associate for the festival, someone who lives in London (or nearby) but is authorized by an Indigenous nation or community to represent them in some capacity. In 2019 the Associate was Stephanie Pratt, Cultural Ambassador of the Crow Creek Dakota Nation. Alongside her at the opening ceremony, the GAFA Arts Collective adapted the customs of the Samoan Ava ceremony to greet invited performers, artists, speakers and other festival participants. Crucially, this involves the pouring of libations honouring the larger-than-human community and ancestors before participants drink from the bowl ceremonially offered to them. Much of this could happen on Indigenous lands. That it happens in London makes it distinctive. Colonialism in its many forms and manifestations is not ignored. ORIGINS is not about decorating the dominant culture with spectacles of diversity, and appropriation is discouraged. In his opening speech, Michael Walling uses words like conversation, equity, justice, complexity and provocation. When he speaks of loss, he does not evoke an imaginary pre-contact purity and subsequent disappearance but addresses the diminishment of all lives and cultures under the continuing impact of colonization. He speaks of London's shameful bankrolling of such colonization. Bringing Indigenous people to London is part of his ambition to 'offer a space for a true diversity of languages, experiences, ideas and actions' in order to deepen a conversation aimed at 'allowing the Earth to become a space that we can all jointly inhabit in a sustainable, just and equitable way' (Border Crossings 2019b: 2). It is possible to see in this a respectful learning from Indigenous people about how to apply Indigenous customary practices to contemporary contexts and, thereby, to appreciate that the interactive patterns of relational empathy have been effectively transmitted.

Indigenous contributors to the ORIGINS programme often continue this negotiation between respecting their hosts and contesting colonization. With considerable generosity and characteristic (somewhat edgy) humour, performers respond warmly to the possibility of speaking back to 'the Empire' and of encouraging audiences to consider the potential of different ways of relating to the world. For example, in the 2019 programme book Madeline Sayet introduces her 'Where we belong' performance (at the Sam Wanamaker Playhouse at Shakespeare's Globe) by saying,

> I share this story to honour [Mohegan ancestors, Mahomet Weyonomon and Samson Occom, who came to London in the 1700s], to offer voice to the many moments when we were all silenced. To remind the world that there is no such thing as the Last of the Mohegans. That not only are we here, but we may be in places you least expect.
>
> (Border Crossings 2019b: 6)

Crucially, her performance arose from the experience of abandoning UK-based doctoral research about Shakespeare, going home and finding that she missed England. Wondering if this made her a 'traitor' she explored ancestral and present-day journeys and relations, exploring 'questions that connect us in a world that seems set on building borders to divide us from one another'. In ways like these, Sayet and other Indigenous participants in ORIGINS offer careful respect to London hosts as well as forcefully sharing their discomfort with past and present colonialisms that diminish efforts towards increasing democracy.

At both Riddu Riđđu and ORIGINS there are frequent references to trans-generational presence and involvement. A parallel youth camp and events at Riddu Riđđu bring young people from different Indigenous nations together. They are intended to encourage younger Indigenous people to take pride and take part in their communities and in wider Indigenous movement. During ORIGINS a number of Indigenous performers spend time in local schools, not only offering talks to convey information but leading workshop-style sessions to enable more experiential and dialogical encounters. In both contexts, educational opportunities (tied in with creative activities) have a view to the longer term and arise from ambitions for increased understanding and dialogue between future generations. In both festivals it is common to hear references to 'the seventh generation' or to taking 'seven generations' into account when considering any activity that might affect the future. As noted already, there are flows – some more complex than others – between celebrating Indigeneity and challenging more dominant cultural norms and processes. However, these youth-focused events might be labelled 're-generative' to fuse different senses of 'generation' in a way that hopes for a more equitable and inclusive future.

Riddu Riđđu and ORIGINS are not only trans-generational and re-generative in seeking to generate the future in the present moment, but they also make ancestors present. In addition to introductory speeches in which ancestors are invoked and/or acknowledged, there are performances in which those who have died are explicitly said to participate. In the 2015 ORIGINS festival, the Zugubal Dancers from Badu Island, Zenadh-Kes (or Torres Strait), brought their mask dances to the British Museum. Some years before, the dance group's director, Alick Tipoti, had seen *Mawa* masks in the museum's collection and told them he would return to dance for them. He gathered and trained a group and made replicas of ancestral masks which could be taken abroad and displayed to uninitiated and non-Indigenous audiences. But a 'replica' of a 'representation' of an ancestor (as these masks could be described) is also the real thing: an ancestor mask (see Altieri 2000; Harvey 2016; also see Whitehead 2013). Thus, at the British Museum, the Zugubal Dancers followed cultural protocols (e.g. not smiling while wearing their masks and costumes) both in their public performance and in their private audience with the older masks in the museum's collection. (Some of the public performance can be seen in the 'Indigenous in London' film, Open University 2016.) For Tipoti and his colleagues, the ancestors are not gone into a distant time or place but are in the dance, the dancing and the dancers. The masks are 'spiritual beings' (Tipoti's translation of *Zugubal*) and 'spiritual ancestors' (or *Muruygal*). They become present and observable as the masks move before and among their audiences, so that performance events potentially transform participants. They transform communities by materializing the presence of ancestors and enact the activity (and acting ability) of masks as animate persons. The definition, institutions and practice of democracy might be deeply affected by taking these trans-generational and other-than-human persons into account.

Riddu Riđđu and ORIGINS both provide other examples of ways in which the larger-than-human world is important to Indigenous people as more than location. Here I cite a conversation by a river. In 2014 the river that flows around three sides of the Riddu Riđđu festival site came very near to flooding. As I watched the river overflowing rocks on which ravens often sit, a local man told me, 'This isn't good for us, but it's a disaster for the trout and even more so the salmon.' He explained that the fish were currently waiting to swim up the river to spawn. They too have their homelands, their Indigeneity. The flow and near ice-cold temperature of the water prevented them. The man asserted that the trout might just find another river. But, he said, the salmon would only return to the river of their birth. If the river flow kept them away, there would be no more salmon in this river. I might have mis-remembered whether it was trout and salmon that are most particular about their rivers. Equally, the man might have been misinformed. My point in summarizing the conversation is that this man appeared to be repeating what other local people were concerned about. (I acknowledge here that it is not only Sámi and other Indigenous people who are concerned for the well-being of fish, rivers and others.) While the threat to fish has clear dangers to coastal Sámi livelihoods – and perhaps to aspects of the cultural renaissance which Riddu Riđđu is encouraging – it was absolutely clear that concern for the well-being, culture and rights of the fish and other river beings was the major issue. No yoik was offered, only deep concern and a sense of regret that human greed had caused this problem. Climate change may be global but at that moment particular fish in a particular river concerned a particular man and his community. Inter-species relationality might be a thoroughly Indigenous cultural emphasis, even a definitive element of trans-Indigeneity, but it is a theme elaborated from many vital local acts and encounters. Perhaps, after all, the man was yoiking.

Festive persons, democratic growth

At Riddu Riđđu and ORIGINS the active presence of Indigenous performers and other participants is already an increase in democracy. A long history of destruction, marginalization and silencing is resisted and contested by such presence and performance. An alternative world is already made in which colonialism and genocide are not the only foundations for performances and other contemporary actions, nor do they strictly delimit the available trajectories of emergent political, ecological and other futures. Nation States are not the only ways to assemble communities and perform belonging and personhood. Voting, electioneering, forming political parties and tax-paying are not the only ways to engage with others in communities.

Chris Hartney's intervention into efforts to define 'indigenous' provides part of a larger picture of sovereignty:

> An indigenous tradition is one that continues to interrupt, problematise, and outright challenge the sovereignty claims of the modernist, post-colonial nation with its own claims of abiding sovereignty. … This [unique political place of indigenous communities] is the holding of claims to sovereignty that precede and may not necessarily be extinguished by the sovereignty of the 'modern' and 'rational' secular state. … The 1933 Montevideo Convention of the Rights and Duties of States legally defines a state as, amongst other conditions, an entity that has the 'capacity to enter into relations with other states.' In light of this, the simplest way to identify an indigenous community is to demarcate a community that is able to enter into relations, sympathies, and solidarities with other self-defined indigenous communities.
>
> (Hartney 2016: 221–2)

As Indigenous sovereignty has not been extinguished, Indigenous polities might outlast Westphalian Nation State constitutions and provide models for their replacement. In the meantime, Vizenor establishes the current importance of cultural creativity:

> The actual practices of survivance create a vital and astute sense of presence over absence in history, stories, art, and literature. 'The nature of survivance creates a sense of narrative resistance to absence, literary tragedy, nihility, and victimry. Native survivance is an active sense of presence over historical absence' and the manifest manners of monotheism and cultural dominance. Native survivance is a continuance of visionary stories.
>
> (Vizenor 2019: 38, citing Vizenor 2009: 1, 162)

Riddu Riđđu and ORIGINS confirm and affirm the contemporary cultural creativity of Indigenous people and present the possibility of new visions and increased liberty. The festivals go beyond 'narrative resistance' to place vision and creativity at the centre of stages. They invite responses not only (even if most immediately) from audiences but also from the embassies and other institutions of those Nation States which fund performers' participation and/or provide gallery spaces and other resources.

The presence of Indigenous people on international stages is already a transformation of a political and cultural world from which they were meant to have been removed – except perhaps as emblems of primitivity, romantic fantasies or savage terrors. Also, the interactions of performers from different Indigenous nations with each other and with their hosts and audiences – usually expressive of 'respect' – illustrate possibilities for diplomacy between communities. But their performances add more. Indigenous performers and those responsive to them create opportunities to evolve democracy to involve the larger-than-human world. Even when this is not the main focus of a particular festival – or of the performances, installations, talks, films or other contributions to them – the widely shared Indigenous notion that humans are not the only persons is resonant and productive. Subtly stated in greetings or powerfully proclaimed from stages, screens and platforms, the pervasive Indigenous understanding that the world is larger-than-human enriches democratic thinking and activism.

Simultaneously, Riddu Riđđu and ORIGINS evoke and encourage the celebration and enactment of relational and dividual ontologies. They proclaim that there are no utterly separate individuals but always relations to be respected. Communities are variously structured and assembled – but always as relations, and always in emergent and never entirely finished, fixed or static forms. Democracy is one label for modes of assembling polities in which there is an ideal (never yet perfectly performed) of forms of participation by an increasing majority of a community. Ideas about what forms of participation are legitimate (voting, protest, representative government, anarchist associations, etc.) have varied and changed. But what interests me here is the contribution Indigenous festivals – and the customary rituals from which many arise – make to understanding 'community'. Questions about what rituals aid the increase and practice of democracy follow from that.

The ideal type (i.e. the ambition teased with and teased out in creation narratives and world-making rites as much as in festivals) is of an all-embracing larger-than-human community of persons (human and otherwise) whose co-inhabitation of a place (or shared emplacement) brings mutual responsibilities (also see Rose 1992, 1997, 2004). When Indigenous performers contribute to festivals they innovate from customary or traditional rites and stories to present – and make present – alternatives to the status quo. Trans-Indigenous, trans-cultural acts translate Indigenous commitments to the larger-than-human community into action. They take knowledge that has already been driven 'deeply into the bone' (Grimes 2000) of Indigeneity by repeated ritualization and narration and improvise performances of many kinds to inject the knowledge and respectful practice of relationality into the body politic of audiences and their communities. In doing so they expand on Grimes's reflections:

> What ritual dynamics might facilitate assemblages that foster justice and the thriving of a multitude of species on the planet? The beginning of a provisional answer is something like: Rituals that include, or are preceded by, at least one

> sustained improvisational phase that stimulates attuned co-acting among the species, and that facilitates self-critical reflexivity.
>
> (Grimes, this volume; also see Grimes 2013).

The trans-customary performances of Riddu Riđđu and ORIGINS, and trans-Indigenous dialogue on them, point powerfully towards the ritually informed achievement of increases in liberty, sovereignty, inter-species conversation and, thereby, a larger-than-human democracy.

Riddu Riđđu and ORIGINS cultivate democratic sensibilities and cultures by encouraging more active participation by Indigenous festivalgoers in their communities, by educating other audience members about the presence and creativity of Indigenous performers and by establishing that 'community' is larger than but inclusive of the human polity. Leanne Howe's statement about stories is equally applicable to rituals and the festival performances they generate:

> Our stories are unending connections to the past, present, and future. And, even if the worst comes to the worst and our people forget where we left our stories, the birds will remember and bring them back to us.
>
> (Howe 2013: 38, cited in Justice 2018: xvii; also see Harvey 2017: 100–1)

In those stories and other acts, democratic relations within the larger-than-human world are renewed.

5

Becoming autonomous together: Distanced intimacy in dances of self-discovery

Michael Houseman

In most large Western cities, hundreds of people attend weekly sessions of collective dancing explicitly aimed to promote 'self-discovery', 'authenticity' and 'connection with others': 5 Rhythms, Biodanza, Movement Medicine and Open Floor, among others (Houseman, Mazzella di Bosco and Thibaut 2016). On these occasions, participants' ability to engage with fellow dancers in a spontaneous, heartfelt, creative manner is unceasingly elicited and displayed. As expected, the physical interactions they have with each other are often deemed to be of exceptional power and eloquence. It is thus noteworthy that those who take part in these practices rarely become close friends or lovers. They may be familiar with the superficial facts of each other's lives, but remain passing acquaintances at best. They are 'consequential strangers' (Fingerman 2009) who, as a rule, tend not to socialize beyond the dance sessions themselves and activities related to them. The extent to which this rule applies varies from one local context to the next (cf. Pike 2017; Mazzella di Bosco 2020). However, what remains constant is a striking hiatus between the intense interpersonal intimacy participants are given to share and the lack of interpersonal commitment that these experiences might be expected to imply. Generally speaking, it is with those with whom dancers feel free *not* to have close relationships, that they develop and demonstrate their aptitude for entering into close relationships with hypothetical others at a further remove.

Moisseeff (2012, 2016c) has emphasized the increasingly important role played by this type of distanced intimacy in the present-day West, notably in psychotherapy and other related practices (coaching, counselling, etc.). Their practitioners are able to become the custodians of their clients' private lives precisely by virtue of the fact that they are not members of their intimate circle. Accordingly, the interactions characteristic of these 'unnatural relationships'

(Moisseeff 2004), although often highly emotional, are oriented not towards developing and handling interpersonal dependencies (as is the case of relations with loved ones and family members) but, on the contrary, towards asserting and preserving personal autonomy. In this chapter, I will be concerned with the workings of this peculiar mode of interaction as an essential feature of what I have loosely identified as 'dances of self-discovery'.

I argue that these practices afford participants with an experience of self-actualization, that of consciously becoming whom one is conventionally prompted to feel one is meant to be: 'spontaneous', 'creative' and 'open to others'. In this regard, these dances fulfil what many see as the defining imperative of contemporary Western individualism, namely the continuous, purposeful construction of the self (e.g. Giddens 1991; Taylor 2007; Le Bart 2008). There is, however, a further complementary aspect to these practices, which is being part of a collectivity made up of such self-determined individuals. Indeed, while dancing, close interpersonal relationships, understood as constantly revised emotional entanglements with particular people, give way to looser, less problematic, higher-order assemblages in which individual self-construction is given pride of place. An anonymized, instrumental mode of intimacy, I suggest, is the hallmark of this particular flavour of we-ness, affording participants with emblematic experiences of the quintessentially modern (post-modern?) prospect of being jointly autonomous. My aim is to explore the performative mechanics through which this model of sociability comes into being.

To do so, I will draw on the practice of Biodanza, whose tag line is the 'poetry of the encounter'. As websites and flyers attest, an explicit emphasis on interpersonal dynamics is what distinguishes Biodanza from other comparable forms of collective dancing. Created by the Chilean Rolando Toro (1924–2010) in the 1960s, this 'human integration system of organic renewal, of affective re-education, and of re-learning of life's original functions' purportedly allows participants to establish 'a connection with oneself, with others, and with life as a whole'.[1]

Talking/sharing circles

A weekly Biodanza session (called a *vivencia*) is led by a 'facilitator'. Lasting about two hours, it usually involves fifteen to twenty participants who are expected to attend a number of such sessions together.[2] Each session is made up of an introductory 'talking' or 'sharing' circle followed by a series of choreographic propositions performed collectively to the accompaniment of music.

Upon arriving for a session, participants greet one another, take off their shoes, change into comfortable clothes and engage in small talk (or not) until being invited to come together. In one series of sessions I attended,[3] participants begin by standing in a circle holding hands; starting with the facilitator, each person introduces himself or herself by name: 'I am Michael.' In the other series of sessions, everyone is seated; the facilitator announces her name and then takes the hand of the person on her right, who then does the same, such that as introductions proceed the circle is progressively joined. The slight pause people take and the insistent way they look around the circle before revealing their name, the animated yet exaggeratedly articulate manner in which names are pronounced, the use of the stilted formula 'I am … ' (instead of the more commonplace 'My name is … '), all contribute to making the situation an exceptional one in which special conditions of presence and expression are presumed to apply. Indeed, saying one's name in a talking circle does not consist merely in identifying oneself to others. It is also a way of showing that one tries to do so in the most authentic and heartfelt way possible. Personal sincerity and exhibited reflexivity are made to go hand in hand.

Participants are then invited to 'share something with the group'. After a few moments people start to speak (there is no obligation to do so). Often, they say how pleased they are to be there and how important these sessions are for them. Here is an example from my field-notes for a circle in which little else was said:

> After a while, Caroline timidly declares how happy she is to be here. Soon after, Sophie, looking around the circle, says how much she enjoys being with this group. She smiles widely at us and some of us smile back. Antonio tells us that he has had a difficult week because he and his wife have had to look after his grand-children. He also reminds us of his advanced age [85 years] and tells us how thankful he is to all of us for giving him the time of these sessions. After a pause, Thomas says that he is going through a difficult time professionally and how much these sessions 'allow him to recharge his batteries for the week'.

Such tributes to the group are unfailingly met with discrete signs of approval – smiles, nods and the like – prompting further expressions of gratitude. Personal disclosure and collective approbation become joined in a self-reinforcing circuit, such that one has the impression that those who talk speak both *to* the group and *for* the group. This impression persists as participants evoke episodes from preceding sessions or, more often, aspects of their daily lives. They do so either to 'unburden' themselves before dancing or to share the fact that they will be 'dancing with' a particular quality or person.

It often happens that a talking circle takes on a life of its own as a motif or affective tone introduced by one person is picked up by others. Consider the following session in which participants disclose feelings of inadequacy and frustration. This often entails the exteriorization of an inner or intimate dialogue in which the speaker's exhibited introspection finds an encompassing echo in the group's manifest attentiveness to the outpourings of one of its members:

> The circle begins with Charles telling us how grateful and pleased he is to be here. After a short pause, Anne, with unshed tears of disappointment, reveals that very few people came to an exhibit of her paintings, and explains how difficult it is for her to find the energy to go on. After a long pause, Boris, in a tear-filled voice that begins haltingly but soon rushes out of control, says that he is going through a hard time 'looking for who I am, trying to know what I want'; he recognizes in himself some of the things his companion (whom he 'loves a lot') reproaches him for, but for others things, he 'just doesn't see it at all', and he 'finds that really upsetting, not to know myself'. After another long pause, Viviane, weeping in rage, explains that she 'has yet again been had by someone because she didn't impose limits', and that she is furious with herself (as is her husband), and that 'it is important that I be myself, and it is so hard for me to do that and not to let myself be dumped on'. Sophie, who is sitting next to her gives her a tender hug and her neighbour on the other side squeezes her hand. Finally, Clara explains that for some time she has been wanting to tell us how much suffering is part of her life, and that her husband, whom she loves, says that she should 'just move beyond it, ignore it and get on with living'. But 'is that a way to live?' she asks. Instead of trying to eliminate this suffering she feels, she prefers to take it on, and to dance with it. She seems at once delighted with herself and deeply moved while announcing that 'this evening I will dance with my suffering'.

When people talk like this, others become unnaturally still and adopt a neutral face, either looking directly at the speaker with softened eyes or keeping their eyes closed as though intently listening. No one interrupts or reacts verbally (to give an opinion, commiserate or offer advice for example), and subjects mentioned in a talking circle are rarely if ever evoked in the informal conversations that precede and follow a session. Participants focus their attention on the person speaking in a benevolent but detached fashion, seemingly mindful not to infringe upon the speaker's disclosures with opinions or concerns of their own. As the talking circle progresses, participants are caught up in a reflexive type of collective empathy in which feelings of self-conscious emotional sharing override the idiosyncratic yet markedly allusive content of what is being said. As listeners they bear witness to speakers' aptitudes for trust and for moving self-expression and self-understanding; as speakers they testify to the group's collective readiness to provide an unfailingly supportive climate. Each is thankful to all for the emergence of an emotionally and intentionally enriched environment in which, during the choreographic propositions that follow, it becomes possible, as Biodanza practitioners say, to 'feel more intensely alive'.

After five to ten minutes, the circle falls quiet. While some participants may feel uneasy about something someone said or regret not having spoken themselves, the dominant sentiment is one of shared complicity and collective self-satisfaction at a job well done, at having given voice to what needed to be said. The facilitator announces that the time has come to dance.

Choreographic propositions

Participants then cease speaking to take part in a series of 'propositions' in which they move their bodies to music. Each proposition (usually ten to twelve in all) is first demonstrated by the facilitator – not as a model to follow, she often points out, but as an invitation or example – before being undertaken by all. Choosing among the wide array of choreographies and musical selections at their disposal, facilitators compose their sessions beforehand in keeping with the group's progress and the session's theme: 'Contact', 'Letting go', 'Joy in one's heart', 'Being the path' and so on.[4]

A session usually begins with an easy-going circle dance while holding hands (grapevine steps to the right). This is often followed by one or more 'walks' in which participants are encouraged to adopt a particularly loose-jointed, springy ('synergetic') step and/or stride around the room embodying affirmative attitudes such as 'being fully present' or 'feeling the joy of life'. They are advised to be attentive to those whose paths they cross, to look them in the eyes and 'to let oneself be affected by them'. Participants may then be invited to take a partner and walk together, and then to change partners, thereby initiating a series of energetic, joyful, sometimes playful propositions most of which entail interacting with others. In a 'rhythmic synchronization', for example, participants pair off and hold hands; facing each other and looking into each other's eyes, they move their linked arms back and forth in rhythm with the music in a way that, in keeping with the facilitator's instructions, their dance 'is led by neither party, but emerges from their interaction'. This first, energetic phase, said to favour a state of 'identity', is followed by a set of slower, gentler, often more sensuous propositions, held to promote a state of 'regression'. Many of the latter exercises (breathing dances, stroking of hands or face, rocking circles, etc.) also entail partnerships of two or more. Towards the end of this second phase, Biodanza's emblematic proposition called 'the encounter' often takes place. Participants are told to move freely around the room while soothing music is playing until they 'connect' with someone and 'enter into a relationship with them'. Such an encounter begins with a 'welcoming look', facilitators explain to novices, that prompts two people to move slowly towards each other until they gently grasp hands; 'depending on how [they] feel', they can then remain gazing at each other, touch each other's hands or arms or progressively move into a long embrace. After a time, as after every proposition, partners solemnly thank each other in silence – a slow blink, a hug, a bow of the head with hands pressed to the chest – before separating to look for others with whom to 'connect'. In the third, shorter phase of a Biodanza session, a small number of 'reactivating' propositions lead to a final, revitalizing circle dance.

The three rules of Biodanza often reiterated by facilitators at the start of a session, especially if newcomers are present, are: (1) enjoy yourself, (2) respect others as well as yourself and (3) no talking. Speechlessness is said to 'favor the use of other modes of communication' and 'make more neurons available for the parasympathetic system governing sensation and emotion'. Facilitators, however, speak a great deal. Before dancing starts they talk about the theme of the session and the overall aims of Biodanza, and before each proposition they provide more specific explanations and recommendations. Among the recurrent motifs of such discourse, along with imperatives to 'rediscover one's spontaneity', to retrieve the creative and expressive qualities 'that all children have naturally', to 'wake up one's body and emotions' and so forth, is the paramount importance of 'entering into relationship with others'.

I have described elsewhere (Houseman, Mazzella di Bosco and Thibault 2016), with respect to dances of self-discovery generally, the learning process characteristic of these practices. Sensory and material cues, the facilitator's words and the example of more experienced dancers all encourage participants to move and act in ways that embody how they feel but also how they feel they should be feeling. The self-contradictory nature of these tacit or explicit injunctions – to be intentionally 'spontaneous', to act 'naturally' in patently artificial settings and so forth – at once heightens participants' self-consciousness and ensures their involvement in recurrent episodes of disorientation and awkwardness. Trying to 'disconnect one's mind' (*déconnecter le mental*) so as to better tap into my 'creative potential', for example, I am dismayed to find myself reproducing the same set of gestures over and over again. This unsettling, self-defeating dynamic is even more pronounced with respect to the 'authentic relationships' participants seek to enact with persons they are ordinarily not close to. Consider something as apparently straightforward as the dance of 'rhythmic synchronization' briefly described above. Partners shift their weight from side to side while swinging their joined hands alternatively backwards and forwards in cadence with the music all the while maintaining eye contact. As the minutes drag on, the movements' repetitiveness, along with the expectation that partners create their dance together, becomes a source of unexpected difficulties. Simply repeating the same movement quickly becomes tedious. Attention wanders and the connection with one's partner breaks down. However, introducing new variations not only makes smooth adjustments between partners more challenging but, contrary to the instructions given, requires that one or the other take a leading role. In such conditions in which defective performance and relational deficiency are closely connected, partners' vigilance towards their dance and towards each other becomes acute; they cannot but own up – sometimes through self-depreciating laughter – to the confusions and misunderstandings that are revealed both in their respective actions and in each other's eyes. Take another, more 'regressive' example of my partner and I as we caress each other's hands over several minutes with our eyes closed while soft music is playing. At one point, I am taken unaware by a rush of erotic attraction or by an equally surprising reaction of repulsion. Although I struggle not to attribute to such sentiments the meanings and implications they might ordinarily have, to reject them as merely intrusive and inappropriate comes up against the imperative to be open to being affected by others.

However, spurred on by the facilitator's directives, the music's tempo, the expressive momentum of one's own and others' movements, as well as partners' good-natured indulgence towards each other's lapses, participants learn to take such momentary setbacks in stride. And as they do so, their efforts are increasingly rewarded by enchanting moments of 'letting go' in which their own and others' dancing, their thoughts and feelings, their consciousness of themselves, of each other and of the group seem to merge into a coherent, flowing whole. During these episodes, potentially dissonant attitudes – flirting, embarrassment, clowning around, and so forth – do not so much cease to exist as they are no longer felt to be problematic. They are, for a time, simply acknowledged as integral aspects of an encompassing and immediately rewarding interactive 'flow' (Csikszentmihalyi 1990). In such moments of grace, participants' routinely shrouded capacity to 'feel more intensely alive' seems to rise to the surface of their awareness to provide them with fleeting 'peak experiences' (Maslow 1968) of whom they are able to become.

Taking part in these sessions proves more difficult for some than for others. Some find Biodanza to be unseemly or just plain boring; having tried it once, they rarely return (see note 5). Others, many of whom become regular attendees, find it appealing but also challenging. Thus, it is not unusual for someone to become excessively agitated, or to stop dancing altogether, or to break down in tears. However, such occurrences are generally considered by all to be part of the ongoing learning process Biodanza puts into effect; the person is briefly and gently taken in hand by the facilitator before being encouraged to join in the dancing once again. Indeed, it is through trial and error, by repeatedly overcoming what are perceived as temporary hindrances, moving from one partnership to the next, at times with a single person, at times with several others, that participants are led to experience what the exemplary yet largely undefined qualities of 'spontaneity', 'naturalness', 'creativity' and 'authentic relationship' might be.

An encounter with oneself …

As we have seen, identifying oneself or recounting an aspect of one's life in a Biodanza talking circle is something quite different from doing so in situations of everyday interaction. Similarly, the relationships participants enter into while dancing are pointedly not the emotionally binding, endlessly renegotiated ties they are familiar with in their daily lives. These 'encounters' or 'connections' take place under highly unusual conditions: as the object of intense reflexive attention, to the accompaniment of music, in the absence of spoken language and in the presence of others. As a result, they easily take on a magnified, self-conscious, almost theatrical quality. Gestures are smoothed out and uncommonly studied, reciprocal gazes are unnaturally steady, physical leave-takings are inordinately prolonged and so on. How should these performances be interpreted? On the one hand, participants do not understand these interactions as phony or fictitious. The emotions they occasion, either while dancing or while being recalled in talking circles, often take those concerned by surprise and are felt by all to be genuine. On the other hand, neither do dancers see these interactions as expressing significant relational commitment, nor do they expect them to lead to lasting ties of interpersonal involvement.

Biodanza participants are engaged in acting out, for themselves and for each other, a conventional (contemporary Western) representation of what an 'authentic' relationship is supposed to be: spontaneous, honest, emotionally eloquent, intimate, caring, pleasurable and so forth. However, these representations are not distanced depictions or hypothetical accounts but personally lived-through experiences. Thus, over the course of weeks and months of practice, participants imbue the exemplary qualities they seek to emulate with their individual sensibilities and behavioural mannerisms. What starts out as an abstract, generic model gradually loses its representational character to become a particular mode of feeling and action, recognizable by the distinctive kinaesthetic and affective experiences it affords. In short, participants progressively come to personify the archetypal values of interpersonal 'connection' they are enjoined to express. In doing so, they develop special, performative *habitus* that both induce and proclaim these personifications: specific ways of moving, of touching, of looking and of initiating and concluding partnerships in which personal inclinations and exemplary dispositions are conjoined.

Particularly telling in this respect is how participants manage that conspicuously interactive organ which is the face. For example, how does one go about gazing into another's eyes – for a full minute, say, while music is playing, while touching without speaking, surrounded by other couples doing the same – in a way that, according to the facilitator's instructions, 'says "I am here"' or 'communicates "unconditional acceptance"'? What is required is neither an impassive look (which connotes a lack of attention) nor an expression that articulates a specific intent (which suggests a strategic posture or a lack of openness), but a sort of uncommitted, self-aware responsiveness. As one facilitator-in-training described it, this 'empathic gaze [...] is at once close and distant. I don't merge [with the other person] and I am not absent [from her]. It's a welcoming, hospitable look (*un regard acceuillant*)'. Participants explore different approaches to melding intimate receptivity and reflexive detachment in ways that do not congeal into a mask. Nevertheless, the facial expressions of accomplished dancers have a definite family resemblance whose regular features include unwavering eye contact (suggestive intensity?), raised eyebrows (unjudging expectancy?), tilted head (playful readiness?) and gentle, unfocused smiling (tranquil benevolence?).

The artful yet pointedly unresolved character of such expressions, and of participants' performative *habitus* generally, bears witness to the refracted or dilated experience of self that Biodanza engenders. The transcendent properties of personhood that dancers are encouraged to embody on the one hand and their own individual patterns of feeling and behaviour on the other are made manifest as mutually reinforcing components of their dancing selves who take on the mysterious quality of being sublime and commonplace at the same time. In this way, Biodanza participants come to be recognized less as individuals seeking to emulate certain cardinal values than as persons capable of revealing these values as heretofore unsuspected aspects of themselves. In other words, to the extent that participants are seen, by themselves and by others, as personifying and not just representing what are held to be the intrinsically worthy qualities of authentic 'connection' (affectivity, caring, vulnerability, spontaneity, etc.), their acting out of these qualities can reasonably be acknowledged as evidence for their own personal capacities to 'connect'.

... through others

Fellow dancers play an essential role in enabling participants to consciously experience their aptitude to enter into relationship with others. This is one of the reasons dancers are strongly encouraged to circulate and try out new partners, whose distinctive ways of moving, of making eye contact, of touching, of showing emotion and so on – all variations within a shared conventional ideal – can provide them with so many complementary interactive experiences of whom they are able to become. As one facilitator explained, 'connecting' with others becomes a wellspring of self-understanding: 'One has an encounter with oneself, an encounter with another, and an encounter with oneself through another [...] what is important is [...] to feel the other and to feel oneself through the other.' Another facilitator once put it differently: "The other is oneself [...] the other is a light, like a flashlight that illuminates me, that reveals me to myself."'

Encountering oneself through another, however, is a reciprocal process. If others act as a given person's resources, each person also acts as a resource for others – as an interactive foil, a source of inspiration, a witness, and so forth. Some propositions, such as caressing one's own face ('as one would wish to be touched') or 'segment dances' centred on particular body parts, are performed alone with eyes closed. However, most of the time, dancers are involved in propositions that require them to assume both exploratory, self-oriented attitudes and enabling, other-oriented ones. Some exercises do this on the basis of turn-taking, with one partner dancing while the other looks on 'in a supportive way'. Other propositions are more elaborate, as when participants are told to stand in 'an open and receptive way' with their eyes closed, while their partners, standing behind them, lightly and rapidly graze parts of their body to induce them to move; after several minutes, the person behind comes around to face their partner in order 'to give them what they need' before exchanging roles. By providing dancers with the means to experience their own capacities for empathy and generosity, such supportive attitudes, like that adopted by listeners during talking circles, can be highly gratifying. Thus, whereas beginners generally come to Biodanza with their own well-being in mind, they progressively come to appreciate how their participation can be helpful to others struggling along their own paths of self-discovery. Increasingly, these two orientations come to reinforce each other, such that for many long-time practitioners, being able to act as a resource for others becomes a constituent aspect of their own self-transformation.

Participants' mutual acknowledgement of their reciprocal enabling roles is an essential component of Biodanza. This is particularly evident in the reverent leave-takings that follow especially satisfying partnerships. Such expressions of thankfulness bridge two opposite inclinations. On the one hand, there is a tendency for partners to abandon themselves in hugs in which the inherent mutuality of touch (touching and being touched becoming indistinguishable) is exploited to the full. On the other hand, encouraged by facilitators' occasional indications that an embrace is perhaps not always the most authentic, appropriate way of connecting with someone, and that hugging a person entails *not* meeting their gaze, partners are careful not to rush into this. As a result, hugging is turned into the consummation of drawn-out processes of reciprocal recognition in which partners, emphatically looking into one another's eyes before embracing, are made self-consciously aware of each other's watchful goodwill. It becomes the sealing of a pact whose collective nature is explicitly expressed during final circle dances. Thus, as participants begin to move together as a single group while holding hands, looks and smiles of complicity begin to blossom, their steps become freer and the circle itself often becomes deformed, buckling in on itself to allow dancers to give each other playful, passing kisses. As participants attend more and more sessions, a trust, born of their shared awareness of having been made aware of themselves through one another grows, facilitating their willingness to convey their aspirations during talking circles and while dancing.

Ritual experiences

As mentioned at the start, Biodanza, 5 Rhythms and other collective dances of self-discovery rely on a mode of interaction – distanced intimacy – also found in contemporary psychotherapy (see also Moisseeff and Houseman in press). However, as Biodanza facilitators are the first to point out, while these practices may have therapeutic effects, they are not therapy sessions: they do not claim to be treatments intended to heal specific psychological or physical disorders. Nor are they esoteric apprenticeships, dance classes, fitness programmes or recreative dance parties. I suggest they be understood as ritual practices, albeit of a type largely overlooked by anthropologists. Unlike more canonical ceremonial activities, these dances are not organized around what Humphrey and Laidlaw (1994) have called 'archetypal actions'. Thus, while certain ways of acting are acknowledged as appropriate (this or that dance step or way of looking or touching), these items of behaviour are not presumed to have value and efficacy in and of themselves. Instead, what are deemed to have such inherent value and efficacy are the exemplary emotional and intentional qualities the dancers' behaviour is enjoined to express and/or bring about: 'spontaneity', 'creativity', 'authentic connection with others' and so on. As in much contemporary Western ceremonial (Houseman 2007, 2016), ritualization pertains here less to the obscure, condensed actions participants perform than to the uncertain, refracted agencies their performances enact. As mentioned, these dances enable participants to take on exceptional, dilated identities in which their embodiment of certain axiomatic ways of thinking and feeling, and their aptitude to undertake and to be affected by this effort are rendered inseparable. In affording participants with the experience of these special, unresolved, short-lived personifications, these practices allow them to become present to themselves and to others as at once ordinary and extraordinary beings.

People's actual thoughts and feelings, because they are volatile, often ambivalent, largely idiosyncratic and directly inaccessible, are generally held to lie beyond the bounds of rigorous anthropological inquiry. This is all the more so where ritual is concerned, for as Rappaport (1979) and others have stressed, one of the features of ritualization is the boundary it establishes between invariant public acts and the vicissitudes of individuals' inner states. Thus, treating Biodanza as ritual entails focusing on the recurrent, observable properties of the practice itself. In other words, contrary to what Biodanza practitioners themselves might expect, description and analysis are concerned not with participants' singular experiences of 'spontaneity', 'creativity' or 'authentic connection with others' but with how such experiences are conventionally elicited and displayed.

There is one definite advantage in recognizing Biodanza, 5 Rhythms and the like as having ritual characteristics. On the basis of anthropological accounts of ceremonial activities generally, we can presume to have a fairly good idea of what these practices can and cannot accomplish. Rituals do not provide answers to problems raised by daily life. At best, they recontextualize particular predicaments in ways that allow answers to be sought more easily elsewhere, by means of the myriad resources humans have at their disposable: intimidation, seduction, logical reasoning, secrecy, storytelling, negotiation, bluff and so forth. Similarly, rituals do not provide realistic models for everyday behaviour. Rather, they act as compelling yet largely unfathomable yardsticks in reference to which participants can re-evaluate themselves, their everyday relationships and their place in the world. Rituals do this by affording participants with conventional yet difficult-to-decipher experiential corroborations of certain axiomatic yet inevitably ambiguous cultural values and ideas. 'Incarnated divinity', for example, is a shorthand label for one such set of values and ideas; 'connection with oneself, with others and with life as a whole' is another. In rendering such ideas and values as performances presumed to have worth and meaning in and of themselves, rituals contribute to their transmission, all the while providing the conditions for their own reiteration. In this way, ritual performance does not so much clarify identities or set things straight as it perpetuates, in a way that makes them particularly difficult to deny, the mysteries and unresolved issues that we hold dear. In other words, ritual promotes the ongoing relevance of certain exemplary cultural values and ideas by packaging them, along with their attendant ambiguities and contradictions, in the form of somewhat enigmatic, yet highly memorable enactments that are hard to argue with (cf. Bloch 1974).

What, then, are the cardinal yet ambivalent values and ideas that are transmitted and renewed in the course of practices like Biodanza? First and foremost, they provide participants with memorable experiences of deliberate self-(re)construction, mediated in this case by bodily movement, emotional expression, music and close physical interaction with others. As mentioned at the beginning of this chapter, engagement in such a process has been heralded as one of the hallmark precepts of contemporary Western individualism. From this standpoint, fellow dancers, like the music played, the exercises proposed and the facilitator's presence, can be appreciated as resources participants make use of in pursuit of this goal. Indeed, the aim of Biodanza is not to encourage dancers to develop interpersonal ties among themselves but to allow them to demonstrate and experience, through each other's intermediary, their promising aptitude for cultivating such ties with others. In short, it is their *potential* for 'spontaneity', 'creativity' and 'authentic relationship' that participants are given to experience during dances of self-discovery and that they are expected to put into effect beyond the confines of the sessions themselves.

It would be abusive, however, to see Biodanza as oriented solely towards participants' ongoing production of their individual 'selves'. There is an undeniable feeling of communal engagement and partnership that develops among dancers. This is made explicit during circle talks, when participants repeat how pleased they are to 'be here' or speak of participants as 'a family' or say how much they feel 'at home' with the group. It is also openly expressed during solemn thank-yous and in the joyful displays characteristic of final circle dances. However, unlike families or homes, this feeling of like-minded community is pointedly not founded on networks of close interpersonal ties with their halting complications of ongoing accountability and negotiation. Instead, it derives from something more ephemeral and less constraining: mutual acknowledgement of the enabling capacities participants willingly assume towards each other and the feelings of personal fulfilment this generalized reciprocity occasions. In this way, Biodanza, like other dances of self-discovery, also provides participants with emblematic experiences of a particular social model in which their mediated self-actualization can be assumed to prosper, namely that of a collectivity composed of independent, self-directed individuals. Such a sociality in which personal sovereignty is paramount is unheard of and even unhoped for in many cultural traditions. However, it is a collective state of being to which many contemporary Westerners might readily aspire: that of becoming autonomous together.

Intimations of a perfect society?

In many respects, the model of 'the social' that Biodanza participants are given to experience dovetails with influential accounts of what contemporary Western society is supposed to be. In psychological terms, dances of self-discovery provide a collective, self-conscious iteration of what paediatrician and psychoanalyst D.W. Winnicott (1965) deemed the necessary conditions for the 'ego-relatedness' underlying the development of a 'true self', namely, the experience of being alone in the presence of someone. He suggests that it is only in an interpersonal environment allowing for such a degree of individual autonomy, prototypically provided by a 'good enough' (as opposed to an overbearing or absent) mother, that the growing child will not become alienated to a 'false self' determined by the expectations of others. Under the guidance of a good enough facilitator, and acting by turns as developing persons and as good enough caregivers towards one another, Biodanza participants afford each other just such a non-alienating interpersonal environment. As one facilitator put it, by inviting participants to interact with others in such a way as to 'recover their childhood proclivities for spontaneity, affectivity, expressiveness, and dance that the process of socialisation and the expectations of society have repressed', Biodanza allows individuals to 'be themselves, to find their identity', to mindfully experience, as adults, whom their 'true self' might be.

A more sociologically informed perspective might see the distinctive sociality of dances of self-discovery as a mode of integration founded on what M. Granovetter (1973) called 'the strength of weak ties'. Those with whom one has strong ties (close friends), he argues, are more likely to be socially involved with one another than those with whom one has weak ties (acquaintances). As a result, strong ties cluster into densely knit 'cliques' of socially homogeneous individuals who, because of their mutual trust, are highly motivated to help each other but who remain isolated from other parts of the larger social field; strong ties favour fragmentation into many small, independent, cohesive groups. By contrast, weak ties form 'bridges' between such groups, providing access to information and resources lying beyond what is immediately available to their members; by linking socially heterogeneous individuals between whom trust is more tenuous, but also less costly, weak ties connect disparate social sectors into a loosely integrated whole. While most weak tie research has focused on the circulation of information between groups, some work has shown that weak ties can also play an important role in group organization. For example, J. Blau (1980, 1991) attributed the exceptionally high morale (and low turnover) of staff of the psychiatric hospital she studied to the surprisingly predominance of weak ties among them. Membership in any given department, committee or clinical team overlapped extensively with many others, interaction being so evenly distributed that cliques were absent and everyone knew each other on a first-name basis. Dances of self-discovery can be appreciated as an extreme case of such a pattern in which the bridging function of weak ties has become the sole basis of group structure. In this light, it is significant that Biodanza participants involved in real-life partnerships studiously avoid any display of their everyday intimacy. Analogously, in the hospital studied by Blau, 'neither homogeneous work groups nor strong friendship relations could be identified', and 'the institution's intolerance of close dyadic ties is expressed by the ritualized avoidance patterns among those who have a sexual or family alliance outside the institution'. This led her to suggest that 'in a complex structure [...] extensive weak networks can remain viable only when close ties are prohibited' (1980: 21, cited in Granovetter 1983: 222). Finally, recalling Biodanza's emphasis on interactions with a multiplicity of partners as a source of self-knowledge, it is worth noting Granovetter's observation, for which he convokes classical authors like E. Durkheim and G. Simmel, to the effect that weak ties, whose inherent heterogeneity acts to promote the construction of a person's ongoing identity in the face of variable interactive expectations, 'are actually vital for an individual's integration into modern society' (1983: 203).[5]

Looking to the field of political science, it is tempting to see Biodanza and other dances of self-discovery as an enactment of 'collective individualism'. This oxymoron-like expression, while difficult to pin down, is often used to evoke a fruitful compromise between individualistic and collectivist paradigms in connection with claims of cultural communality.[6] Recalling philosopher R.B. Perry's suggestion that '[American] individualism is a *collective* individualism – not the isolation of one human being, but the intercourse and cooperation of many' (1949: 9), historian Y. Arieli, for example, maintains that 'since Jefferson and Paine, this "collective individualism" has signified for the American people the essence of their social system, of their national identification' (1966: 176). Similarly, in her analysis of South Indian cultural nationalism, Barnett uses 'collective individualism' to distinguish a Western 'abstract individualism' from a more holistically derived form in which 'each self [...] represents and embodies a particular cultural tradition bounded by the collectivity of similar selves' (1976: 163). In still another context, E. Poljarevic has qualified the pursuit of authenticity by young Egyptian Salafis as 'a form of collective individualism' (2012: 139) in which commitment to the idea of community (*umma*) and an intense focus on individual morality go hand in hand.

The political dimensions of Biodanza, while not entirely absent, are played down, and participants' shared white middle-class identity remains largely unsaid. Hence, the collective individualism it brings to mind resonates above all with the growing usage of this expression as a largely undefined yet positively connoted label for socially sensitive free-spiritedness. It has been used in this way in connection with activities as ideologically divergent as counter-hegemonic activism – for example Soon (2010) on political bloggers in Singapore,[7] Dobernig and Stagl (2015) on urban food cultivation in New York City – and the '"me-to-we" mentality shift amongst Chinese adolescents' reported by the Pepsi Cola company to justify their new nationwide 'Voice of Next Generation' campaign (*China Daily*, 2 April 2009). The trendy, conspicuously Western fields of fashion and design provide additional if somewhat caricatural expressions of the vital connection between individual initiative and collective feeling, as attested, for example, by the Butter Boyz modelling crew's self-affirmation that they 'don't follow rules like wearing pink on Wednesdays – they celebrate their collective individualism instead'.[8]

The wide-ranging correspondences and affinities briefly indicated above suggest that the social ideas and values that Biodanza and other dances of self-discovery put into effect are precisely those that underlie much contemporary Euro-American thinking about society. The imperative of personal autonomy in the face of possible alienation by others, the usefulness and integrative potential of (weak) ties with consequential strangers, the ongoing tension between personal fulfilment and collective sentiment are all essential aspects of what Elias (1991) has called a 'society of individuals'. From this point of view, one of the advantages of convoking 'collective individualism' in connection with these dances is to emphasize the degree to which both of the notions this expression brings together are to be approached not as natural givens but as cultural productions, upheld among other things by ritualized undertakings such as dances of self-discovery. Indeed, by enacting a happy reconciliation between individual precedence ('an encounter with oneself … ') and collective interdependency (' … through others'), these practices consecrate these qualities as dichotomous poles whose interplay is presumed to be constitutive of any social life worth living.

Conclusion

Biodanza, 5 Rhythms, Movement Medicine and the like can thus be seen as the ritualized vehicles of the cardinal cultural values of self-actualization, on the one hand, and of a sodality of distanced intimacy that honours it, on the other. As in the case of rituals generally, these ideas and values are given new life and handed on not in the form of unequivocal understandings but in the form of memorable, partially unresolved experiences upon which disparate yet somewhat overlapping personal meanings are inevitably imposed. Thus, while it is sensible to assume that those who participate in these dances take these cultural expectations away with them, they do so, and translate them into action, in a largely idiosyncratic fashion, in keeping with their individual dispositions and the particular circumstances of their respective lives.

Although dances of self-discovery are statistically limited, they are in no way marginal. They do not pertain to a fringe element of the population (whose specific 'needs' they are supposed to meet), but are part of the multifarious set of culturally characteristic, collective practices regularly pursued by contemporary Westerners of almost all walks of life to 'understand' or 'rediscover' whom they 'really are'. Thus, many features of these dance sessions resonate with other popular practices of mediated self-(re) construction as found in New Age movements, Contemporary Paganism and Personal Development ventures, but also in more mainstream activities such as psychotherapy, various well-being techniques, coaching, advertising, reality TV, stardom and the reading of self-help books. In this light, it is not unreasonable to see Biodanza and other such initiatives as providing a readily observable and therefore privileged access to the workings of non-institutionalized, grassroots practices whereby the axiomatic precepts of contemporary Western society, together with their attendant ambiguities, are being continually reshaped and passed on.

6

Walking pilgrimages to the Marian Shrine of Fátima in Portugal as democratic explorations

Anna Fedele

Since we cannot rely on the government, we can only trust that Our Lady will help us.

(Portuguese pilgrim, informal interview, May 2016)

Based on intensive fieldwork in Portugal in occasion of the centenary celebrations of the apparitions of Our Lady of Fátima (2016 and 2017),[1] this chapter explores the experiences of Portuguese Catholic pilgrims walking from their hometowns to the Marian shrine of Fátima to attend the annual celebrations of the Marian apparitions in May and October. I argue that in a historic moment in which the Portuguese face economic difficulties that have forced many of them to emigrate and in which the state is incapable of guaranteeing real democracy offering a solution to the strongly polarized distribution of wealth, these pilgrimages appear as strategies to reaffirm grassroots forms of solidarity and democracy.

I explore how embodying desired social changes through rituals and ritual objects that form part of the pilgrimage can have empowering effects for the pilgrims. Following Catherine Bell (1990, 1992, 2009), I consider ritualization as a 'strategic mode of production' that is intended to change a set of social categories by creating a shift in dominance among a set of symbols in a way that sanctions parallel social changes in the non-ritual world (Bell 1990: 304). As Bell observes, ritualization addresses core contradictions between cultural ideals and current conditions. Through ritual it is possible to redefine and reconceptualize these contradictions through the use of symbols, ritualized objects and the ritualized body. In this way rituals can become vehicles of resistance and subversion.

I am also influenced by other scholars in ritual studies such as Ronald Grimes (2000, 2006), Graham Harvey (2005), Michael Houseman (2007, 2010) Sarah Pike (2017) and Jone Salomonsen (2002, 2003), who have analysed the potentialities of rituals as catalysts not only for personal but also for social change, central topics of the REDO research project from which the chapters contained in this edited volume originate. Analysing walking pilgrimages to Fátima, I argue that embodying social change through rituals can open the way to social and political transformation.[2] During rituals another world becomes possible, being ritually enacted and embodied by ritual practitioners. I show how these in-group journeys to Fátima and the rituals and ritual objects created by the pilgrims help them to come to terms with the current scenario of social and economic crises in Portugal. Through their sacred journeys they reassert values of solidarity and democracy on a micro (personal and group) level as well as on a macro (national) level, reactivating also the engagement of local public institutions. Through the detailed description of one ritual object, the pilgrims' walking stick, we will see how the performative qualities of ritual resources achieve their potential as forms of personal and political empowerment in a country that in 2016 had the highest percentage of emigrated population in Europe.[3]

Our Lady of Fátima and 'Her' pilgrims

As scholars focusing on Marian devotion and apparitions have shown, the narratives about Marian apparitions are complex and constantly evolving in close relationship with the historical and political contexts (e.g. Perry and Echevarría 1988; Zimdars-Swartz 1991; Christian 1996; Claverie 2003). A contested local apparition site during the First Portuguese Republic, Fátima gradually became the most important national pilgrimage site (Zimdars-Swartz 1991; Fernandes 1999; Barreto 2002; Reis 2007), until it eventually developed into a centre of global Catholicism (Cadegan 2004; Duque 2017; Franco and Reis 2017), attracting Catholic pilgrims from all over the world but also other Christian as well as non-Christian pilgrims (Lourneço and Cachado 2018; Fedele 2020; Cavallo and Fedele 2020). For reasons of brevity, I will introduce here only a summary of the narratives offered to visitors through the official leaflet distributed by the sanctuary, through its website, and by the most popular books about the shrine and its origins.

In 1917, three shepherd children, Lucia, Francisco and Jacinta, reported having seen Our Lady, who told them to come to that place (*Cova da Iría*) each following month on the thirteenth day. The shepherds reported seeing Our Lady on every subsequent thirteenth of the month (with a small change of date in August) and the apparitions culminated in what is known as the miracle of the sun. On 13 October 1917, hundreds of people gathered to attest to the sign that Our Lady had announced 'would make all believe'. Although no accurate statistical data are available, it was reported that hundreds of people saw different changes in luminosity, shape and positioning of the sun. The Lady also declared that she was Our Lady of the Rosary and for this reason the rosary, the most important ritual object related to Marian devotion, acquires yet another layer of importance in the case of Fátima. The different layers of meaning constructed around Our Lady of Fátima during the last 100 years are complex and entangled with the local and international political context along with successive interpretations of sister Lucia, the only surviving visionary. They also need to be understood in the context of the increasing importance given to the figure of Mary as well as of rising occurrences of Marian apparitions since the end of the nineteenth century (e.g. Christian 1972, 1996, 2011; Warner 1983; Perry and Ecevarria 1988; Zimdars-Schwartz 1991; Claverie 2003; Orsi 2010). The following historical overview cannot therefore be exhaustive and offers only the most important elements to situate the devotion of the Portuguese pilgrims described here.

After almost ten years of debates around the authenticity of the visions, with the beginning of the Portuguese military dictatorship in 1926, an auspicious period for the devotion in Fátima started. Eager to distance itself from the anticlerical positions of the Republican period, the new government endorsed Fátima as a patriotic altar. On 13 October 1930 the bishop of Leiria, José Alves Correia da Silva, officially authorized the cult to Our Lady of Fátima and during the *estado novo* the flourishing of the pilgrimage site continued. The identification of the Portuguese population with this shrine became clearly visible when Our Lady of Fátima was crowned as Queen of Portugal in 1942. Her golden crown had been made with pieces of jewellry donated by Portuguese women to thank for Our Lady's intercession in avoiding Portugal's participation in the Second World War. Through the figure of the Queen of Portugal a strong link between the Portuguese state and the Portuguese population was created.

From the 1940s onwards Fátima increasingly acquired an international visibility. Gradually replicas of the statue of Our Lady were created and consecrated as pilgrim statues that started travelling around the world. In the 1960s and 1970s, in the context of colonial wars, Fátima emerged as a kind of promised land of hope and safety for the men sent to Africa to defend Portuguese supremacy over its colonies. After the revolution in 1974 the new government adopted a moderate position. Our Lady of Fátima increasingly became an international symbol of anti-communism through the spreading popularity of the three secrets of Fátima, as well as Pope John Paul II's interpretation of his survival of an attempted assassination on 13 May 1981, as a consequence of the intervention of Our Lady of Fátima.[4]

In 2016 and 2017 with the celebration of the centenary of the apparitions in Fátima, the visit of Pope Francis and the sanctification of Jacinta and Francisco, the relevance of this shrine as a high place of global Catholicism was sanctioned once again. Through the constant attention of Portuguese media, the preparations and the celebration of the apparitions in 2016 and 2017 became a national event, implicating even the participation of the president of the Republic. The walking pilgrimages on 12 and 13 of May mobilized an unforeseen number of Portuguese men and women who walked from their hometowns to Fátima from all over Portugal, paralysing certain parts of the country and requiring the development of a huge apparatus of assistance and security.

For the pilgrims participating in the walking pilgrimages explored here, Our Lady was first and foremost what Her name said, 'their' own divine Lady/Mother and many of them referred to her as 'the Mother of all Portuguese'. Many of them knew little about the three prophecies or of Fátima's link with anti-communism and they rarely referred to political meanings. When I deliberately asked questions with a political background, they had little to report and their answers seemed genuine. Even when speaking to pilgrims who had developed their devotion during the colonial wars, they reported that their personal devotion was mostly related to giving thanks for having safely come home from the war.

Walking pilgrimages in group

Although most people in Portugal are still Catholic, there has been a constant decline in church attendance that reflects trends in other countries of Southern Europe considered as traditionally Catholic such as Italy and Spain (Vilaça 2006; Mapril and Llera Blanes 2013). However, walking pilgrimages to Fátima still attract huge numbers of pilgrims twice a year, requiring the intervention and support of national and local entities.

As pilgrimage scholars have shown, Marian apparition shrines are arenas for the creation of competing discourses (Eade and Sallnow 1991). They can act as catalysts for feelings of *communitas* (Turner and Turner 1978), allowing the pilgrims to experience a sort of extra-worldly and non-hierarchical fellowship, but they can also be used to promote nationalistic politics (Claverie 2003; Eade and Katic 2017), voice religious criticism (Claverie 2003; Fedele 2013, 2014a, 2014b), give space to ritual creativity (Bowman and Valk 2012; Fedele 2013, 2014a), allow multi-religious devotion (Bowman 2012; Albera and Couroucli 2012) or visit a religious heritage site (Isnart 2012) and engage in different touristic and economic activities (Badone and Roseman

Figure 6.1 Group of walking pilgrims on their entrance into the sanctuary. Picture by Anna Fedele.

2004; Reader 2014; Coleman and Eade 2018). In Fátima all these and more different dimensions are present to different extents. Here I will focus on one specific kind of pilgrim: Portuguese pilgrims walking in organized groups from their hometowns to Fátima usually in May and October, to a lesser extent in August and sometimes during the remaining months of the apparitions (June, July, September) (Figure 6.1).

Many Portuguese are used to going to Fátima during the year by car or bus with their family. For many Portuguese informants going to Fátima is like 'going to visit my mother'. As one woman from the North of Portugal explained to me: 'Whenever I must drive south and pass by, I have to stop in Fátima, even if it is only for some minutes, to say hello to my Mother. If I drove by my (biological) mother's place I would also stop to greet her.'

Twice a year, in May and October there is a major pilgrimage that is widely broadcasted in the media and involves a lot of organization on part of the firefighters, local churches and other associations. The pilgrimage in May, to commemorate the first apparition on 13 May 1917, is the most important and is considered as a nationwide pilgrimage during which pilgrims from all over Portugal make their way by foot from their hometown to Fátima. They usually walk in groups, together with people from their same village or area, and carry with them banners with the coat of arms of their municipality and/or the patron saint of their parish church. Most of the time they walk along public roads, because, unlike in the case of the Camino de Santiago (Frey 1998), alternative footpaths rarely exist. Only skilled pilgrimage guides know all the shortcuts to avoid the terrible heat emanating from asphalted roads on sunny days, as well as the danger of passing trucks and cars. Mortal accidents have led over the past twenty years to the increasing use of reflective vests that have now become visual markers of pilgrims arriving by foot, distinguishing them from the other pilgrims in the middle of the crowded sanctuary.

The image that media usually convey is that pilgrims from all over Portugal are making their way to Fátima, giving witness to the strong faith of the Portuguese. The huge efforts of the Scouts,[5] NGOs and other volunteer associations are praised as demonstrations of national solidarity. Along the path, pilgrims often sleep in community rooms, fire stations or other shelters offered to them for free by local groups or individuals. The pilgrims can rely on several entities to provide support with the purpose that everyone arrives safely to Fátima. These are critical times due to the increasing numbers of pilgrims walking by foot – which were particularly high in 2017 because of the celebration of the centenary and the consequent visit of Pope Francis.

The operations in the field involve several organizations. These usually are national or local entities and non-profit organizations that support the pilgrims for free. These entities include civil protection authorities like the National Guard, the fire department, field hospitals, but also local Catholic and philanthropic organizations. They can easily be recognized by the pilgrims through their uniforms, marked vehicles, tents or stands, strategically positioned along their paths. Their main purpose is to prevent the pilgrims' physical exhaustion, since many of them set out poorly equipped and with no previous physical preparation or training. They provide medical and sanitary assistance, mainly nursing, first aid, physiotherapy and massages, podiatry, psychological support, baths, rest places, distribution of water, small meals and so on. Scattered along the path, there are other organizations related to other social areas like sports and insurance, advertising their brands offering reflective vests, sport drinks or energy bars to the pilgrims. The great majority of the human resources are provided by volunteers from different parts of the country belonging to Catholic organizations or Private Social Solidarity Institutions (IPSS).

I will focus here specifically on one pilgrimage group and on one *cajado* (walking stick), analysing in detail its multiple meanings and exploring how these are embedded in the life story of Teodora, a woman in her late fifties who lived in the Lisbon area. The ways in which Teodora described her pilgrimage experience and in particular her *cajado* summarize effectively the experiences of other Portuguese pilgrims. The *cajado* can be considered the symbol par excellence of pilgrims to Fátima. Analysing its components, we gradually untangle the complex forms of solidarity that are at stake. As we will see the *cajado* condenses forms of solidarity related to family ties, but it also fosters a sense of union with past, present and future pilgrims as well as with the country as a whole.

For the analysis of the *cajado* I also draw on the experiences and interviews I made in another group, coming from the North of Portugal, that placed a particular emphasis on the use of this walking stick. First, I will introduce the group with which Teodora walked.

Teodora's group and their *cajados*

Having wished to do so for many years, Teodora joined a group walking to Fátima in October 2016. This group started from the greater Lisbon area. It was led by Rita and accompanied by David Soares, who worked as my research assistant for one year.[6] I met the group during their following pilgrimage in May 2017, re-encountered them in May 2018 and had informal conversations with Rita as well as with other committed members of the group.

Apart from David, in October 2016 Rita's group was composed by seven women aged between 20 and 69. Rita usually organized pilgrimages in May as well as in October and groups used to be mixed and more numerous for the pilgrimages in May but the rituals they made on their way to Fátima had been the same over the last years. In May 2017 the group was larger than ever before (around thirty pilgrims) and women were still the majority as in most pilgrimage groups. In October 2016 all of Rita's pilgrims described themselves as Catholics, although they often had quite different approaches and were in some cases quite critical of the Catholic Church. They had different social and cultural backgrounds, most of them were divorced and all had jobs or were retired. Rita was fifty years old. Her husband had a floating low income and she could not work due to an incurable disease. She started organizing pilgrimages with a group from her parish centre in 2004 and kept running pilgrimages twice a year, even if the groups she led were no longer related to that parish. She considered her role as a pilgrimage leader as a mission that she carried on despite increasing difficulties due to her health problems.

This group of ladies was supported by João, an experienced pilgrim in his sixties who drove the so-called 'support car' (*carro de apoio*) following the group. One or more support cars or vans were used by all the organized pilgrimage groups I came to know, and as in the case of João, the driver was considered as a particularly important member of the group. Since a child João frequented the church. He used to be an alcoholic and beat his wife and son. His son left the house as soon as he could and only recently started to talk with him again. João's wife is ill and in need of continuous medical assistance. He now takes care of her, asks constantly forgiveness to Our Lady for his sins and is relentless in helping others. In the support car he seems to have found the perfect conditions for what he perceives as his mission: he takes care of the luggage, food, water, backup and logistic material, ensures the safety of the group pinpointing its presence on the road, makes arrangements for shelter each night and negotiates with the authorities in the sanctuary to organize the participation of the group during the huge celebration of mass on May 13 and October 13.

Other support car drivers I talked to described their tasks as part of a sort of mission they were doing for the group. They often acted as coaches, encouraging the pilgrims who felt they could no longer continue, helping to solve the conflicts that inevitably arose when the pilgrims were particularly exhausted and cheering up the group with jokes. Two men in their thirties who accompanied a women-only group in August 2017, and had been supporting the same group for several years, described themselves as the 'psychologists' of the group who listened to the difficult stories that often lay behind the pilgrims' decision to walk to Fátima.

Even if they did not walk to Fátima, these drivers were usually considered as pilgrims *honoris causa* because they played a key role in promoting the sense of community and solidarity within the group. For this reason they were allowed to join the group on its entrance walk into the sanctuary.

The sharing times, held daily once a shelter had been reached and dinner was over, were an important moment of the pilgrimage. Although these moments had been prepared and were guided by Rita, they also happened without guidance, through the support of the most committed members who helped to create a space that felt safe for sharing personal experiences as well as the pains and troubles at home. Each member was free to give voice to her needs and eventually to reshape the rhythms and contents of these moments accordingly. Usually, Rita would propose a trigger question or an activity that would create new forms of participation, setting the tone as she started opening up to the group about her personal situation. In those moments, pilgrims perceived that they all had a voice and were allowed to express themselves as they liked (words, hugs, tears, jokes) and to support each other as each pilgrim eventually ended up sharing his or her personal difficulties. In other pilgrimage groups moments of sharing were less structured but happened spontaneously, after a common prayer or during and after the evening meals. Leaders, support car drivers and experienced pilgrims usually acted as facilitators of these sharing moments and as one pilgrimage leader put it: 'By the end of the pilgrimage even the most shy and reserved pilgrim has revealed the reason of joining the pilgrimage, so that the group then helps a bit to carry the burden.'

The spontaneous solidarity that emerged, and that led even people who were relatively or totally new to the group to open up, has been described in the case of other collective pilgrimages (Turner and Turner 1978) as well as in the case of pilgrims walking on their own or in smaller groups who meet other pilgrims along the way (Frey 1998). What is particularly interesting about these Portuguese pilgrimages is that they offer the possibility of a renewed mundane sociality as well as of reconfigured national identity.

Displays of solidarity in Rita's group continued throughout the pilgrimage with meals brought by pilgrims who were not able to walk in the October pilgrimage but used to join Rita's group in May for the most important celebrations of the year in Fátima. These committed pilgrims were considered as 'being all part of the same family' and when they did not walk to Fátima, they provided lunch and dinner for their pilgrim family members. These dynamics of solidarity within Rita's group mirror those I observed in other groups coming from all over Portugal. On their arrival to Fátima many pilgrims who had walked in a group for the first time described the support they had received and explained that they felt they had now acquired a new family. The food the pilgrims ate along the way had often been brought over by family members or former pilgrims or had been sponsored by villagers who could not join the group because they did not get days off work or had physical problems. The meals were therefore a celebration of community and solidarity that were shared, along with other moments of the pilgrimage, through Facebook, WhatsApp and other social media with family members, former pilgrims and with the whole local community of origin. In a more concrete sense these meals also allowed pilgrims, many of them with low incomes, to eat freshly prepared food without the need to spend money eating in restaurants.

Either among the pilgrims or the wider supporting community involved, there were Portuguese migrants who lived abroad, having been obliged to leave their country to find a job. For them these pilgrimages represented a way to reinforce their link to their country of origin. Some migrants who could not join the group participated in the experience indirectly, for instance, by paying for food or material needed along the road or following and encouraging the pilgrims through social media. They then usually visited Fátima with their family during their vacation in Portugal to attend the celebrations of the 'pilgrimage of the migrant', held each August. The important role that pilgrimages to Fátima play for expatriot Portuguese and the annual 'pilgrimage of the migrant' cannot be explored here in detail, suffice it to say here that I came to similar conclusions as those advanced by Policarpo Lopes in the case of Portuguese migrants living in France (Lopes 1992). The pilgrimages as well as the devotion to Our Lady of Fátima represent for migrants a way to come to terms with the wounds caused by their departure as well as to mantain links with their family members left behind and their homeland.

Rita's pilgrims in October 2016 all lived in Portugal and their life narratives were enacted during public as well as private rituals of the pilgrimage, displaying distinctive ways of what it means to be Catholic that were not perceived as clashing. This personal and creative way to adapt and reinterpret Catholicism

Figure 6.2 *Cajados* placed on the floor in the area close to the chapel of the apparitions for the closing moments of the pilgrimage. Picture by Anna Fedele.

emerged as well in other groups I accompanied (Fedele 2020). As in most groups I observed, not all of Rita's pilgrims used a *cajado*. Those who had one did not necessarily use it all the time. Sometimes left in the support car, the *cajados* were always used when arriving at Fátima and entering the area of the sanctuary, the moment that for almost all the pilgrims represented the most important and final passage of the pilgrimage (Figure 6.2).

The sticks were usually decorated with different ribbons and objects that had often been added throughout the years. Some elements were personal, while others might be common to the whole group (like the violet ribbon with the angel in Teodora's case below). Sometimes these objects might have an almost self-evident meaning that was easy to guess for outsiders, as in the case of a pacifier, usually recognized by observers as a way for giving thanks to Our Lady for the birth of a baby. In other cases, the meaning of an object could only be understood by talking with the pilgrim. In any case the full meaning of each object of the *cajado* was deeply embedded in the pilgrim's life story. This becomes evident if we consider the objects chosen by Teodora to decorate her *cajado* and the accurate description and analysis she made of it.

Teodora and her *cajado*

Teodora worked in a Flag House as a manufacturer, she was divorced and had two daughters, the oldest was married with two kids and the other one was single. She also considered her niece as a daughter because she had looked after her when she was a baby and since then they had bonded and become inseparable. Teodora had been visiting Fátima by car or bus for many years but this was the first time she joined an organized group and walked the 150 km/93 miles from the wider Lisbon area to Fátima during five days.

She had a strong bond with her family and had decided to go on a pilgrimage for the first time with this group to give thanks for the blessings her family had recently received. Portuguese pilgrims usually go to Fátima to give thanks for a vow (*promessa*) that has been granted or to ask for the fulfilment of such a vow (see, for instance, Gemzöe 2000; Pereira 2003; Fedele 2017, 2020).

Since childhood, Teodora had attended church and as time went by she had reshaped her notion of religion making it more syncretic especially after she had started practising yoga. Teodora had her own way of experiencing the pilgrimage and did not always necessarily agree with the Vatican, an attitude shared by many other walking pilgrims (see Fedele 2020). With age, Teodora had developed fluid retention in her legs that made them heavier and she became tired very quickly. She had revealed herself a very determined person during the pilgrimage, eager to reach Fátima and overcoming all physical difficulties.

Teodora had been preparing with care her *cajado* that should help her to overcome the challenges of the long walk. She explained:

> My *cajado* carried symbolic things of mine. Well, in fact the *cajado* in itself was already symbolic. The stick belonged to my daughter who is part of the Scouts, when she went to catechesis (…) she brought the stick that my mother had prepared taking off its bark (…) it came from a tree we have there in our village (…). My mother took off the bark so that my daughter did not get hurt. (…) already the fact that it had been taken and peeled by my mother was a reason enough for carrying it with me. I asked my daughter for permission, the stick was in my house, and she agreed. She had already put on the stick a *dezena* (small rosary of 10 beads) and a transparent rosary. I left those there, I added the ribbon (*fita*) that we had been told to add (by the pilgrimage leader), a small ribbon that made it easier to get hold of the stick or to add a handkerchief if necessary. And then I had some spare white ribbon that had been used to involve the (dress) hanger of my daughter's wedding dress. This was another symbolism. And finally, I added a small ribbon (*fitinha*) coming from my job

> (in a flag factory). A ribbon that is half green and half red that was related to Portugal. Therefore, I also went with the intent (*fito*) of asking for Portugal. So that Portugal could be happier and that all people can be happier and that there can be a better social situation for all of us. (…) After the pilgrimage Rita gave me a violet ribbon (…) with a little angel (*anjinho*) that she gave (to each pilgrim), the ribbon (related to the ritual) of the guardian angel. This ribbon had flowers on it because we decorated this ribbon with little flowers. Along the way I stole a little rose, mine was a real rose, it still smells of rose, the little rose of Teresinha (saint Teresa of Lisieux), I love these roses. The stick still smells of roses (2 months after the pilgrimage), how amazing, I came across these roses and it smells of roses, wonderful, spectacular! (Personal interview conducted by David Soares, with written consent from the pilgrim, original names changed).

As we can see, there are different 'symbolisms', as Teodora called them, related to the *cajado*. Each of these corresponds to different layers of meaning as well as to different places, family members and social roles played by Teodora throughout her life. This timeline even reaches the moment of the interview because the roses still smell. Let us briefly explore the different layers described by Teodora and how they relate to ways of creating and manifesting links of solidarity at different levels:

1) The stick in itself comes from a tree from the village of her maternal family. Like many Portuguese Teodora left the rural area where she grew up to live and work in Lisbon, where most of Portugal's economic and social activity is centralized. The stick coming from a tree therefore represents her roots in a rural Portugal where Catholic devotion and celebrations have more importance and influence than in the larger Lisbon area or in other more urbanized spaces.
2) The peeled stick relates to her mother and is handed down through a matrilineal line of care. The grandmother carefully prepared the stick so that it could help the niece while walking, marking also her belonging to a certain place and family.
3) The decorations added by Teodora's daughter during her Scout activities with a small and a regular rosary. The rosary is the most important ritual object in Marian devotion and as we have seen above there is a strong link between the rosary and Fátima devotion.
4) The wedding ribbon expresses Teodora's joy and pride for the marriage of her daughter, also mentioned earlier in the interview and closely related with her vocation to be a mother and grandmother.

5) The job ribbon with the colours of the Portuguese flag represents Teodora not only as a mother and grandmother but also as a working woman who is concerned not only about her closest family's well-being but also about Portugal, which she describes almost as a person ('so that Portugal could be happier'). She also describes the Portuguese population as a sort of extended family ('all of us').
6) The guardian angel ribbon emerging from what was probably the strongest ritual celebrated during the pilgrimage to foster and consolidate solidarity within the group.[7]
7) The roses related to Sainte Therèse de Lisieux, a French saint known also as the saint of little things, that is of foremost importance for Teodora because it is closely related to her life story. The roses are one of the most important symbols related to this saint as is the smell of these flowers. (de Blic 2011)

Through Teodora's *cajado* we can see that, as one pilgrimage leader from the North put it, on a group pilgrimage to Fátima 'you never walk alone'. Pilgrims walking in a group are accompanied by their fellow pilgrims but also by other persons who are not physically with them but whose presence can be felt. Like Teodora, pilgrims often do not walk for themselves; they set out to give thanks or to ask for help for their family and/or for their friends. They tend to describe their pilgrimage group as a sort of extended family. The family links become particularly visible on the group's arrival to Fátima where previous pilgrims are often waiting to join the moment of arrival and common prayer in front of the chapel of the apparitions. One pilgrimage leader, for instance, used to greet pilgrims from previous groups who joined the group in Fátima shouting enthusiastically 'hello family', thereby emphasizing their special status and their belonging to the community of pilgrims. Pilgrims often felt that through their journey they were in some way walking for their whole family at home. This presence became visible through elements fixed on their *cajado*, pictures they carried with them inside their wallet or backpack as well as through the candles they lit or the wax figures and flowers they offered at the sanctuary, often following the specific requests and indications of friends and family regarding the number and size of these candles and/or offerings. In some cases, especially when the group had a strong connection with the local priest in charge of the parish, who usually blessed the group upon their departure, the pilgrims felt that they were also walking for their entire village or, if they came from a town or city, for their entire parish. The place of origin is usually clearly shown on the group

T-shirts worn by pilgrims (see Figure 6.1) on their arrival and the priest as well as other villagers sometimes meet the group in Fátima.

The pilgrims also feel supported throughout their effort by their family and wider community. As we have seen, the stick that served as a support for Teodora on her difficult way to Fátima is linked to her maternal line of descent. She felt the support of her family also through shawls that belonged to her mother and daughters that helped her during particularly challenging moments of the pilgrimage.

Relational networks

As we can see these walking pilgrimages involve the construction of complex relational networks (Turner and Turner 1978) as well as the condensation of different modes of relationship (Houseman and Severi 1998) and solidarity. The relationships involved are those among the pilgrims walking together but the web gradually expands including also the family members (dead or alive) of each walking pilgrim as well as former pilgrims and finally the entire Portuguese nation, including those who were forced to leave the country and to migrate, usually to other European countries of North America. The links of this web are not only symbolic, but they are also visible through the social media and they become tangible when family members, friends, neighbours or former pilgrims provide food along the way or even join the group on their arrival to Fátima. These webs of relationship help to reinforce the pilgrims' feeling of belonging to their own family as well as to the extended family represented by the other group members and often also by their local community. In a wider sense these webs also encompass all Portuguese pilgrims making their way to Fátima by foot as well as all those professionals and volunteers who support the pilgrims along the way and on their arrival. During the celebration of the main ceremonies on 12 and 13 of May and October, the different components of these webs become visible because they participate in the official ceremonies. The medical volunteers as well as the members of the police or the army who helped the pilgrims, for instance, are allowed to carry the statue of Our Lady of Fátima during the solemn mass celebrated on May 13 and October 13. During this same mass the groups of walking pilgrims wearing their group T-shirts can carry their own banners and representations of Our Lady (*andor*) receiving a special place in the procession that accompanies the statue of Our Lady.

I also interviewed one Scout leader who was in charge of ensuring security during the celebrations of May 13 as well as four members of an association of volunteering doctors and nurses supporting the pilgrims. They all perceived their activities as part of a sort of patriotic mission and described with pride and joy their experiences of carrying the statue of Our Lady or other salient moments of their experiences of support for pilgrims. One female doctor commented: 'If things in Portugal would always be like this, with the same degree of collaboration and organization, things would be very different.' Other pilgrims and members of the pilgrims' support system expressed similar feelings contrasting their Fatima experience with the lack of solidarity and governmental support they perceived in their everyday life.

The pilgrims acknowledged the help they received along the way through the extended national web of non-profit support system and although they criticized certain aspects, suggesting how support strategies could be improved, in general they were proud of the recognition the government gave to their walk through the deployment of such a complex structure of support.

This kind of walking pilgrimage to Fátima is considered something so special and characteristic of Portugal that pilgrims sometimes are granted extra days off work for their journeys or are allowed to take days off in a period when this would normally not be possible.

Pilgrimages and democratic explorations

Even if they are sometimes also criticized or ridiculed, Portuguese walking pilgrims are usually portrayed by the media as some sort of national hero. This was especially true for the pilgrimages in May and October 2017 for the celebration of the centenary.

During their journey to Fátima the pilgrims feel that they are acknowledged, supported and protected as individuals by the Portuguese state. This feeling contrasts with their everyday experience of successive governments that have been incapable to guarantee real democracy, offering no solution to the strongly polarized distribution of wealth. This already difficult situation further declined after the economic crisis that started in 2008 and exacerbated the process of massive emigration. Through their pilgrimages and through rituals and ritual objects such as the *cajado* the pilgrims enact and display the kind of solidarity and support they would like to receive from their local community and more widely from their government. They experience these sacred journeys as empowering experiences that show them that another more democratic and caring society is possible. As the Queen of Portugal, Our Lady of Fátima also becomes a sort of personification of Portugal as their Motherland, a divine, national Mother that helps them whenever the government that should be in charge of taking care of them fails to do so, as the pilgrim in the opening vignette clearly explained.

The support the pilgrims receive from different public institutions as well as from national NGOs and other entities also provide examples of grassroots solidarity and sustain the pilgrims in their hope that their wider national family will rise from the ashes with the divine help of the Queen of Portugal.

In contemporary Portugal, the dramatic consequences of the economic crisis and its impacts in terms of massive emigration, as well as on an evident deterioration of social care structures and the quality of life, represent a difficult challenge for the Portuguese of the lower and middle classes. During recent years the governments in charge have failed to provide appropriate solutions and often try to downplay the gravity of the situation, refusing to fully acknowledge (yet another) difficult passage in the story of modern Portugal. Pilgrimages to Fátima allow the pilgrims to express and share their difficulties related to this historical moment in Portugal as well as to develop forms of solidarity and democracy that make them realize that another world is possible. Through what I have described in the title as 'democratic explorations', the pilgrims enact and experience different modalities of being together, supporting each other inside the group of walking pilgrims but also in the wider group formed by their family members and by former pilgrims. This kind of grassroots communitarianism sometimes also continues after the pilgrimage among the most committed members of the group who remain in touch and regularly meet to plan future pilgrimages but also to support each other or simply to celebrate their community. Although I would not go as far as suggesting that these pilgrims end up creating a sort of antistructure in the Turnerian sense (Turner and Turner 1978), we have seen that during the pilgrimage many of them describe at least some of the features of Turnerian *communitas*. They no longer feel isolated in a country facing severe economic problems but as members of a wider community that encompasses the pilgrimage group but also the wider web analysed before that eventually extends to the entire Portuguese nation.

Following Bell's analysis, I view these sacred journeys as allowing pilgrims to experience a new sense of belonging to a local as well as wider, national community. These pilgrimages also help to reinforce old and new forms of solidarity establishing a sense of democracy where all are equal and there is one leader but all can decide together. This does not imply of course that there were no moments of frustration, refusal to follow common rules, critique or anger during such a physically and emotionally challenging enterprise as the pilgrimage. However, upon their arrival to Fátima pilgrims usually manifested a strong sense of belonging and many of them expressed their wish to join future pilgrimages or were planning to help or share future pilgrims in some way. As one experienced pilgrimage leader enthusiastically said: 'Once a pilgrim, always a pilgrim', meaning that walking to Fatima was an experience that changed a person and usually led her to repeat the experience in some way, joining the group of pilgrims on their next walk, catching up with them on their arrival or visiting the shrine with family and friends.

Experiencing and promoting solidarity and democracy through pilgrimage

Throughout this chapter I have explored national pilgrimages to Fátima, focusing on the ways in which these journeys offer opportunities to promote feelings and notions of solidarity and democracy among the pilgrims on a micro level (pilgrimage group, family members), but also to experience and envisage new forms of solidarity and democracy on a more macro, national level. I have briefly analysed the aspects (support car and driver), moments (sharing) and rituals (guardian angel, lighting of candles) related to the progressive creation of a sense of belonging to a single group of pilgrims, sometimes even described as a family and to the perception of a wider, Portuguese national family safely situated under the protection of Our Lady of Fátima, the Queen of Portugal.

Analysing Teodora's *cajado*, we have seen that it condenses the micro and macro levels of solidarity and democracy experienced by the pilgrims because it refers to the family of origin of the pilgrims, the pilgrimage group as a new extended pilgrim family and finally to Portugal as a national family. The reference to Our Lady of Fátima helps these pilgrims to envisage a different 'healed' family as well as a different, thriving and 'happy' Portugal in a historical moment when this kind of national change seems an almost impossible task.

Following Bell's analysis (1992, 2009), I have argued that these national pilgrimages foster new forms of participatory democracy, based on respect for individual differences but also on the community of pilgrims' needs. Pilgrimages to Fátima emerge as ways of mobilizing material as well as symbolic resources in response to economic and social crisis because pilgrims learn and experience new ways of supporting each other as well as of giving voice to their personal problems feeling the support of others.

On a macro level, these sacred journeys help to reassert national values related to solidarity and democracy because they reactivate the engagement of national and local public institutions as well as a wide array of NGOs and other organizations reasserting the values of solidarity and democracy that are perceived as central to the Portuguese national identity and its strong Catholic roots. They allow pilgrims to reinforce and create forms of solidarity and to express a need for social and economic change in Portugal, waiting and hoping, against all odds, for some kind of redemption.

Acknowledgements

Research for this article was funded by FCT/MCTES (the Portuguese Foundation for Science and Technology) as part of the strategic research plan of the Centro em Rede de Investigação em Antropologia (UID/ANT/04038/2013), as part of my activities as an FCT investigator (IF/01063/2014) and as part of the HERILIGION project from the European Union's Horizon 2020 and IF/01063/2014/CP1233/CT0001 research and innovation programme under grant agreement No 649307. I thank David Soares for his collaboration as a research assistant and for gathering the ethnographic material that provides the core of this chapter. I am grateful to Marion Grau, Ronald Grimes, Graham Harvey, Michael Houseman, Sarah Pike and Jone Salomonsen for their useful suggestions. Giulia Cavallo, who worked as a postdoctoral fellow as part of the HERILIGION project, provided useful feedback as well as important updates about the pilgrimage in May 2019.

7

The interreligious Choir of Civilizations: Representations of democracy and the ritual assembly of multiculturalism in Antakya, Turkey

Jens Kreinath

This chapter discusses the intricate relationship between ritual and democracy in the context of interreligious relations in the Turkish province of Hatay. The findings presented here are drawn from ethnographic research conducted on the Choir of Civilizations in the city of Antakya based on interviews during the summers of 2012 through 2014. By design, this choir, founded in 2007, is intended to represent the diverse religious traditions in the city of Antakya in the form of a musical kaleidoscope of religious coexistence. Thus, it performs songs drawn from the various religious communities locally present: Jews, Orthodox Christians, Armenian Christians, Catholics, Turkish Sunni and Arab Alawite, the latter two being the major religious majorities of Hatay. To better understand the significance of the choir, some background information is necessary. At the choir's formation, it consisted of about thirty to fifty members, that grew growing over the years to about 150 choral members in 2014. Many founding members of the choir knew each other from years of living together in the old town of Antakya, where there are different churches, various mosques or shrines and a synagogue all located within the realm of one or two square miles. The first members of the choir consisted of the educated elite, who had a unique interest in supporting the culture of interreligious tolerance and respect among the members of their society. Although the Choir of Civilizations neither performs rituals in the strict sense nor serves as a public entity to formally represent democratization processes, it can provide valuable insights into the intertwined dynamics of ritual practice and democratic discourse in the public sphere in Hatay.

History of the Antakya Choir of Civilizations

Initiated on the occasion of the annual tourism week in April 2007 under the name 'Rainbow Choir', the choir was renamed only weeks later and officially founded under its current name as the Antakya Choir of Civilizations (Turkish: Antakya Medeniyetler Korosu). In direct consultation with the leaders of local religious communities who served as the initial board members and in close collaboration with the Ministry of Tourism and Culture, the choir was institutionally placed under the care of the governor of Hatay. With generous financial and institutional support from the government, the choir gained instant access to the most valuable resources and networks. Based on its success, it was subsequently coined as the exemplary emblem that best showcases the multiethnic and interreligious culture of Antakya.

In fact, advertisement of the plurality of diverse religious communities was the major aim of this initiative. In preparation for the week of tourism, the head of the directorate of cultural affairs considered and collected ideas regarding possible ways to brand Antakya for purposes of advertising its unique culture of religious coexistence. Instead of a specific delicacy, product or site of tourism through which other regions of Turkey are branded and advertised, the idea was that Antakya could best be represented through the dynamics of its religious culture. Within two weeks, leaders of the choir were appointed and started working with members of the religious communities to collect musical pieces of the different religious traditions. These were to be sung at the reception for the opening of the Week of Tourism in April 2007. On this occasion, the choir gave its first concert in the Archaeological Museum of Antakya. After the official name change in May 2007, the Choir of Civilizations gave its first public concert during celebrations of Pentecost in May 2007 at the Orthodox Christian Church located in the centre of old town Antakya.

The first concert outside of Hatay was held during the celebrations of the year of St. Paul in 2008. In Tarsus, the birthplace of St. Paul, the concert of the Choir of Civilizations provided a ceremonial framework for celebrations at the square of the main church. With members of each religious community singing songs from their own liturgical or musical tradition, this concert provided the first venue for the choir to visually and acoustically represent the religious diversity of Antakya during a festival held to celebrate the heritage of the Christian minority in present-day Turkey.

The concert in Tarsus was important to the identity formation of the choir as much as it marked a turning point in its history, during which the choir decided to abandon the idea that each religious community would sing only the songs from its own tradition. From then on, it established the practice that all members of the choir would sing all songs together. Additionally, all members of the choir would wear a uniform liturgical costume during the concerts and, except for religious headgear of men and women, would discard any other traditional garb through which the members could otherwise be identified in their religious identity. This concert in Tarsus also fostered the idea that the choir could spread in one voice the message of Antakya's religious peace and coexistence.

Soon afterwards, the choir began to perform outside of Turkey's borders beginning with an invitation to give a concert at a summit of the European Union in Paris. As many members of the first generation of the choir still vividly recall, in 2009, the members of the choir were informed about the concert on the very same day. The choir flew in the private jet of the then prime minister Recep Tayyip Erdoğan to Paris, gave a concert at the EU assembly and flew back to Antakya that evening. This was one of the most memorable events for those members of the choir who were able to participate. Another significant concert was given at the Assembly of the United Nations in New York in 2011. After being nominated for the Nobel Peace Prize during the same year, the choir performed at the European Parliament in Strasbourg and gave numerous concerts in European cities like Berlin, Oslo and Rome. In 2012, the Antakya Choir of Civilizations performed in Washington, D.C., followed by a concert tour in various towns in Germany. Most of these international tours were – as I was told by the choir members – organized and sponsored by the network of the Gülen movement in the respective cities and towns. Along with tours to international destinations, the choir continued to perform in Antakya and throughout Turkey.

Interreligious soundscapes of Antakya

Visitors to Antakya recognize that the public sphere in the old town district of Zenginler is characterized by a unique sonic or acoustic environment or 'soundscape' as 'the sonic environment, the sum total of all sounds within any definitive area which surround us as a result of certain historical, technological, and demographic processes' (Schafer 1993; see also Thompson 2002, 2; Ingold 2007, 10–11; Samuels et al. 2010, 330), that indicates the interreligious relations of this part of the city. Due to the close proximity of churches and mosques in Antakya's old town, it is at times possible to hear the ringing of church bells along with the call for prayer as it is common in this region

(Borsay 2002: 94–5; Bandak 2014: 248–50). It is in this context of the sonic environment of an interreligious soundscape that the Choir of Civilizations has recently had its own house: the House of Civilizations. This house with its high walls and spacious courtyard was formerly built and owned by Armenian Christians. After being abandoned for years, it was completely renovated in 2013–2014 in an antique Ottoman style and dedicated to the work of the Choir of Civilizations. The architecture of the House of Civilizations, with the high ceiling of its rehearsal rooms and a tiered platform at the eastern end of the elongated wide-open courtyard, provides a soundscape of its own. Due to architectural design, the soundscape is shielded from many other sounds that could disturb its peacefulness. The high stone brick walls act as a shield against the sounds of the surrounding streets and create a space of relative silence in the courtyard. Although the courtyard buffers the urban soundscape, it is possible to hear aerial sounds like the call for prayer and the church bells of the Orthodox Church. The medium-size stage at the eastern end of the courtyard is designed to give open-air concerts during the late spring and through the late summer months. The two rooms in the back of the house are primarily used for the choir's rehearsals, with one specifically designed for the choristers and the other for the instrumentalists, but they can also serve as a meeting space and for concerts during the rainy winter months. They both have very high ceilings and the only windows they have face the courtyard. The Choir of Civilizations also accentuates the interreligious soundscape of Antakya by blending different local styles and traditions into a unique performance of religion and music. In doing so, it serves as a sonic medium to initiate, signify and maintain the dynamics of interreligious relations in Antakya. It established itself as an auditory medium in the transformation of diverse religious and musical folk traditions through their performance on stage (Shannon 2004; Ingold 2007; Born 2011). Particularly the aim of bringing the message that peaceful interreligious coexistence is possible on stage brings the forms of religious coexistence as practised by locals in everyday life through social life, political debate and economic interaction onto a new level. Framing these musical styles and religious traditions as a message of interreligious peace (Robertson 2010) carries this message by musical means beyond the borders of the city.

Although the choir produces this interreligious soundscape primarily on stage, the soundscape the choir produces is perceived by the members of different religious communities differently (Dağtaş 2012; Kreinath 2019a). Through the songs alluding to a different set of soundscapes, the audience is able to perceive these as different soundscapes interacting with one another on stage. The local influence of the choir and its musical performances involves its contribution not only to the religious soundscape in Antakya but also to the sensory effects it has on its members (Kellogg 2015: 433–4; Laack 2015; Wilke 2019). It enables the members of the choir to experience and appreciate the musical features of other religious traditions while nevertheless empowering the latter to interact with one another musically and ritually, not only during rehearsals and performances but also in the course of social interaction outside of the choir's direct vicinity. In this regard, the Antakya Choir of Civilizations cultivates a new sensory aesthetic of religious music and thus contributes to the formation and transformation of a civil society as it fosters respect and courtesy through the ritual interactions of its musical performances (Dağtaş 2012). It does so by allowing its members from different religious communities to interact with one another through the religious aesthetics of sensory perception during their joint performance of religious songs.

Through the adjusting of musical scores, members of the different communities adjust to the different musical styles and religious aesthetics ingrained in the various traditions that are represented in the choir and only come into play through its musical performances (Born 2011: 380; Faudree 2012: 520; Laack 2015). The choir rehearses the songs not by using musical scores but rather singing by ear. The texts that the choir uses that are not in the Turkish language are transcribed by using Turkish phonemics. In light of this, one can recognize the variations that are taking place in the choir's production of an interreligious soundscape. Musical instruments used in the concerts reflect to a certain extent the local musical traditions. These include the *bağlama*, a traditional Anatolian string instrument, the *ney*, a long reed flute used for traditional Sufi music, the cello, the guitar, the violin and the flute, as well as the shells and the drums. The use of electronic percussion during the concerts as an aesthetic device is foreign to the musical performance of local religious traditions and adds a layer of contemporary mundane reality. To untangle the dynamics of interreligious relations at play in these performances, it is necessary to develop a clearer idea of the musical and social assemblages these performances put into effect.

The choir's repertoire of local musical traditions

The songs performed during concerts were chosen from a repertoire of religious songs collected by the leaders of the choir who met and consulted with the leaders of the local communities represented in the choir. The repertoire consisted in 2013 of about thirty-five songs, which are sung in changing combinations during different concerts. Even though the religious communities represented in the choir do not have the same forms and styles of musical traditions, the repertoire was intended to represent at least some traditions of every religious community participating in the choir.

Over the years, various songs were added or removed depending on the priorities of the conductor and preferences of the choir's members. The actual selection of songs from this repertoire always depends on the time, place and occasion of the concert and is made anew by the conductor every time. As a guiding principle, however, the programme for each concert consists of a mixture of Jewish, Armenian, Orthodox and Catholic Christian, as well as adaptations from the Sunni and Alawite Muslim tradition of Qur'an recitation. While some songs chosen at any given concert are part of the standard repertoire, other songs are only chosen for the respective occasion. Usually one song in particular is chosen for each concert to reflect on the local tradition of the city where the concert is given and to better connect with the anticipated audience.

The repertoire of the Choir of Civilizations was adopted from existing local traditions as practised within the religious communities. However, while the local Jewish and Christian communities have a considerable musical tradition, such equivalents do not exist among the Sunni and Alawite communities (Kreinath and Sarıönder 2018). The repertoire of the Choir of Civilizations includes many songs from local folk music traditions or from other well-established musical traditions more widely known throughout Turkey (Stokes 1998). Besides, the choir also adapts to local customs, as it sings all songs from the Christian tradition homophonically instead of polyphonically as well as in tonic scales and tempi that are different from those used in Jewish or Christian religious services.

Aside from the specific selection of religious songs for the individual concerts, the overall structure of all concerts in principle follows a previously determined sequence. All concerts open with the ninth Symphony of Ludwig van Beethoven, known as 'The Ode to Joy', which was adapted as the Anthem of the European Union and identified as an emblem for civil engagement and political participation, and all concerts end with the 'Memleketim', a popular folk song widely known in Turkey. Both songs frame every concert and provide – aside from songs selected to represent the tradition of the host city or community, which often can be mundane – a clearly secular framework within which the religious songs from the various traditions are performed.

The way in which the songs of the different religious traditions are arranged into a sequence and sung collectively along with the accompanist musical instruments creates an interreligious soundscape through the amalgamation of different harmonic styles and traditions. The songs that became most popular throughout its history include the 'Eladon', 'La El Baruh' and 'Hava Nagila' from the Jewish tradition, which appear as recurrent elements in the concerts. Preferred choices for the concerts also include the 'La Rabbal Kuvvat' taken from the Orthodox Christian tradition and the 'Sari Gelin' and 'Sasna Şaran' implemented from the Armenian tradition. Similarly, the 'Hallelujah', 'Jubilate Deo', as well as 'Laudate Si' are songs most commonly employed from the Catholic musical tradition. The songs that are taken to represent the Sunni Muslim tradition are 'Bülbül Kasidesi', 'Salat-i Ummiye' and 'Erler Demine,' while 'Yine Dertli Dertli' and 'Demedim Mi' as those songs taken from the Alevi and Sufi tradition. All these songs by design create musical soundscapes, and through their performance on stage, they represent the different religious soundscapes in which they are traditionally embedded. The sequence in which the songs are sung during the concerts is aimed to create an acoustic environment, where each of the songs reflects and inflects the various soundscapes that the choir aims to represent.

Aesthetic design features of the Choir of Civilization

Aesthetically, the choir transgresses various traditional distinctions between the liturgical and musical use of religious songs as well as the religious and secular function of a concert hall or church. To sing religious songs of worship and prayer as part of a musical concert implies a conflicting frame of reference by reframing the intended meaning of religious songs within a secular context (Handelman 2004; Kreinath 2019b). This also changes the interaction between the choir and its audience within the soundscape that is created through the concerts.

The concerts are supported by lighting and background acoustics. An arrangement of the stage, with religious and secular symbols displayed in the background before which the choir performs its concerts, supports the perception of the interreligious soundscape that the Choir of Civilizations creates. The concerts are all well-choreographed and the visual design of the stage is usually very strong. Considering the choir's beige silk robes, the compositions, the instruments played and the lighting of the stage, the musical performances simulate a form of religious worship. Even though the choir performs at both religious and secular locations, the concerts are always aesthetically designed to create an experience of religious peace and spread the message of tolerance through musical means, as it is also known from other contexts (Clark 2010; Robertson 2010; King and Tan 2014).

The blending of religious traditions in the design and composition of musical performances uses various forms of interreligious aesthetics. Although the concerts are framed as cultural performances of religious songs and conducted in often predominantly secular settings, the combination of traditional religious music with elements of local folklore gives the design of these performances a religious character. In doing so, the choir shapes its own culture of religious coexistence among the members, and through their joint performance, the choir's members are all perceived as serving the One God of the Abrahamic religious tradition (Bandak 2014; King and Tan 2014).

In the communal and public enactment of singing songs that otherwise serve religious and cultural functions within the different religious communities, it demonstrates that the Jewish, Christian and Muslim members of the choir are willing to jointly praise the same God by singing songs that originated in their different religious traditions. In doing so, the Choir of Civilizations creates a new form of religious worship that is ambivalent about its religiosity and secularity, aesthetically transgressing such frames of reference (Kreinath 2019b). By being at the same time religious and secular by nature, it cultivates, embodies and shapes a form of interreligious coexistence in its own way. Regardless of how it represents the actual religious diversity of Antakya, no religious symbols that would exclusively be identified with one of the represented traditions are displayed on stage.[1] It is primarily by means of religious songs that an aesthetic soundscape of interreligious coexistence impacts how the dynamics between the three Abrahamic religions are perceived and how the musical performances of religious songs contribute to a peaceful coexistence (Shannon 2004).

Negotiating religious traditions and the message of the Choir of Civilizations

One of the most significant design features of the Choir of Civilizations is that the members of different religious communities sing songs together that are – to differing degrees – central to religious worship in synagogues, churches or mosques. The main reason for the decision to sing all songs together was apparently an aesthetic one. Because the religious groups were unevenly represented in their musical traditions and in number, with some communities consisting of just five members and others more than four times that size, the volume of the smaller groups was considered not strong enough to have the desired impact to make this project worth continuing within that format. This decision, which was made by the conductor, led to considerable discussion among the members of the choir and the leaders of the respective religious communities about which songs were acceptable to be performed by all members. Some members initially could not accept singing songs from other religious communities due to dogmatic reasons or simply because they felt odd or uncomfortable performing and representing the musical traditions of religious communities other than their own.

Overall, this discussion assessing all songs for whether or not they would be acceptable or at least tolerable found that with the exception of some few folklorist songs, almost none of the religious songs were uncontested. As recalled by many of my interlocutors, this phase in the initial formation process was experienced by many members as quite challenging and personal, as the members of the choir were asked to do something they had never done before: not only to tolerate the beliefs of their fellow members from other religious communities but also to actively engage in some of their religious traditions and cosmologies. This process was intense for a lot of members, as the very act of talking about one's religion or religious beliefs in public is quite a sensitive issue for most natives of Antakya. Religion is, by most, considered a private issue, despite its virtual presence in everyday life (Kreinath 2019b).

In the end, the choir as a whole ended up with some major revisions to the repertoire of the choir's songs. Whereas before numerous songs of the other religious communities were tolerated simply for matters of respect and non-interference, now the situation was considerably different. Those who would sing songs of praise and prayer from religious traditions other than their own would voice and thus actively represent these traditions. With the decision for the whole choir to sing the songs of other religious traditions, the minimal consensus of all members involved needed to be reached, and this affected the selection of the songs that were available for further consideration.

The choir assembled a catalog that was generic in their message relating to the praising of God while at the same time excluding dogmatic differences, particularly those attached to the names of figures central for the respective beliefs like Ali or Mary (Kreinath 2014, 2019a). This decision can be seen as unique in the formation and shaping of interreligious relations. The assemblage of songs of different religious traditions that are sung by all choir members thus has a significant impact on the message the choir is able to transmit (King and Tan 2014). Even though not all religious groups represented in the choir have the same form of musical traditions, as discussed above, the repertoire was invented to give every religious group its share in the choir. As the members of all religious communities started to sing the songs of combined religious traditions and wore uniform attire for the concerts, the audience would not be able to distinguish or identify the religious affiliation of the choir's members. This procedure helped to overcome religious division among the choir members by erasing their differences and creating a form of group membership unique for this choir.

Although the concerts are framed as musical performances from the different religious traditions and indiscriminately conducted in secular and religious settings, the combination of traditional religious music with elements of local folk music gives the performance a ritual design (Kreinath 2016). Since some of these songs are integral parts of liturgical traditions as performed by some communities in their religious services, the musical performances gain a semi-religious character while they are usually performed on a stage or in a church setting.

The mission of the choir and its musical and religious composition

When the Antakya Choir of Civilizations was founded, its explicit aim was to advertise the peaceful coexistence of different religions in Antakya through musical performances. Its mission to bring peace to the world – as it was subsequently articulated – assumes that peace in the world depends on the peaceful coexistence between the different monotheistic religions. It is stated by numerous informants that the concerts of the Choir of Civilizations demonstrate peaceful coexistence by affirming that members of different religious communities not only sing together the songs of their traditions but also express their common belief in the One God that conjoins the Jewish, Christian and Muslim faiths based on the shared soundscape's capacity to animate an imagined community, 'aggregating its adherents into virtual collectivities and publics based on musical and other identifications' (Born 2011: 382).

The main message of the choir is that all Abrahamic religions worship the same God and hence the similarities between the Jewish, Christian and Muslim religions are emphasized. The message is embodied through the assemblage of songs that are sung within the frame of the choir's concerts. Since most of the songs have a specific function in the local religious communities, the singing of these songs still reflects and performs their religious functions for the members of the respective community even if these songs are sung on the stage of a concert hall.

The production of the interreligious soundscape shapes the perception of religious dynamics between the different religions involved. It is the unity of these communities that is highlighted and in the end the choir embodies and enacts a form of interreligious worship as they praise together the unity of the same God. In doing so, the choir is shaping its own form of religious practice. The leader of the choir even stated in an interview with me that the choir is an instrument of God to bring peace to the world. Advertising the plurality of diverse religious communities was one of the methods for this approach, and it serves as a major motivator for interreligious engagement. At the opening of a concert, the choir is always announced as representing the three monotheistic religions and its six denominations in Antakya.

Social dynamics in the transformation of interreligious relations

The Choir of Civilizations presents a unique example highlighting the dynamics of interreligious aesthetics that emerge by conjoining musical and ritual elements that otherwise do not exist together. Due to the transformation of the interreligious relations among the members of the choir, formations of social relations as they occur through the work of the choir can be analysed in terms of ritual. The membership in the choir is defined by three criteria. One criterion for participating in the choir is membership in one of the religious communities. The second criterion is that one needs to have been born in Antakya. In addition, minimal vocal skills are the third criterion for the admission to the choir. The membership in the choir is decided by a committee; and new members of the choir are selected annually in September.

The internal structure of the choir as it currently exists explains some of the dynamics of interreligious relations that have already been analysed. There is a clear distinction of the roles and hierarchies established in the choir, which is also reflected by the salary that some of the members receive. The conductor deals with all business related to the work of the choir, including the arrangement and organization of the concerts as well as the rehearsals and concert performances. He also deals with the media and is the only person in the choir who is authorized to give interviews. The conductor has a staff of numerous voluntary assistants who take care of all related administrative responsibilities in particular with regard to the arrangement and organization of concerts that are performed outside of Antakya. Although the choir is a lay choir based on the commitment of voluntary choristers, professional instrumentalists are hired and paid per concert. The work of the choir is usually accompanied by eight to ten instrumentalists. Overall, the instrumentalists themselves are mostly music teachers or professional musicians who make a living by playing music. Other than the instrumentalists, none of the regular choir members receive a salary or an honorarium, although travel and housing expenses during travels for the concerts are covered. At times, the choir is even accompanied by a well-known soloist who is paid an honorarium.

The instrumentalists are from within the musical profession, usually with respective academic training. With the exception of the priests and imams, all other choral members are lay persons from different social strata and religious communities in Antakya. Although participation for the choir members is voluntary, the conductor clearly has a list of preferred choristers who are invited to join the international concerts based on experience and degree of commitment. The degree of commitment required to be a member of the choir often only permits students, retirees or teachers who could make special arrangements with the school authorities to participate in the choir activities on a regular basis. Participation in the choir is particularly attractive for teachers, students and younger members of the society due to the fact that the choir is very successful and established. However, numerous students I talked with had to give up their role in the choir due to their commitments to their future careers that are not in the field of music.

This commitment to the choir was centralized in that most of the original members had a unique interest in fostering and supporting the culture of interreligious tolerance and respect among the members of their society. The vast majority of the 150-member choir is Sunni, while other groups are minimally represented with at times only one or two members. As dictated by the choir leader, religion and politics are topics that are not allowed to be talked about in the House of Civilization. Interestingly, some of the younger members informed me that they did not know which religion many of the other members are a part of and that this is not something discussed, which seems to be a norm among the members. Privileges (received by members of the choir selected for international travel and similar to those issued to diplomats) particularly irritated the members who were either not included in the travels or permitted to join the choir. Although the choir aimed to keep a considerably low profile with the intention of being a lay choir, the members grew to serve as cultural and religious ambassadors of Antakya's peaceful coexistence and were recognized as local celebrities.

Political implications of the Choir of Civilizations

The choir dwells in the cosmopolitan image of Antakya with its portrayal of peaceful coexistence and is used for advertising the city's faith tourism and interreligious pilgrimage (Doğruel 2013; Prager 2013). Beside invitations from different foundations and organizations to perform at social gatherings, cultural events or religious festivals, the concerts were sponsored by local and regional businesses, which considered such events to be public outreach as a welcome opportunity for charity and advertisement. The instant success of the choir can be attributed to the continued support and endorsement of various local religious organizations. Through backing from local networks of the social, political and economic sectors of the civil society in Antakya, the choir gained wider public recognition and was considered one of the most successful civil initiatives in Antakya.

Since its inception, the choir's success exceeded the founders' expectations and, over the past few years, the fame of this choir has transcended the Turkish borders. This success was greeted with mixed responses from various segments of the society – mainly among those people who worked as professionals in a religious, cultural or educational sector or dealt with music and folklore in various ways, leading to suspicions and rumours about the surprising success and seemingly unconditional support by the Turkish government. The choir's public recognition also became a particularly sensitive issue since other choirs and cultural initiatives that were founded with the intent to further strengthen interreligious relations and forms of religious coexistence did not receive such generous support from the government, nor were they so closely tied to the economic sectors of the business world and regional tourism industry.

The choir's public appearances were followed by the local media and always covered in local newspapers and broadcasted on local television stations. These achievements not only impacted the general perception of the choir but also shaped the public appearance of the choir and its members. Aside from some critical reports in some leading and well-established newspapers in Antakya that shaped the public discourse on the choir, the broad public coverage and media attention also created social and religious dynamics in Antakya that led to the formation of new initiatives and the foundation of new choirs – partly in critical response to the broader controversial perception of the choir.

Although none of the political events – which marked some of the major turning points in recent Turkish national and international politics – immediately impacted the work of the Choir of Civilizations, the dynamics these events unleashed in local and global politics that also played out on regional and local levels impacted the long-term mission and mobility of the Choir of Civilizations in the arena of representing interreligious relations of Hatay both at home and abroad. Since the external dynamics that impacted the Choir of Civilizations themselves align to different notions of democracy and governance while employing their own sets of rituals, the comparison of how ritual and democracy relate to one another in other more distinct cases, like the Gezi protests in 2013 and the attempted military coup in 2016, helps illustrate how the Choir of Civilizations is positioned in the context of local and regional dynamics.

Even though the leader of the choir claims to stay out of discussions about religion and politics by not taking any particular position, the choir is loyal to the current government according to its leader. The leader clearly stated that the choir performs whenever and wherever it is invited by the government or any other social, cultural, religious, political or economic organization or foundation that supports its mission. However, some critics of the choir say that they are too closely tied to the current government and that it would vanish if a new government were elected. The stance of the choir's leader and conductor to stay out of matters concerning religion and politics is perceived by some not only as simply opportunistic or tactical but also as dangerously naïve and highly controversial. By not taking sides or by remaining silent on religious and political issues, the choir is perceived as being content with the government. This position is understandable since the choir is financially and logistically dependent not only on the governor of Hatay but also on the president of Turkey, who had a hand in its instant success. These strategies were questioned by members of different religious minorities and political opposition groups who have suffered from the politics of religious and ethnic division that have increased in Turkey since 2013.

Conclusion

This chapter addresses the limits of rituals shaping public discourse and democratic participation. The main objective of the research project *Reassembling Democracy* was to determine how far rituals are or can become a cultural resource for democracy. My case study concerning Antakya's interreligious Choir of Civilizations suggests that the ritual dimensions of the choir's work only have a limited impact. As argued, the Antakya Choir of Civilizations aimed to represent the religious diversity of this region by dwelling on the public image of the city's multiculturalism and cosmopolitanism. Composed of members of the three Abrahamic religions, this choir could be perceived as integral to the representation of religious coexistence, as it performs religious songs on a concert stage, thus presenting features resembling ritual elements of religious worship.

It could be assumed that a thorough study of the internal and external dynamics of interreligious coexistence in the civil society as reflected in the composition of the choir would provide some interesting ethnographic evidence and some considerable ground for studying ritual as a cultural resource of democracy. Focusing on the agenda of the Antakya Choir of Civilizations – that is to perform songs of different religious traditions on stage with a choir composed of members of different religious communities – the case study was designed to address the main question of our research group, Reassembling Democracy: 'Can rituals also contribute to enhance democracy or to change society?' Even though my general answer would be affirmative to the research objective, the specifics of my ethnographic evidence do not allow me to come to such a conclusion. It was integral to the argument presented in this chapter to specify the factors that accelerated or blocked certain internal and external dynamics that led to the branding of the choir. However, the main model on which the choir is based is a representational one, which takes the mere presence of different religious communities in the choir as being sufficient to index the religious coexistence in Antakya. Put otherwise, it is believed that it is sufficient to perform concerts with the appropriate songs and members of the respective communities to be effective in making changes in supporting interreligious peace.

The Antakya Choir of Civilizations makes every effort to represent interreligious peace through the interface of concerts. Other than the transmission of the general image of religious coexistence as practised in Antakya and represented in the choir, no attempts are made to enhance democracy or change society. It is the image of representation that matters most for the Antakya Choir of Civilizations, and the concerts are given on invitation by any special interest groups, businesses or any governmental or non-governmental organizations. The internal dynamics of social and religious relations among members of different religious communities may contribute to the unity and cohesion of the choir. However, the social hierarchy within the group indicates the social dynamics within the choir that might counter the public image that the choir is supposed to convey.

Part Three

Commemoration and resistance

8

The ritual powers of the weak: Democracy and public responses to the 22 July 2011 terrorist attacks on Norway

Jone Salomonsen

On Friday afternoon, 22 July 2011, a bomb in Oslo destroyed a government building and killed eight people. Police quickly closed off all the downtown streets and asked people to go home and stay indoors. Soon text messages started coming from young people at the Norwegian Labor Youth's (AUF) summer camp on the Utøya Island, an hour outside Oslo. Kids reported being hunted and shot by a tall, white Norwegian man dressed as a police officer as they were screaming and running for their lives. It took seventy long minutes after the first message was sent until the real police arrested the thirty-two-year-old Norwegian Anders Behring Breivik. By then he had killed sixty-nine people, the youngest only fourteen years old.

Norway is a small country with only 5 million inhabitants. A lot of people knew someone who knew someone who was at the summer camp on Utøya. We were shocked, and many felt powerless, weak and confused. People hid in their homes, continually watching television to get the latest news, trying to understand. But by early evening some started to think and act differently. They walked to Oslo Cathedral to put down flowers and light candles in the town square bordering the church. Rumours about the flower 'ceremony' spread, and more and more people showed up. On Monday 25 July, more than 200,000 people gathered with flowers in their hands, creating what was later known as 'an ocean of roses' (see Figure 8.1). For several weeks, massive gatherings marked a togetherness, solidarity and a different kind of 'love of country' than did Breivik's nationalist feelings and violent acts. In the years that followed, memorials for the victims of Breivik's attacks tried to capture the spirit of these powerful and inclusive non-violent gestures.

Figure 8.1 The Ocean of Roses, Oslo Cathedral. Source: http://static.vg.no/uploaded/image/bilderigg/2012/07/21/1342889615890_239.jpg

This chapter moves from a descriptive analysis of Breivik's ideology and mission to an account of three cases of ritual imaginaries intended to counteract them. These are the Ocean of Roses that arose in downtown Oslo, a multi-workshop for young adults at the Norwegian Centre for Design and Architecture (DogA) in the fall 2014 during which participants proposed a number of memorial designs and an actual memorial site, *The Clearing*, built at Utøya in 2015. The questions asked by the chapter concern what is created by ritual and what these particular rituals tell us about ordinary people's ritual competence and sense of democracy. Hannah Arendt's (1998) conceptualization of the political as distinct from the social, and her attendant opposition between *demos* and *ethnos*, as well as Chantal Mouffe's (2002) distinction between the political and the pre-political, is used to interpret the findings. Ritual, specifically the ritualized creativity of 'the weak' that became manifest in post-2011 Norway, is revealed to be both a gate that leads from community to democracy and a fence that stands between them. Such ritual, I argue, is conceptualized not so much as a political means for building stronger democracies but as a pre-political tool to secure democracy's precondition: an egalitarian people capable of accepting others' humanity and rights.[1]

Breivik's mission: A fascist revolution – first terror, then cultural wars

When Anders Behring Breivik conducted his carefully planned terrorist attacks he wanted to 'kill' Norway as an open, democratic society. From his perspective, he killed in order to save the nation from multicultural decay and the slow extermination of the white race due to Muslim invasion and feminist Norwegian women's betrayal when marrying non-Aryan migrant men. His attack was both a declaration of war against liberal democracy and a spur to Norwegian men to wake up and join his ultra-nationalistic battle for the country (cf. Salomonsen 2013, 2015, 2017). Although he spent eight years of his life in single-minded and systematic preparation for war, he conceived of himself as a consecrated Templar who was only executing orders. Thus, he drew on powerful symbols and the rhetoric of so-called magical rites to prepare, stage and legitimize the 22 July massacre as a possible sacrifice, his sacrifice, and to be proud that he was willing to die as a martyr. Then, at the opening of his trial on 17 April 2012, he greeted the court with a raised arm and a clenched fist – the fascist 'heil'. Finally, towards the end of his opening statement, he proclaimed:

> Multiculturalism is an anti-Norwegian and anti-European hate ideology … We, the indigenous people of Norway, are now in a situation where we are losing our capital [Oslo] and our cities … Responsible Norwegians and Europeans feel morally obligated to see that Norwegians are not made into a minority in their own country … The attacks [22 July 2011] were preventive attacks in defense of Norwegian culture and my people. I acted from the principle of necessity on behalf of my people, my religion, my ethnicity, my city, and my country.

What exactly is Breivik's religion, and what kind of society is he propagating? Just hours before his attack, Breivik published a much-studied online manifesto, *2083 – A European Declaration of Independence*, where he calls for a violent change of European political realities. He also posted a ten-minute video in which he urges radical nationalists in Europe and the United States to 'embrace martyrdom' and to join him in defending ethnic rights to a homeland. The video shows him dressed as a Knight Templar, wielding a large sword and calling for a return to the zeal of the medieval Christian crusades.

Breivik grew up in a secular, democratic society with the Lutheran Church as the hegemonic, state church of Norway. Historically, the church has always been closely linked with Norwegian culture and society. Until the 1990s, for example, the church refused to marry gays and lesbians or employ them as ministers if married. Then, after twenty years of intense debate, it changed its own theological understanding of marriage (in 2007) and quickly developed a new, inclusive marriage liturgy. In 2017, almost 71 per cent of the population was still affiliated with this majority church even though less than 4 per cent attended Sunday worship on a weekly basis. And 88 per cent of those who lose a loved one choose a funeral ceremony under the auspices of the Church of Norway (Høeg, this volume). This way of 'doing church', a fairly stable pattern, may be related to what Grace Davie has termed 'vicarious religion': religion as performed by an active minority on behalf of a much larger number (Davie 2007: 22). The majority may approve of what the minority is 'doing' or regard church as important to maintain the moral fabric of society. A Norwegian with this paradoxical relationship to church will downplay personal belief and call herself a 'cultural Christian'. Breivik is no exception.

In his manifesto Breivik argues that religion is necessary to society and therefore also to successfully building a new society. But the Church of Norway is not the one he chooses. Not only does it support social democracy, it also endorses multicultural, feminist, homosexual and trans-religious practices. He calls instead for a return to a strong, unified Catholic Church, the way he imagines 'it must have been' before the Reformation: an aristocratic house with one will and one sword. Only such a militant church can be at the head of the non-pluralist, homogeneous, patriarchal and traditional society he wants to re-construct. Yet, in a typically Norwegian way, Breivik felt the need to explain that he was not really a 'believer' but merely identified with church as a 'cultural Christian'. Pages 1360–3 of his manifesto reveal that he has in fact two religious identities, as both a cultural Christian, relating to his Norwegian citizenship, and a cultural Odinist, relating to the heritage of his Norwegian ancestors.[2] His emphasis on European Christianity may have been strategic, as Odinism is too local and ethnically limited to Northern Europe.[3]

When Breivik reappeared in public in 2017 (to accuse the state of Norway with having imposed inhumane prison conditions) he had resolved this apparent religious knot by purifying his thinking and taking sides. He announced that he was no longer a Christian but simply an Odinist. Furthermore, he had embraced National Socialism as his version of fascism and dedicated his life and work to the deceased Norwegian NS-leader Vidkun Quisling in a ceremony in his prison cell. He had also changed his view on tactics, he said. He now distanced himself from terrorism as a method. In 2012, after the Greek right-wing party *Golden*

Dawn won more than twenty seats in the Greek parliament through the regular electoral system (twenty-one national candidates, as well as two in the European Parliament), Breivik gained new trust in peaceful methods to transform society.[4]

It needs to be emphasized that in Breivik's case, the term 'fascism' does not denote a concrete regime but points to a hybrid, religionized, ultra-nationalist ideology that criticizes the society we live in based on a very approximate vision of what should replace it. Historian Roger Griffin has introduced the concept *generic* fascism to explain thinkers like Breivik. Generic fascism has three characteristics: belief in collective regeneration and rebirth of society after full collapse or deep crisis; practical politics anchored in myths of a past golden age and in work for its retrieval; nation understood as an organic entity of ethnically interlinked peoples and patriots, governed by a monarchic-hierarchical principle (Griffin 1992). Thus, while fascism aims to deconstruct democracy and create something completely different, it can also use the democratic political system to mobilize voters and gain power legally and through slow reform, and then destroy this system later on. This typically modern, intellectual and reform-friendly version of fascism seeks political change through cultural wars, not military ones, and makes use of a *meta-political* strategy to do the more 'spiritual' work of bringing about political change by modifying people's awareness and culture.[5] This 'option' was not acknowledged by Breivik until 2017. Chantal Mouffe (2002: 63) seems to warn us of this type of fascism when she reminds us of the interplay of two different traditions in modern democracy: on the one hand, the classical democratic, communitarian tradition of equality and popular sovereignty, and, on the other, the liberal tradition and rule of law and individual liberty that protects minorities from oppressive majority rule.[6] In the resurgence of Radical right movements today, communitarian egalitarian ideals are typically foregrounded while liberal rights such as rights of assembly, rights to freedom of speech, sexual rights and reproductive rights are attacked.

From this perspective, terrorist acts are to be understood not as political acts but as preparatory to the breakdown of democratic society. Indeed, following Hannah Arendt, true political acts do not seek to create a tribe or ethnic culture but rather a civil society and a new, constituted people that come together as *demos*. Politics deal with the coexistence and association of different people in the contemporary and in the open, not with society as a hereditary, tribal unified totality or as a secret club where those who do not fit, such as the youths at the Norwegian Labor Youth summer camp at Utøya, are weeded out. From this point of view, Breivik had no real political project but was merely articulating a yearning to return to a kin-based, patriarchal unity inside a tall, ethnic fence – a project helped by his guns, the internet and the microphones he had access to during his trials.[7]

The ritual powers of the weak

I approach people's gathering in the streets to protest Breivik and mourn the dead as an instance of ritual. Why ritual and not just a social event? Sociologist Emile Durkheim (1995) saw ritual as a socio-religious tool. The work of religion was to create social cohesion and unify its practitioners into 'one single moral community'. Ritual was the tool with which this miracle could happen and social bonds be forged. In this light, ritual acts to preserve existing social realities, not to protest or explore other possible worlds. Durkheim probably assigned this power to rites because their underlying symbolic imaginaries were borrowed from small tribal societies and from what he understood to be the elemental forms of religion, universally. Thus, the social was perceived as a unified totality, and rites were seen as expressive of this totality, providing meaning and consolidating moral community. In this sociological tradition, ritual underlies the social, its ground or supportive wall, not a productive anti-structure in which alternative worlds might be created and visited. In short, in the end, the aim of ritual is political. When Breivik refers to 'my religion' and points to the necessity of returning to religion to be able to build a new society for 'my people', he leans on this powerful sociological matrix and its allegation that ritual/religion facilitates bonding and group building within society perceived as One – traditional or modern – and without which there would be no stable societies.

The problem with Durkheim's conceptualization of ritual is that the social is collapsed into the political. By making this 'category mistake' both authoritarian fanatics like Breivik and utopian religious or social movements may fuel their dreams that a new world order can be created by social means, by merely living 'as if' or by changing consciousness or by dropping a bomb, and that working through the slow democratic public assemblies and political institutions is not a necessity. Another effect of making this 'category mistake' is that the more generative side of ritual itself is easily displaced and attributed to art, play or psychology. This generative dimension of ritual refers to what is commonly called its subjunctive mode, its 'what if' mode of creativity, and ritual's ability to invert or bring into being new possibilities through its own inner potentialities and subversive dynamics (Handelman 2005).

To help scholars distinguish better between two very different forms of appearing together in the social, anthropologist Victor Turner (1989) split the category of ritual into 'ceremony' (the actual) and 'ritual' (the possible). While ceremony might be about both *social* cohesion and the harnessing of the *political* powers to rule, only ritual can facilitate the enactment and articulation of collective *aspirations* aimed at transformation and change. The secret tool of ritual to achieve 'change' is its interstitial and processual character, its framing and sequencing processes. Through the ritual process, a person or a group is transported from structure to a liminal space and back to structure – a process which in itself can create major 'before' and 'after' experiences. Thus, the liminal is essential and key to this definition of ritual. According to Turner, it is in fact only liminality that can constitute (time-limited) zones of creativity, subjunctivity and communitas (Turner 1979: 469).

Turner was aware that the powers of ritual in liminal space can also be subversive. When he coined the expression 'the (ritual) powers of the weak' he referred to ritualized, social critique performed by stable categories of people, such as 'women' and 'outlaws', directed against the strong and mighty (1979: 478). I disagree with Turner that the contextual 'weak' in ritualized space represents a stable social class or position and that the situated powers of the weak are necessarily intentional, self-conscious or directional. Ritual can evolve spontaneously and even surprise its participants. By gathering together in the streets of Oslo, 'the weak', victims of terrorist threats, 'grew strong' and produced a sense of taking back control over their daily lives. But to the extent that such acts produced 'meaning' they did so not because of people's explicit intentions to manifest criticism, but through a need to be with others, to comfort and be comforted, which took place through the gathering itself.

In the Ocean of Roses, both modes of rituality were present, both ceremony and ritual, with one mode evolving into the other, without clear beginning or end. I am interested here in what was created by these two modes of ritual in the Norwegian post-22 July responses and also by what this response says about people's ritual competence.

The Ocean of Roses in the streets of Oslo, 2011

The immediate counter-response to Breivik's horrific killing was the small condolence ritual in the early evening of July 22, which quickly evolved into a strong mobilization of togetherness, solidarity and protest. Some explained their participation as springing from a need 'to come together', others that they felt a need 'to act': 'I had to do something' (*jeg matte gjøre noe*). The act of leaving one's home and 'coming together' with other Norwegians one did not know in unprotected space in downtown Oslo could include other smaller acts such as picking or buying flowers, writing a personal condolence letter, fixing up an old teddy bear, bringing chocolate or asking the children or the neighbours to join in. All the objects would be placed in the streets, although some of them were intended for the dead, some 'for my little country' (Norway), while others could be more political in character, diagnosing the situation.[8]

On Monday 25 July, almost half of the capital's population (more than 200,000) attended this silent condolence ritual, and the flowers and other objects they brought grew into what Norwegians called an 'ocean of roses'.[9] The event was attended by the royal family and Prime Minister Jens Stoltenberg, who said, 'The answer to violence is even more democracy, even more humanity. But never naivety.' He encouraged the crowd to dress up the whole city with their flowers, as a protective shield and as an expression of love. The Ocean of Roses spread out and its dense materiality flowed into more streets, squares and parks, and touched buildings associated with Parliament, the Norwegian Labor Party and Labor Union, as if a coordinated body in motion, and peaked at Oslo Cathedral.

Oslo Cathedral opened its doors to the 'push of the ocean' in a way that has never been seen before. The streets continued materially into the middle passage of the church and people circulated in and out for weeks. On the town square bordering the church, the gathering grew, its density standing in contrast with the quiet atmosphere that reigned. People behaved as if at a funeral or as if at church. They greeted newcomers with a nod, perhaps a smile and whisper, by giving them space, but in the absence of loud talking. These simple gestures were enough to create a sense of 'love' and 'solidarity' experienced and attested by thousands of people, and the red rose became its symbol. At the same time, these actions were more than symbolic expressions of something else. They were, in themselves, embodiments of peace with unknown others, expressing great trust and therefore also great vulnerability. People stood side by side with others they did not know and were not afraid of being stabbed.

I have already suggested that both ceremony and ritual, the two modes of rituality, were present in people's response in the streets of Oslo, each leading to the other. The more political aspect of the gathering, the ceremonial, obviously spoke back to Breivik and to the world, 'we are not your people', simply through the gesture of forming a large ritually structured 'body' that positioned 'itself' respectfully in front of important political and ecclesial institutions. In doing so it confirmed Norway's democratic constitution and Christian-humanistic heritage. At the same time, this structured body was transformed into *communitas* (a liminal form of togetherness) when it turned inward on itself, processing people's fear and grief at having lost fellow humans and their own sense of security. Ritual was in this case contemplative, opening up space for a new experience of togetherness, love and solidarity primarily characterized by an attentive collectiveness. Silence was privileged; so were material, individual expression and movement. Ronald Grimes repeatedly reminded participants in the REDO project from which this volume arose that ritual in this sense 'springs up in the cracks created by disasters'. In this mode, rituals are not the performances of the 'as is' of democratic society or of the perfection of business as usual but, to use Turner's formula, enactments of collective aspirations of 'what if's'.

The 22 July protesters' massive presence at the edge of Oslo Cathedral was clearly part of their bodily statement against Breivik, not a witness to suddenly becoming 'more religious'. They also gathered in and around the cathedral because church represents a well-known space of sanctuary and safety, and because church is where they marry, baptize their children and send off their dead. Indeed, this unusual close interaction between church and people should rather be perceived as an invitation 'to be received' or 'to be held', which refers to primary acts of hospitality, love and healing. We do not know precisely how people interpreted the invitation of an open Cathedral, but we know that thousands of people every day accepted it and walked in, lit candles, wrote prayers, touched things, looked at the art, listened to music, often joined in the singing, walked out and came back in. Generative ritual is not primarily about belief but about participation in what it creates, being willing to experience it.[10]

According to Judith Butler's critical reading of Arendt (Butler 2015), when bodies come together 'in alliance in the street', the act produces more and other than what mere conversation does. It enables people to create a physical memory *in each other* through acting together, both by being physically close and as vulnerable individuals. While this is true, ritual in its subjunctive mode is more than bodily alliances in streets. It is a process that brings us 'out' of ourselves, acts on us and imprints us, skills something in us, then brings us back. We may therefore ask, what was being rehearsed and skilled in the streets of Oslo? An answer is: letting the other press her or his living, bodily image onto me, into my personal space, and tolerating their unique existence with me.

The multi-workshop for memorial design at the Norwegian Centre for Design and Architecture (DogA), 2014

Inspired by global social movements and their notions of 'democracy in action', but also by Judith Butler's ideas of how street assemblies imprint themselves on participants' memories, the REDO project staged a three-day workshop in October 2014 to learn more about how young adults experienced 22 July 2011. We invited people aged 18–30 to participate in open conversations and discussions with each other and with us in the rented venue DogA in Oslo.

These self-recruited participants were also asked to help design a fictional memorial site that they felt would embody the spirit of their own and of other people's response to Breivik's terror. The workshop was in part inspired by the 2013 survey conducted by the official Norwegian *Artistic Plan for Memorials after 22 July* (KORO), in which people were asked what words they associated with the street assemblies following 22 July and what words they hoped future memorials would be able to evoke. In the REDO project, however, we not only wanted to learn how small groups might negotiate the terms in which best to express their emotional experience of public responses to Breivik; we also wanted to see how they could collectively convert their responses into a material, architectural image by designing a fictional memorial.[11]

The event was organized according to *charette* principles, a planning method used by green architect Frederica Miller and urban planning activist Audun Engh. With their help we constructed a methodology in which 'charrette' was transformed into a 'multi-workshop' of five specific tasks to be collectively resolved in five different rooms. Thus, we were interested not only in what small groups of young adults would say but also in how different environments could influence their engagement and response: what can safely be said in what kind of space?[12]

For many of these young people, assembling in front of the cathedral and in the streets of Oslo after 22 July was a radically new experience. Specifically, they were amazed at being part of *creating* something new. Although individuals were free to express what they felt on paper and other materials placed on the ground, there was no preaching. Nor were there leaders or instructors, although silence was the tacitly obeyed rule. The assembly had no stable borders, ebbing and flowing with the changing number of people present, its flow structured by streets and walls. Finally, it was devoid of explicit religious and/or political symbols except for the red rose which represented both love and a passion for justice.

A majority of Norwegians responding to the 2013 KORO survey reported that the words 'love', 'solidarity', 'grief', 'reflection', 'hope' and 'peace' best captured their post-22 July experience.[13] The conversations in our workshop did not contradict this, but more emphasis was placed on inclusion, community, safety, contemplation and space for individual needs. The experience in the streets seemed to have created in and of itself a form of ritual resourcefulness, both to express resistance and to form a new type of floating community. Discussions revealed a need in young people for contemplation, with opportunities both for silence and for individual processing while at the same time being part of a group, a community. When in the streets, they had felt that they 'gave' love and solidarity to strangers and that they 'received' a sense of belonging in return. For a few days, they experienced a transformed city in which it was safe to stand close to strangers. All of them were certain that love and solidarity is the glue of society, although many were aware of fear lurking just beneath the surface. They are afraid of racism and xenophobia, of Breivik's ideology, of what might happen if trust is undermined and fear encouraged, and if people started acting collectively on the basis of fear and not community sentiment.

It also became evident that young people lacked venues where they could talk about 22 July. They felt that both high school and college/university had failed to deal critically with Breivik's ideology in class. Neither their fear of extremist ideology nor their experience of showing 'love and solidarity' to strangers was ever discussed in connection with democracy or freedom of speech. Nor did teachers reflect with them on the nature of the acts in the streets of Oslo and elsewhere. (Were the acts manifestations of a sudden democratic assemblage? Were they instances of genuine ritual?) Educational research had already documented that Breivik's ideology was not sufficiently discussed in Norwegian schools and that more education in democracy was needed.[14] But no research had yet documented the need for young adults to be able to understand the *nature of the acts* in the streets of Oslo, which implies knowing how to discern democratic assemblage from genuine ritual. To develop this skill set, students would need to be taught not only democratic theory but also ritual theory. The young at DogA were able to critique what they felt was lacking in democratic education. But they were not aware that the 'other' side to their experience in the streets could also be conceptualized and that their own ritual competence therefore could also be educated.

The most important work accomplished in the multi-workshop was participants' design of an imaginary 22 July memorial site, visualized to be located at the end of a hiking trail that goes through the recreational forest surrounding Oslo. We asked them to decide on its structure and components and to describe the experiences that they hoped their design would elicit from the 'hikers'. All three groups began their work by the participants being taken directly into a subjunctive ritual mode by means of a 'walking guided meditation'. As she does in all her creative architectural design work, Frederica Miller began by asking the young to get up and walk alone in the room, in a pattern they just make up as they walk. She then asked them to imagine going back to the past, to a past time of walking, to observe their surroundings, to remember, then to stop and share their 'experience of the past' with another person. Then she asked them to continue the walking, but now into an imagined future, to remember and to share. And finally, they were asked to walk in the present, and again, to remember and to share. The group then sat down at a table with Frederica and basically told her how to sketch a 22 July memorial site, taking clues both from their experiences in downtown Oslo in 2011 and from their imagined walking in the past, future and present at DogA in 2014. In this way, the memorial designs they proposed derived at once from their personal phantasies, their invented memories of walking together in time and their actual memories of 22 July.

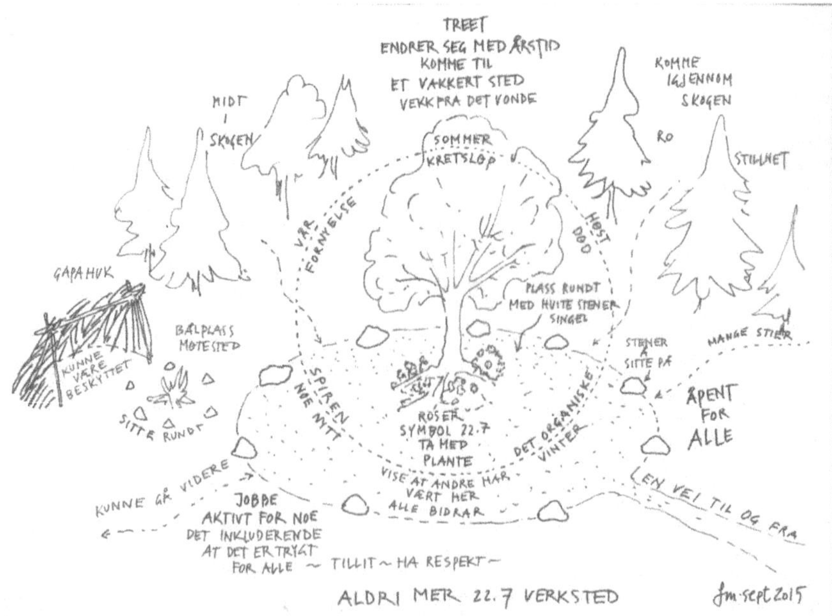

Figure 8.2 Imagined memorial design, multi-workshop, DogA. Photo by Frederica Miller.

All three workshop groups used memories from the Ocean of Roses as a template for their imagined memorial and were united in insisting that a memorial should be able to host people of different cultures and religions. Also, they thought, it should take the form of a circle and with a number of openings so that anybody who walked by could enter in many different ways and also leave whenever they wanted. Some details varied. Some groups placed a beacon in the middle of the circle, others placed a tree that could also become a tree of hope if people hung objects and written messages on it. In all proposals, the memorial site either had a hearth or a water source close by. Many named this place a 'clearing in the woods' as they were trying to explain its 'feel'. The designs were not monumental but allowed for action, enabling people to do something 'in it' or while 'being there'. They were grounded in a ceremonial structure with the form of a 'wide open' circle within which people could remain silent or engage each other by means of the objects and symbols at their disposal, thereby allowing ritual acts to emerge.

The convergence of the participants' designs is remarkable. But it is difficult to know if this is due to similar experiences from the streets and their bodily imprints or if the walking-meditation was formative. Ritual in its subjunctive mode is meant to act on us, skill something in us, before it brings us back. If we ask what was skilled through the DogA experiment, toleration, playfulness and trust stand out. Willingly participating in an on-the-spot walking meditation signals toleration and playfulness. Agreeing to invite 'the other' into one's own personal space through speaking about and listening to 'fantasy memories' signals trust. These values are echoed in the proposed memorials' material design and statement, 'wanting to share' sacred place with the other.

The Clearing memorial site at Utøya, 2015

There are a number of striking similarities between the memorial design proposed by young people during the REDO multi-workshop at DogA and the actual design (by 3RW Architects) chosen and made public several months later for a private memorial at Utøya. In both cases a unifying circle defines a space designated by the same name: 'the clearing' (in the woods). This should be interpreted as evidence that the youth at DogA and those linked to Utøya – a training ground for political activism and participatory democracy – share overlapping cultures with respect to ritual imaginaries that feel inclusive and safe and that connect with other living beings.

According to the architects who won the competition, their design tries to address the duality of Utøya as both a unique natural site and the scene of horrific crime.[15] In this duality, nature represents hope, and the memorial clears a space in nature to establish community and to give shelter and protection from the weather. It is meant to highlight the fact that nature has no memory of Breivik's killing and is already healing from the scars and wounds of 22 July 2011. When a big tree in the forest dies, an organic process that we know as a clearing begins. The memorial forms this clear spot, free from violence, free from history. The Clearing is shaped into a circle by means of four pine trees and a heavy metal ring hanging from the trees and into which the names of the dead are carved. Inside the uneven circle is a garden of bushes and herbs meant to attract life from the surrounding environment, including butterflies, not least of which is the mourning cloak. Life lost is to be remembered with the smell and vision of new life, and the fact that the ring broken by the names of the dead makes all the difference.

The 'Memorial Committee' at Utøya that chose this design regards it to be both sophisticated and unpretentious: 'No matter what social, cultural or religious affiliation, you can feel welcome here.'[16] The memorial, which is both non-religious and trans-religious, was crafted with voluntary work from parents and survivors and opened 22 July 2015. Many families who had lost their

Figure 8.3 The Clearing memorial site, Utøya. Photo by Jone Salomonsen.

children in Breivik's massacre were present, mostly adults. All carried flowers. The prime minister said a few words. Then silence. No music, no talking, no singing. People walked slowly around the metal ring and put down flowers under the carved-out-name of their lost child. Some stuck flowers into the name carved into the ring itself. The flowers form a new ring under the metal ring. The slope above the ring has benches and seats. It invites mourners to rest in contemplation with memories and stunning views of the sea, the sky, the birds, the trees and the beautifully made memorial site. The same ritualized patterns that unfolded in the streets of Oslo are repeated here: silence, whispering, kindness, togetherness, roses, small movements, circles.

Utøya is a campsite on a small island and is in many ways already always a liminal space. But within it, different modes of rituality have been put in place. From the architects' point of view, it was important to build the memorial in a place where nobody was killed and which materially and symbolically could harvest all the riches of nature for its design. However, it is just as important to be aware that the old gathering site for political speech and discussion, concerts and rallies is a three-minute walk from the memorial site. These two places are connected by a border of trees and flowers that demarcate two different modes of rituality: on the one hand, the political, ceremonial meeting grounds for assembly that can instantly shift into a loud, singing crowd that creates a deep sense of bonding and community; and on the other, an intimate, spiritual memorial site inviting individual and collective commemoration and open to ritual.

The presence of the memorial is a constant reminder that democracy is not a given but must be defended and its supportive social institutions strengthened. Still, these two sites, the one linked with the political, the other with ritual, are complementary, and it is important not to confuse them. It is ritual, as a time-limited tool of the social, which may be supportive of democratic politics, not the other way around. Ritual rehearses our common humanity while politics contains our wildest disagreements and offers civilized tools to come to terms, despite conflicts.

The political, the pre-political and democracy

In 'The Human Condition', Hannah Arendt distinguishes between public and private spaces and their respective structural logics. A public, democratic space is a political space open to continuous talking and listening, to opposition, confrontation and endless debate. These free contestations take place among people who are free citizens and who constitute a *demos*. Such public space is in principle different from the socially constituted and ordered household of the family, the church or the welfare state. Arendt believes that these latter spaces are generated from the hierarchical principles of *ethnos*, meaning kinship and lineage-based organizational principles. To better identify the essential difference between the public-political and the private-social, Arendt points to the Greek *polis*:

> In Greek thought, the human capacity for political organization is not only different from but stands in direct opposition to that natural association whose center is the home or household (oilier) and the family. [...] The foundation of the *polis* was preceded by the destruction of organized units resting on kinship, such as the *phratria* – derived from brother and meaning brotherhood and kinfolk, which was a social division of the Greek tribe (*phyle*)
>
> (Arendt 1998: 24).

Arendt builds her argument in reference to Fustel de Coulanges's *The Ancient City* where he argues that the religion of the family and the regime of the city represent two analogous forms of government. The paterfamilias, like the authoritarian monarch, is a king in his own terms; both are leaders of (continuous) social units. The political, however, argues Arendt, is constituted differently. It is an assemblage of free and equal citizens who regularly come together to discuss and resolve conflict, legal issues and other mundane affairs on behalf of society (and themselves). It is a time-limited assembly, a *thing*. To compare the household rule with political governance is thus a category mistake.

It is a well-known fact that women, slaves and strangers-immigrants were excluded from the polis of Greek society. They represented its constitutive outside; only free Greek males had dual citizenship in both private and public spheres. In recalling this, Arendt's point is simply that a political public space is not built on domestic structures, on variations of *ethnos*, but constitutes something radically new, people as a temporary 'gathering together' a *demos*. An ultra-nationalist desire to dismantle liberal democracy, to put up fences and return to *my kindred*, is therefore basically a desire to dismantle the *demos*, the constructed people of a nation state, and to return to king, fürer, church, family, a closed community or to the one head/one body symbolism of authoritarian mass movements. In short, the political does not resemble a home and familiar consensus is not its goal. To criticize democracy is therefore tricky since a desire to leave the political and return to the social can also mean returning to the hierarchical orders of the patriarchal household and its resort to violence to force obedience.

Political scientist Chantal Mouffe builds on Arendt's distinctions between public and private but recasts the spatial limits of the political when she argues that the 'political' *is* the potential antagonistic inherent in all social relations – in the parliament as well as at the dinner table. It operates in both public and private spaces and manifests as strong disagreement when decisions are to be made. Democracy, she argues, is a way of organizing human coexistence in a context which is always conflictual exactly because of this ever-present 'political'. The aim of democratic politics is thus to create the institutions through which this potential antagonism (hostility and strife) can be transformed into agonism (a community of disagreeing citizens) and enable pragmatic decisions to be made on matters of concern. Yet, she warns, if we want democracy to actually work, citizens must pay allegiance to two basic norms (or political principles): (1) all humans have equal worth, and (2) all human rights are universal rights since they are inborn and not relative to culture.

Mouffe is critical of consensus decision-making in new social movements because it may cover up the realities and dangers of antagonism. She is also critical of deliberative democratic theory and the belief that we can create societies that are no longer concerned with collective identities or distinctions between us and them. For her, good democratic governance requires a plurality of social units and *demoi*. At the same time, she urges us to imagine and experiment with new forms of association in which pluralism can flourish and where the ethical capacities for democratic decision-making can be enhanced. However, she defines such experimentation as belonging to the 'pre-political', as opposed to 'the political', which is the work of transforming antagonism into agonism and of facilitating deliberative and sensible decision-making.

Mouffe's concept of the pre-political is helpful for thinking about the outside of democratic politics. However, I suggest, it is less productive to think of the pre-political as limited to imagination and experimentation, set apart from the political, than it is to see it as closely entangled with it. In other words, if she is correct in thinking that democracy begins in a shared allegiance to ethical norms, the necessarily cultivated human ability to pay allegiance in this manner can only be developed in pre-political social domains. This idea joins up with concerns expressed in the 2014 government report on Norwegian culture (the *Kulturutredningen*) regarding a new political trend in Norway in which people tend to split into activist subgroups and only engage with those they already agree with politically. Historian Francis Sejerstad regards this tendency as a problem for democracy since political debates and disagreements must take place within, not outside of, a community constituted horizontally and in conscious acceptance of differences and disagreements – which is his definition of democracy. The remedy against this political trend, he writes in *Kulturutredningen*, lies in the 'pre-political sphere', in phenomena called 'cultural meeting places'. The report argues that inclusive 'cultural meeting places' have a civilizing effect and can help a community of disagreeing people to come together across the real divisions in society. Ritual is not mentioned in this report, but the elusive ritual work in the streets of Oslo after Breivik's deadly attacks were such cultural meeting places for those who participated. In the meeting, pluralism flourished and ethicality was practised and enhanced.

As documented in this chapter, the pre-political is not only a remedy to the political. In a democratic society they are interdependent. Instances of the pre-political in which ritual played a major role were not only the Ocean of Roses but also the DogA memorial proposals, including the ritualized tools (walking guided meditation) used by the architect to open up creativity and a sense of pre-existing interrelatedness. The two kinds of ritual spaces at Utøya bear witness to the same.

But part of the skill of performing a ritual in a democratic society is to make sure that ritual really ends and to be aware of this fact. Otherwise ritual can become a totalitarian way of life and impose utopian or nativist norms onto politics, or be a battlefield for the never-dormant antagonistic forces. This demand for ritual closure necessarily means that an experience of 'togetherness' ends when ritual ends. For an experience to take hold and be 'crafted' onto the body as rhythm, feeling, knowledge, disposition or memory of alterity, ritual must be repeated again and again. Thus, ritual *in this take* is a major cultivating tool of 'bodies in alliance' in a plurality of places. It imprints a physical memory of close inter-relations with the not-me human other of the 'built community'.

Conclusion: Ritual and democracy

Democratic theorists such as Hannah Arendt and Chantal Mouffe argue that politics is about agonistic confrontation and negotiation in a context which always will be conflictual. Democracy is a way of organizing human coexistence that leaves behind kinship based on *ethnos* as a model for politics and builds instead a new body politic, the *demos*. This does not mean that society should not be concerned with collective identities. Mouffe insists that if people want effective democratic self-governance they need to be citizens with rights and duties under a nation state and in *addition* belong to at least one other civil association, a local *demos*. In such associations, she says, pluralism can flourish and ethical capacities for democratic decision-making be enhanced. The work and experiments of these associations are said to be outside of democratic politics and therefore belong to the pre-political. At the same time they are instrumental in cultivating human allegiance to the two foundational norms that are a precondition to democratic governance: human equality and human rights.

As conveyed in this chapter, egalitarian ritual plays an important, yet underestimated role in the cultivation of democratic dispositions. Ritual is not an organization but a cultural *tool* with which people gather into a certain ritualized mode and for a certain reason. Neither is ritual democratic per se. It becomes part of democratic culture through its particular enactment in place, through how it is constructed and done.

The two formations, the noisy negotiation of democracy and the quiet space of condolence, memorial and walking meditation may seem to be mutually contradictory to the demands of living collectively and at the same time individually in modern society. Democracy begins in the experience of social battle and political disagreements. It does not reflect unity but provides a framework and a method for fair discussion, negotiations and distributions of power, obliged by a notion of inborn human equality and right. Democracy is therefore not a goal in itself but a continuous and unrestricted process towards better solutions.

Ritual, on the other hand, begins in the experience of life and of pre-political fellowship and inherited and invented traditions. Its formality, modesty, festivity or silence may seem to break with the forever open, democratically negotiated traditions, even though ritual too invites participation. The process may be prescribed or improvised. It nevertheless takes people into places and processes where they are forced to see the other, without argument, including those who do not belong to their own in-group. Ritual intends to build or confirm community and therefore society. That is why it also needs to end. Because if our social life becomes a single ritual event, without open conflict and debate, society becomes totalitarian.[17]

9

The flower actions: Interreligious funerals after the Utøya massacre

Ida Marie Høeg

On Friday afternoon 22 July 2011 extremist right-wing political attitudes led to acts of terror that took the lives of seventy-seven people in Norway. Seven victims died when a fertilizer bomb packed in an illegally parked vehicle exploded outside government office buildings in downtown Oslo. One hour later, sixty-nine mostly young people were fatally shot on a small island 24 miles outside Oslo where 650 people were gathered for the annual social democratic youth camp.

This chapter examines the funeral ceremonies of three Muslim adolescents – Mona Abdinur, with a Somali background, and Bano Rashid and Rafal Jamil, with a Kurdish background – who were victims of the terror attacks at the youth camp on 22 July 2011 on the island of Utøya. The important question in this context is: Did the terror attacks and the subsequent interreligious funeral ceremonies create a community of mourners? Inspired by actor-network theory and material semiotics, I will explore a ritual object that became dominant for the participants in their ritual response to the attacks during the three funerals: flowers. The mourners brought cut flowers with them when they joined the torchlight procession in Oslo (Høeg 2015) and placed them in and outside churches and at spontaneous shrines that were created in cities and towns all across Norway (Høeg 2013). Not surprisingly, there were also many flowers at the local funeral ceremonies for the victims. They were not only brought by young people from the Labour Youth movement; other participants also came to the funerals with cut flowers. Those who did not bring flowers to the funeral acted or refused to act with the flowers present at the funerals, flowers which were ordered by the victims' friends, family, organizations and so on. These ritual responses to the terror attack, where the flowers were a distinctive part of the rituals, prompt the question of whether the cut flowers functioned as ritual participants in their own right and furthermore worked as relational entities in the funeral assembly. If so, did the flowers operate under some restrictions in these local empirical settings, potentially not only enhancing but also disturbing interactions between the attendees? Based on films, hundreds of photos and in-depth interviews with organizers of and participants at these three funerals, I will argue that once the flowers were assembled within various practices and then shaped within relations, they were more than representations of personal sadness, national solidarity and political commitment. The flowers opened up a ritual relationship between the participants. Even though the plurality among the attendees led some to refuse to interact with the flowers, the funerals' democratic openness to the performance of various ritual actions with various entities did not exclude the restrictive attendees from these multicultural ritual assemblies.

Funeral culture and changing cultural conditions

In the three interreligious funerals the participants mirror the heterogeneous society that the terrorist aimed to attack. Anders Behring Breivik, a 32-year-old ethnic Norwegian, did not specifically target Muslims. Rather, he targeted the Norwegian Labour Party for being too accommodating to Muslims and too tolerant of multiculturalism. The terrorism he perpetrated was not only an attack on the immigration policy that the Labour Party and its youth organization represented. It was first of all an attack on Norwegian democracy which had welcomed a culturally pluralistic society. The terror attacks highlighted the tensions within the Norwegian majority society relating to cultural plurality and integration, a society in which Muslim immigrants, in particular, have found themselves under scrutiny and widespread suspicion.

Two social factors are significant for understanding the cultural context of the interreligious funeral ceremonies in Norway: firstly, the growing pluralization of religions and world views, and, secondly, the stronger position of individuals vis-á-vis church authority when it comes to performing funeral ceremonies. These factors are important social conditions to take into consideration when trying to understand the complex social context the burial rituals were embedded in.

Since the end of the 1960s, when labour immigration and family reunification from non-Western countries started, Norway has developed into a culturally plural society where different religious traditions and communities are represented. In recent years, immigration has accounted for most of Norway's population growth, not only in the capital but also in the rural areas. Currently, the total number of immigrants amounts to 17.3 per cent of the population.[1] Even though the attitudes towards immigration and immigrants have tended to be more positive over the last fifteen years,[2] a large number of Norwegians are likely to feel that the government is doing a poor job of managing immigration and integration. The majority of Norwegians are also worried about the increasing level of xenophobia. The terrorist attacks in Paris and Copenhagen, the recruitment of foreign soldiers and the fear of parallel societies contribute to these concerns (Brekke 2015).

Due to migration, particularly of Muslims, the most visible change in Norwegian society over the last generation has been the growth of non-Christian minorities. Muslims are at the centre of the current controversy over cultural diversity, integration, democratic rights and ethnic and religious identity, which puts pressure on institutional systems. In spite of the huge amount of attention Muslims receive in the Norwegian press (Døving and Kraft 2013), they represent a small minority of the overall population. No more than 3 per cent of the Norwegian population is affiliated with a Muslim community (Statistics Norway),[3] and an estimate based on the immigrants' countries of origin sets the group 'Muslims' at just about 4 per cent of the population (Østby and Dalgard 2017).[4]

In Norway, as well as the other Nordic countries, many people turn to the familiar religious institutions to observe the traditional rites of birth, coming of age, marriage and death. The Lutheran majority church, with strong links to the state, plays a dominant role in the Nordic funeral culture (Høeg and Pajari 2013). In 2018, 71 (70.6%) per cent of the population was affiliated to the Church of Norway and 88 per cent of all deceased had a funeral ceremony under the auspices of the Church of Norway. The declining prestige of the ministry, falling membership rates and the church's shrinking influence have had an impact on the Lutheran Church members' approach to the ecclesiastic rites of passage. A small, but steadily growing group of people tend to use private funerals, and bereaved families are demanding more democratic funeral ceremonies, including the right to contribute to developing ceremonies conducted by the church (e.g. introducing popular songs, family members making the memorial speech, decorating the coffin, asking an artist to perform, etc.).

The ongoing process of individualization and cultural diversity in Norwegian society has led to the acknowledgement of pluralism at public cemeteries through multi-faith expressions and articulations. The cemeteries are in a process of re-branding and re-framing earlier policies that previously favoured the Church of Norway and demanded that dissenters and people with other religious affiliations adapt to Christian norms and rules of funeral culture (Rygnestad 1955). Funeral cultures with and without reference to religious cosmologies now give cemeteries not only a pluralist but also a more democratic look. There are very few private cemeteries, so public graveyards are in a process of providing separate space for Muslims, as well as for some other faith-based communities, where they can conduct their funeral ceremonies and design the grave (Døving 2009).

The transformative aspect of rituals: Entities acting out relational forms

To consider the specific ritual contexts in which human and non-human entities are related, we need a reorientation which leads to a more dynamic comprehension of the multiplicities of *the social*. The French professor of Science Studies Bruno Latour's contribution to social science is his idea of seeing the social as association. Latour convincingly argues that human activities are only one part of the associations that constitute the social collective. To fully understand what collective existence has become, he argues that it is necessary, aside from considering the circulation and formatting of traditionally conceived social ties, to detect other circulating entities than just the human ones (Latour 2005: 233). Accordingly, he calls for the tracing of new connections and new associations produced by entities which are not human and have not always previously been included in 'society'.

Rituals connected to death stand out from other rites of passage as they do not only relate to an embracing cosmological and social system but also have a very practical purpose – to inter or cremate the human remains. From a practical point of view, these are sufficient ritual actions – they provide a grave or places to spread ashes. The functional aspects of religious and secular rituals connected to death are important if we are to understand how non-human and human entities contribute to the enactments of realities. The performative approach of actor-network theory and material semiotics helps to clarify the formation of entities (artefacts, materials, technology) which takes place within practices (Mol 2002; Law 1999: 162). It provides fruitful perspectives for understanding the performativity in the funerals not as static structures but as structures with transformative aspects. This assumes that the non-human entities have to be understood in relational terms (Law 1999; Moll 2002). In the study of interreligious funerals, the perspective on the interplay between individuals and materiality is further developed with inspiration from ritual scholars who have a relational approach to ritual action. They state that rituals are the key to the act of relation making (see Bell 1992). Pointing out that rituals embed individuals in groups and in the performance of relations, they have a specific focus on constructed relational networks and relational configurations (Houseman and Severi 1998; Moisseeff 2017). This prompts the question of how relational forms are acted out in these rituals and whether non-human entities can be perceived as 'living beings' in these networks.

The practice of rituals has become associated with the dynamics of transformation and empowerment. Funeral rituals, as other rituals, encompass social actions which display, construct and promote power relationships. The dynamic and transformative aspect of funeral rituals helps to elucidate the ongoing formation which is enacted through ritual actions. The funerals' entities may act as 'mediators' that shape and affect the content of the funerals, which they transmit, rather than merely acting as tools for transmission or as 'intermediators' (Latour 2005: 39–40). Latour's concepts of mediators and intermediators are used to show how the non-human entities have the power to enact and affect the outcome of the interreligious funerals. The mourners, and the emotional enactment of these funeral rites, make them a potent force for social construction: in performing ritual activities, they challenge existing power structures. The human and non-human entities may have agency to establish contact and cooperation between the participants. In this respect the trajectories of the flowers and their potential as material entities are in a position to establish relations between the dead and the living and between the networks of bereaved people.

I have undertaken ethnographic fieldwork to develop an empirical study based on the assumption that the world has to be understood from the bottom up. I visited the places where the ceremonies took place, interviewed people who took part in them, and people who planned and performed in them, watched films and studied photographs of the participants. When exploring the rituals and their interreligious nature, I did not see the flowers as an analytical entity, I was more focused on the participants and their relational actions, how the actors performed the ritual actions and their relation to those they performed the rituals with. When examining what orchestrated the ritual actions, I saw that many entities were present. The participants framed their actions with objects to shape the ritual contexts and thus I was curious about the relational role of materiality in the rituals. I decided to study and describe the flowers in these multicultural ritual contexts and see if this could be a way of exploring the social relational network enacted in the rituals. It was somewhat astonishing that the flowers stood out as acting entities when considering that several ritual traditions were in play. Before moving on to explore the use of flowers in the funeral ceremonies, I will give a more detailed description of the ceremonies themselves.

The interreligious funerals

Mona's, Bano's and Rafal's funeral ceremonies were not mainstream Muslim funeral ceremonies according to the religious tradition of their families or the way most Muslim funerals are conducted in a Norwegian context. The ceremonies were interreligious in terms of actions from Muslim and Christian funeral traditions and also ritual actions which hardly represent any religious tradition but encompass symbols and artefacts that are becoming more and more common when death and bereavement are being ritually marked.

These funeral ceremonies do not pre-exist before they are performed. The structure did not exist prior to these events, they were a work in progress – thought about and imagined, but not anchored in established structures. The interviewed organizers of the ceremonies describe a process that did not assign roles and functions to these temporary elements. They could not lean on local, regional or national arrangements, institutions or networks for organizing such burials. The organizers explain that the terror actions called for new structures. People from different communities and organizations had contact with each other and worked together on the funerals. Thus, new networks of actors arose. Formally, the ceremonies were organized by secular and religious institutions cooperating together.[5] Geographically, the funerals took place in three areas near where the girls lived with their families (west coast, Egersund, eastern Norway, Oslo and Nesodden). Mona's funeral was held in a Muslim field at a cemetery in Oslo, Bano's in the local church and afterwards at the Muslim field in the local churchyard and Rafal's in the auditorium in the local school. To the extent that the ceremonies were planned in advance, the three girls' families were the ones who decided or confirmed external ideas and arrangements for the rituals. According to the organizers, Mona's mother wanted to have *salat-ul-janaza* at the cemetery and not at the Mosque. She also wanted a representative from the Somali community to hold a speech. Bano's parents wanted the Muslim funeral director to hold a speech in the church and asked him to ensure that only the closest family members lowered the coffin. According to the clergywomen and the Muslim funeral director, the parents' wish was to have a Christian funeral ceremony in the church and afterwards a Muslim funeral by the graveside so they could address Bano's two identities – the Norwegian and the Kurdish (Tronvik 2011a: 445).

The funerals were national events. Prominent people took part and contributed at the funerals. At Mona's funeral the Norwegian prime minister and his wife attended, at Bano's the Foreign Minister was present and at Rafal's the Justice Minister and the Iraqi ambassador attended. At these funerals, as in the funerals of the other victims of the terror attacks, the ministers made speeches. In addition to the ministers, at Mona's funeral, a representative of the Somali community and the leader of the Labour Party made speeches by the graveside. At Bano's funeral, the former local leader of Labour Youth, Bano's cousin, the funeral director and the clergy made speeches in the church. At Mona's and Bano's funerals the *salat-ul-janaza* prayer was led by an imam by the grave and afterwards the coffin was lowered and the graves were filled with earth, with some of the participants praying by the grave. All three had memorial assemblies in public buildings.[6] For Rafal, the memorial assembly was arranged by the local authority prior to the ceremony for those directly affected. For Bano and Mona, the family invited all the participants to the memorial assembly.

The ritual arrangements for Rafal did not encompass the regular Muslim obligation to pray *salat-ul-janaza* or the custom to pray by the grave. She was buried in northern Iraq, where the local religious customs were observed. In Norway, the Labour Party, on behalf of her family, was responsible for the memorial service and made the arrangements together with the local authority, the Salvation Army, the Church of Norway and the Muslim community in the town (Egersund). Men and women from the organizing institutions made speeches together with representatives from Labour Youth, the Labour Party and the Iraqi ambassador. Even though the burial was not part of the ritual, the memorial ceremony had several of the same ritual actions and objects as Christian funerals, with flower garlands, commiserations directly addressed to the deceased, clergy who made speeches, sing-alongs and praying of the Lord's Prayer. The place for Rafal's memorial ceremony was continuously discussed with her father on the phone from Iraq. It was also his desire to include the Salvation Army (with which the family had a close relationship), Muslim communities and the Norwegian Church in the planning and implementation of the ceremony.

The ritual assemblies were complex and comprehensive. The performing of the two funeral ceremonies and the memorial ceremony forms an association between heterogeneous people of different ages, genders, religious beliefs, political preferences and values. The associations consist of participants who were connected and people who did not have any personal relations to each other or to the deceased. The people who attended the three ceremonies were schoolmates, teammates, friends, neighbours, family members, teachers, politicians, sports coaches, ethnic peers, Kurds and Somalis, clergy, deacons and leaders of Christian and Muslim congregations, Muslim funeral directors and Muslim undertakers, leaders of the Islamic Council of Norway and Muslims who were complying with their obligation to participate in funeral ceremonies and pray for the dead. The shape, size and combinations of associations made the group boundaries uncertain and therefore the social aspect was intricate.

The ritual interactions were not necessarily thoroughly planned or well arranged. According to some of the people who were asked to make speeches, they were not supplied with an explicit aim, not even the expressed intention of cooperating across religious, cultural or gender divides. The Muslim congregations' and the Muslim undertakers' desire to fulfil the Islamic obligation to make the time between death and burial as short as possible meant there was a tight time frame for the development of Mona's and Bano's funerals. The wish to hold the memorial ceremony close to the time when the funeral took place in northern Iraq also left tight time margins. Spontaneous and planned ritual actions from different religions together with actions which in character are not strictly religious or secular were performed. In these rituals we saw particularly young people and females as ritual agents. The Imam and the clergywoman in Bano's funeral who walked side by side out of the church to the grave did not, according to what they say, plan this action; it just happened.

The interviews conducted with adolescents and adults taking part in these rituals reveal an intricate interaction with a juxtaposition of funeral ritual practices. The informants expressed that they had little experience of other burial practices than those of the religious or ethnic group to which they belong. They clarified that it was just natural for them to gather and take part in the funeral ceremonies regardless of whether they were familiar with the funeral ceremony or not. Whether or not the ritual actions came from a Muslim, Christian or other tradition was of secondary importance. The main thing was to attend, to show the bereaved families respect and compassion and to express grief. This does not mean that the rituals were without conflicting emotions.

The funerals did not only express love or compassion but also included actions which indicate that there were conflicting opinions among the participants. One of the attendees in Mona's funeral saw that some of the Muslims who came to perform *salat-ul-janaza* were unhappy about the physical contact between men and women, involving handshakes and hugs. The Bishop of Stavanger felt that it was not appropriate to say the Lord's Prayer at Rafal's memorial ceremony, such as the dean did. In referring to Bano's funeral, clergy in missionary organizations expressed in editorials and letters to the editor that mixing Christian and Muslim preaching is a questionable action.[7] The minister who conducted the funeral ceremony in the church defended what evolved when she and the Imam led the funeral procession to the grave together: 'Thus, a bridge was built between two separate rituals' (Tronvik 2011b: 41).

The agency of flowers: Flowers transform interactions

Flowers occupied a central position in the 22 July memorial events. People brought flowers to local memorial sites around the country. In Oslo, the planned torchlight procession on 25 July turned into a flower parade. The red rose as the symbol of the Labour Party along with roses in other colours and other kinds of flowers were continuously raised in the air during the parade. Flowers were also highly visible in Mona's and Bano's funeral ceremonies and Rafal's memorial ceremony.

Some will say that there is a strong vitality in flowers. They demand attention and also appeal to several senses. When humans act with flowers, various forms, colours, fragrances and textures of the flowers are displayed. Flowers have always been an integral part of cultures. In various traditions flowers have been associated with worship, celebrations and festivals, but also with death rituals. However, how the ritual is 'translated' is based on a social interactional process which constructs common definitions and meanings. What the participants experience they enact as important. Thus, meaning is relational and performative, and a subject of change. The social interactions between the participants and flowers in the funeral rituals may be seen as an assemblage produced relationally with the vitality to express meaning to the collective of mourners.

Flowers are obvious objects in all Norwegian funerals, Christian or not. In Muslim funerals in a Norwegian context flowers are increasingly present. In Mona's and Bano's funeral ceremonies and Rafal's memorial ceremony the flowers were more than representations of emotions, symbols and identity. They were not static objects but seem to have had a social role to play. The flowers appeared in almost every funeral action, and the participants acted with them. The Labour Youth members brought red roses with them and many other young people brought white roses. During Mona's and Bano's funeral ceremonies the participants kept the roses in their hands. When the graves had been filled and the observant Muslims who had been standing a while by the grave turned away, the young people and adults approached the grave and placed their roses on the soil. In Rafal's memorial ceremony the roses were put in vases on the stage when the young people entered the school auditorium.

The agency the flowers had for composing the memorial rituals connected to 22 July gave the rituals a particular structure. Apart from the rose as a symbol of 22 July itself, other flowers played a vital part in the rituals. The Christian funeral habit of mourning bouquets and garlands decorated Mona's and Bano's coffins, and for Bano, also the church room prior to and under the Christian funeral ceremony. Mourning bouquets and garlands, as mentioned above, were put on the stage in Rafal's memorial ceremony. The Muslim undertakers received many calls from florists about where they should deliver the flowers for Mona's funeral. They were told to send them to the hospital from where he could carry them to the cemetery. He wrapped the coffin in the carpet with quotes from the Quran, which is the Muslim custom, added the Somali flag, which was a wish from Mona's family, and decorated the coffin with flowers from the florists. The flowers for Bano's funeral were transported to the church. Together with the photo of Bano, and the Kurdish and Norwegian flags, the Muslim undertakers placed them on and near the coffin, on the altar, on the floors and other places in the church where there was room for them.

Flowers in the ceremonies demonstrated that a mourning community is not a pre-existing entity that expresses itself via a fixed set of actions but is rather a formation that comes into being through the circulation and use of shared mourning actions. These funerals reveal that the mourning community is not complete. The flowers had an active role: they acted as 'mediators' in shaping the mourning community. When the hearse arrived at the cemetery where Mona was going to be buried, the funeral director pushed the button to open the back door of the vehicle. As is the custom, several of the Muslim participants stood by ready to fulfil their religious obligation to carry the coffin. But in this case, the many flowers disturbed the first attempt to enact this obligation. They had to change their actions. Before they could start, the Muslim undertakers had to move all the flowers away from the coffin. Then the observant Muslims lifted the coffin out of the car and put it on the catafalque which was standing beside the baldachin. And then again, before the speeches and prayer could start, the undertakers put the garlands on stands and placed some on the coffin's three sides and on top of the coffin. Participants who had garlands and bouquets that had not been transported in the hearse then approached the coffin. They placed them in the same direction as the funeral director had done – towards where the gender-mixed group of attendees was standing. Then the speeches started from the pulpit placed beside the coffin and afterwards the *salat-ul-janaza* prayer was performed, directed towards the decorated coffin.

Usually when there is a funeral procession from the chapel or church to the grave, the undertakers ask the participants, with the exception of the closest family, to help carry the flowers from the chapel or church to the cemetery and open grave. The participants pick a random bouquet or flower garland, or the undertakers give them one on their way out of the chapel/church. Bano's funeral was no exception. The flowers were to be used to decorate the grave and whether the bereaved were used to this custom or not, they took part in the shared action. All the flower arrangements and all the single roses the young people had brought with them were part of the funeral procession. As the clergywomen and the Imam walked side by side down to the grave, the undertakers ensured that the church was emptied of the flowers.

In a Christian funeral the participants usually lay down flowers around the open grave. The sexton is the one who will later fill in the grave and place the flowers on the soil. Generally, the bereaved family and others do not see the filled grave decorated with fresh flowers. If they are able to visit the grave the next day, they will see an unflattering view of the fading flowers. This time, at Bano's and Mona's funeral the participants were the ones who decorated the filled-in grave. They kept the flowers in their hands during the *salat-ul-janaza* prayer. After the burial prayer the participants took the bouquets of flowers and garlands to the filled-in grave. Other adults and young people also approached the grave to place their roses on the soil. At Mona's funeral ceremony, her mother kneeled by the grave and started to pray. Immediately, Ingrid Schulerud, Prime Minister Jens Stoltenberg's wife, stepped up to her, held around her and comforted her while she prayed. The young people stooped to place their flowers. They were standing around the pair, praying or just standing there with their flowers. While the Muslims who had performed their religious obligations were leaving the cemetery and Mona's mother was finishing her prayer, those who had not yet placed their flowers did so. It started to rain but the young people remained. When they were the only people left, they gradually moved away from the grave on their way to the reception.

At Rafal's memorial ceremony, where there was no coffin and no soil, flowers still were present. They greatly influenced the visual impression of the ceremony and gave it the image of an ordinary funeral ceremony. The organizer and participants had filled the stage with flower garlands and bouquets with mourning bands, which were put on supports in the same way as is done at funeral ceremonies in chapels and churches. The entire ceremony was filmed and the recording was later given to the family. Although the bereaved family was not present and could not smell nor see the beautiful flowers on stage, and all the roses that the young people had brought with them, the flowers opened interactions between the participants and the family. The organizers wanted to give the family not only the film from the memorial ceremony, which they could keep, but also the flower objects. One of the organizers collected all the bands and commiserations which were tied to the flowers. He also collected all the commiserations from the local memorial site in the centre of town. He gave all these objects from the ceremony to the family when they came home from Iraq. Thus, the delivering of commiserations was more than an action that could serve the memory of the ceremony. Indirectly the flowers mediated relationality between the family and ritual participants.

Conflicting flowers

Flowers are not universal objects for the expression of grief. In Muslim funeral cultures flowers may be placed on the coffin, and flowers or branches from a tree or bush may be placed on the grave. In the Muslim communities in Norway there are contradictory attitudes about using flowers in a Muslim funeral. The Muslim funeral director for Bano's and Mona's funerals will use flowers in Muslim funerals from time to time even though this is not part of his cultural background. He was often asked by bereaved people whether flowers were appropriate in a Muslim funeral. When we talked about this Norwegian/Christian custom he pointed out that people will always adapt to the surrounding culture. The longer they live in the country, the more the funerals will be characterized by Norwegian customs. He particularly felt that this applied to the second and third generations, with little connection to their parents' or grandparents' homeland.

The large quantity of flowers among the participants at Mona's funeral sparked debate. One of the Muslim participants said they had many discussions in the Mosque about flowers in funerals. Even though he believes there is nothing wrong in having flowers at a funeral, he responded with surprise at Mona's funeral. He had never seen so many garlands in a Muslim funeral before:

> Flowers and garlands are a very unknown Islamic tradition. Then someone began to say: Okay, one thing is that we have accepted that you [non-Muslims] are here, because it's a part of her life and so on. But to mix traditions, this is very undesirable. Some of the Somalis began to talk amongst themselves about this at the funeral.

The Muslim participant knows that flowers are a marker of religious and cultural belonging. He points to some of the tensions that are linked to national and religious identities, and the need for some Norwegian minorities to maintain strict borders that make Muslim culture different from Christian and other religious cultures. For other participants, it is a collective action that marked affiliation to the broader mourning collective. The collective encompasses different people with different cultural backgrounds and different experiences, with different death and mourning cultures. None of the other Muslim participants I interviewed had negative attitudes to flowers. Some of them actually brought flowers to Bano's and Mona's funerals and to Rafal's memorial service on their own volition.

Reassembling the social

Mona's and Bano's funeral ceremonies and Rafal's memorial ceremony reflect some of the dramatic effects of the acts of terror. While this terror was motivated by hatred of Muslims and defence of a Christian homogeneous society, the funeral ceremonies expressed opposite cultural tendencies. People belonging to different ethnic groups came together and the death rituals and spaces from different funeral traditions mobilized joint actions. Understanding interactions where people with different cultural backgrounds gather and contribute to the funeral ceremonies requires a reorientation of social theory. Rather than asking which of these objects count as ritual objects or sacred objects, which ones are mere disposal material and which ones are implements actively used in the rituals (see Grimes 2014: 268), it can be argued that the objects can work in tandem with the people involved.

The dynamics of these funeral ritual actions place emphasis on the contribution to the enactments of realities. The ongoing formation of power which is enacted through ritual actions is not only shared between the participants but also between participants and entities. These mediators are objects that help the performativity. In this study, mediators are used to examine how entities alter their contributions in three funeral ceremonies and how they acquired agency to affect interactions.

The funeral ceremonies express an ongoing social formation that is handled and performed within actions. Each represented heterogeneous ritual actions within a Christian and Muslim framework: they combined some actions and added others, shared some entities and were exclusive when it comes to the other. In these ritual processes with several ritual leaders, participants with different relations to the deceased had weak scripts. No one had control over the ritual, as would be the case in a mainstream Christian or Muslim funeral ceremony. In these settings there were several scripts and some parts did not have a script at all. The participants were observant, following each other or just acting according to the circumstances. For some this meant following the guidance of the ritual leaders or the group of people they were connected to or what they were used to from other funeral ceremonies. In this open and uncertain ritual process, the cast of participants in the actions involved the relations of human and non-human actants. Following the funeral ceremonies' 'pathways', the flowers were not passive objects.

In one way or another the cut flowers and design bouquets had a fragrance and an appearance, but first of all they seem to call for action. They acquire the agency to trigger emotions, interact in predictable and unpredictable ways and establish an atmosphere of collective mourning. They were brought, carried and placed, but not by every participant. During these three funerals the participants were acting or refusing to act with the flowers. However, when participants acted with them, this assemblage seems to take the initiative. Instead of representing something, the flowers were relational: the participants and flowers created interactions.

The participants who acted directly with the flowers were people who knew the deceased and were related to them through school, a sports team, neighbourhood relations and/or the Labour Youth movement. However, the flowers did not only act in ways that all the participants regarded as positive. As mentioned above, some of the Muslim participants who attended the funeral had religious obligations to perform, and the assemblage in Mona's funeral of human and non-human entities (e.g. soil, rope and shovels) was disturbed by a foreign entity. The funerals they were accustomed to worked fluently with a 'correct' assemblage of mourners and coffin, rope, shovels and soil, but not flowers. In their opinion the assemblage of flowers and participants was inappropriate. The flowers were not to have an effect on death, grief or dignity. What transpired was that these foreign objects started to work as mediators.

For these participants it was important to reject the actions of flowers, so they refused to act with them, which can be interpreted as a means to destabilize the relations between the flowers and the participants. When they refused to take them out of the car, or to decorate the coffin or fill the grave with flowers, or even touch them, they tried to disempower the flowers from the funerals. When the ritual leaders – the imams, the Islamic undertaker and his staff – did not interfere with the interactions with the flowers, the flowers' transformation continued. They occupied time, influenced the ritual performance and were the subject of performance. Even though this group of Muslim participants did not interact with the flowers, they had to relate to them. More precisely, they had to pay attention to them, and wait for and watch those who enacted the flowers. The assemblage of participants and flowers transformed the ritual.

The funeral ceremonies took place in a context where several anti-authoritarian rituals were performed. The huge ritual response to 22 July with torchlight/rose processions and great numbers of people tending spontaneous shrines all over Norway can be understood as an anti-authoritarian protest against the terrorist's authoritarian behaviour. The terror attack and the three local funeral ceremonies paved the way for under-represented groups to take an active part in the ceremonies. The assemblage of flowers, young people and women, Christian, Muslim, secular and other religious traditions helped to shape the practice of interreligious funeral ceremonies. The enactment of flowers was performed by people who in traditional Christian and Muslim funeral ceremonies usually are submissive ritual actors with few enactments. Even though the large number of flowers escorted an assemblage with an exceptional age range and mix of genders and religions, did the flowers disturb a democratic openness? On the one hand, the flowers inscribed these assemblages within mainstream Christian celebratory tradition, which the observant Muslims were definitely exposed to. On the other hand, the flowers were not the only entities that were enacted and worked as relational entities in the ceremonies. Yet, the observant Muslims were not subordinated to local values which excluded them from every assembly.

The funerals' heterogeneous assemblage demonstrates that face-to-face interactions in funerals have the potential to be prime movers in an increasingly culturally diverse society, challenging the authority and relevance of 'mainstream' funeral ritual managements. Actor-network theory is a useful tool for studying processes and actions where the actor's own actions make a difference (Latour 2005: 253). Thus, these funerals during a politically tense period show that the actions involved are not lacking in substantive political critique. In a national crisis situation that prompts interreligious funeral ceremonies, the actants seem to be more transparent and easier to follow than in traditional funeral ceremonies. In this chapter actor-network theory has been used as a tool to study the rituals in all their richness and complexity. Generally, it was possible to embrace much more of the original setting. I could follow and describe many other human and non-human entities that functioned in a network of face-to-face ritual actions in the particular situations. Perhaps the social relations could have been held together by more and other networks than I have examined. The participants and ritual organizers were enrolled in a group with a number of interventions with several possible and contradictory calls for regrouping. Relating to one group or another is an ongoing process made up of uncertain, fragile and ever-shifting ties.

Attending funeral ceremonies in the framework of Christian or Muslim traditions requires interaction (like all other funeral ceremonies). The small contingent of Muslims in Norway and their short history here means that there are few traces of Islam in Norwegian culture and the barriers to acting in these arenas seem to be irrelevant for most people. In these three funeral ceremonies caused by terror and the terrorist's motives for the acts of terror, one outcome could be a reduction of the barriers against Muslim burial. The same is the case for the majority of Muslims who were introduced to the Norwegian majority culture's funeral tradition that involves the use of flowers. These funerals mobilized people where interaction between the mourner and the flowers was socially transporting. The focus on the loss of a young life, the mourning and the feeling of being threatened that the terror created did not allow the alien religious acts to become a barrier to attending the ceremonies but instead brought people together in joint actions.

10

Dealing with death in contemporary Western culture: A view from afar

Marika Moisseeff

One of democracy's fundamental features is that it allows for the expression, in the public sphere, of different perspectives on issues and events affecting the community. As I will try to show, rituals are one of the means whereby individuals are able to express their emotions publicly on the basis of the distinctive places they occupy with respect to particular events. In order to deal with foreseeable disruptive events affecting particular individuals or groups, such as births or deaths, society makes use of institutionalized rituals that allow those concerned to share these experiences in accepted, conventional ways. On such occasions, those who come together to acknowledge the event in question manifest their feelings as a function of their respective positions (Moisseeff and Houseman forthcoming). In the case of unexpected, exceptionally large-scale events that affect the community as a whole, such as terrorist attacks or natural catastrophes, democratic structures are put to the test. The positions occupied by those involved – immediate victims and their close ones, perpetrators and their close ones, as well as various others – cannot be conflated, and the emotional reactions of these disparate parties, although potentially standing in opposition to each other, must nevertheless be publicly taken into account, even in the absence of institutionalized commemorations.[1] In this chapter, I will consider institutionalized rituals dealing with individual death in the European past and in other-than-Western cultural contexts, on the one hand, and in the contemporary West, on the other, to propose a comparative perspective for thinking about collective, ritualized but as of yet institutionalized responses to such large-scale disruptive events.

I do so from the standpoint of an anthropologist who has worked in an Aboriginal community in South Australia (Moisseeff 1999, 2017) and who is also a clinician having shared mourning experiences with people from a variety of cultural backgrounds. I hope this can help us to better understand what is at stake in the aftermath of the sudden, unexpected mass massacres that have occurred these last years in Western countries, the individual and collective reactions they have provoked and the grassroots and official initiatives undertaken in response to them.

Let us first note that although it is often said that in the West death has become 'taboo',[2] the fact is that it constantly makes news headlines, figures prominently in fictional works and has become a subject of utmost importance in social debates and legislation (e.g. bioethic laws, palliative care and more generally, ends-of-life concerns including access to euthanasia). Similarly, Westerners are regularly incited to work through processes of grieving and remembrance. The 'psys' – psychiatrists, psychologists, psychotherapists and so forth – are the ones who are expected to help people with this work. This development, I have suggested, is directly related to changes in how personal identity is conceived (Moisseeff 2012) and to the subsequent delegation of the management of bodies to the medical establishment (Moisseeff 2013a, 2016a, 2016b).

Most people in the West today are born and die in hospitals and other medicalized institutions, whereas barely a hundred years ago most were born and died at home. This cannot but have had a major impact on mortuary practices. As documented by ethnographic research, treatments applied to bodies by medical staff are highly ritualized.[3] However, those closest to the deceased are generally allowed to play only a very peripheral role, when they are not excluded out of hand. This gives people the impression that death has been 'deritualized' (e.g. Michaud-Nérard 2007). Moreover, since the end of the nineteenth century, corpses have been increasingly taken in hand by specialized personnel working in spaces from which the profane are banned. Thus, what has been made invisible is not so much death as the decaying body itself. This state of affairs contrasts sharply with what anthropologists observe in other societies, where the corpse's presence is central both to the organization of funerary rites and to the regulation of the emotions of those close to the deceased.[4]

As a framework for a cross-cultural perspective on mourning proceedings, I propose to envisage 'death' as an event involving three types of phenomena: (1) the presence of a corpse, (2) the emotional reactions of those close to the deceased and (3) collective representations of pain, loss and dying. I will try to show that whereas in many societies studied by anthropologists these three types of phenomena tend to be treated together in the course of collective funerary rituals, in contemporary Western societies, they tend to be treated independently of each other in distinct places. This dissociation, I suggest, is part of the Eliasian 'civilizing process' linked with the emergence of democracy in Western countries.

Anthropologists generally describe those having shared a close intimacy with the deceased as 'mourners': spouses, children, parents, siblings. As Van Gennep noted as early as 1909, mourners, notably the spouse, acquire a special status that situates them between the living and the dead, the deceased in particular. However, unlike the deceased who must at one point relinquish the society of the living to join the community of the dead, those close to the departed must return to the community of the living after having been partially excluded from it for a period generally lasting between one and two years. Often, a distinction is made between primary funerals, that is, mortuary services centred on the corpse, and secondary funerals that, where they exist, can take place months or years later when the deceased is deemed to have become an ancestor.

In order to provide a multifaceted comparative perspective on death and mourning in contemporary Western societies, I start by looking at mortuary rites among the Aboriginal Australians with whom I work.[5] I then turn to a performance of mourning among the Kaluli of Papua New Guinea that is in many respects comparable to a secondary funeral, then to a brief account of the lifting of a widow's mourning prohibitions among the Beti of Cameroon and finally to mortuary practices in twentieth-century rural France, before returning to the management of death in the contemporary West.

Current funerary rites among Aboriginal Australians

In Aboriginal communities I am familiar with, when someone's death is made known, those close to the deceased, the mourners, begin to scream; some of them hit themselves on the head, arms or shoulders, inflicting deep wounds that leave lasting scars. More traditional members of the community set up a camp outside their house – the 'sorry business camp' – where the mourners stay, along with members of their extended family who often come from far away after having been informed by telephone of what they call 'bad luck'. Less traditional mourners remain in their house, but are also immediately joined by members of their extended family many of whom 'camp out' at their place. Those who don't sleep on site come almost every day to spend time with the mourners and to bring food and drink.

These large-scale family reunions are thought to be crucial for the comfort and reassurance family members must provide for each other. Those most affected by the death expect their close relatives to be united with them in their grief, and, reciprocally, such persons ardently want to show their solidarity concretely by accepting to be emotionally and physically affected and by displaying this.[6]

Old women, who are not among the deceased's close kin and who are responsible for Aboriginal traditions, take on the role of 'weepers' until the body is buried: they lament loudly in chorus in a conventional way when each new person arrives at the sorry business camp or enters the mourners' house. This wailing lasts several minutes during which the newcomer shakes hands with those close to the deceased, sometimes embracing them in a gesture of mutual compassion. Visitors inquire in a low voice about the circumstances of death and the arrangements made, before moving on to other, everyday matters.

The mourners' and visitors' meals, like the organization of the funeral, are handled not by the mourners themselves but by the dead person's in-laws. The day before the burial, neighbours and in-laws prepare a light meal that will follow the burial.

Certain family members prepare a eulogy that will be distributed and preciously kept. In it, the deceased's family members, living and dead, are mentioned by name, and significant events in his or her life are recalled. Such a eulogy can become an extensive biography, especially in the case of adults who have played an important role in the community. Here is an excerpt showing the importance given to the relational identity of the deceased:

Molly Lennon

Dearly loved daughter of Indulkulta [her mother] (deceased), Edward Lennon (Ted) [her White biological father] (dec.) and Charlie Mara Muka [the Aboriginal father who raised her] (dec.)

Beloved wife of Malcom McKenzie (dec.)

Loving mother of Kenneth, Donald, Angeline, Molly (dec.), Beatrice, Margaret (dec.), Vivianne, Malcom, Heather, Alwyn, Rex, Deirdre and Regina.

Much loved baby sister of Jenny Stewart (dec.), Tom Cramp (dec.), Franck Mike (dec.), Special sister to Ray Lennon (dec.), Ronnie Lennon, Ruby Jones (dec.), Barney Lennon (dec.) & Tom Brady [all are biological or classificatory brothers & sisters]

Dearly loved daughter in-law to Fred and Jessie McKenzie (both dec.)

Much loved mother in law to Margaret, Maudie (dec.), Rex (dec.), Andrew, Johnny, Dorothy, Raymond, Irene, Heinzy, Deborah and Leonie [here are listed Molly's children's successive spouses]

Dearly loved Grandmother and Urnda [great grandmother] to all her grandchildren, great grandchildren and great, great grandchildren.

> Dearly loved Aunty, Sister, Sister in law and Nanna to all her Luritja/Yankantjatjara and Adnyamathanha families [Aboriginal communities to whom she and her husband were affiliated]
> Loved by all who knew her.

These days, the corpse is entrusted to an undertaker who also organizes the burial. Funeral home staff accept that Aboriginal family members participate in preparing the body (applying make-up, doing the person's hair) and come for lengthy visits with the deceased up until the moment of burial. They also agree to keep the corpse for a much longer period of time than is usual for non-Aboriginal Australians. Indeed, it is important that as many family members as possible be present at the funeral.

On the day of the burial, the mourners dress up in formal clothes, such as black dresses, skirts or pants with white tops. The corpse is exposed in an open casket inside a Christian place of worship chosen by the family. Indeed, as a result of the widespread missionization of the Australian Aboriginal population, present-day Aboriginal funerals always take place, at least in part, according to a Christian liturgy. Upon entering, mourners and weepers gather in front of the coffin. The weepers launch into their laments, whereas female mourners begin to cry loudly, at times screaming, some of them giving the impression of being on the verge of fainting or of wanting to throw themselves into the coffin, while others hold them back. After a time, the celebrant appears, and everyone sits down. The sermon that follows is interspersed with well-known Christian hymns sung by all. Messages from those unable to come are read out loud.

The casket is then sealed, occasioning a new explosion of tears and wailing by the weepers and the mourners. It is carried out not by funeral home personnel but by male members of the deceased's family (sons, nephews, brothers-in-law).

Everyone makes their way to the cemetery in a long slow cortege, on foot or by car. Once there, they walk silently together to the gravesite. As the casket is lowered into the grave screaming and crying erupt once again. The widow, or a sister, or a daughter may seem to faint or to throw herself onto the coffin. It often happens that musicians close to the deceased start playing guitar and singing his or her favourite songs. Finally, each person throws a flower or a handful of earth onto the coffin and shakes the mourners' hands.

After leaving the cemetery, everyone gathers in a community meeting place where small sandwiches, cakes and soft drinks have been set out on tables. Leading up to the burial, participants follow the mourners' emotional lead; however, after this tipping point it is those less close to the deceased who set the affective tone to which the mourners are called upon to comply. Thus, the atmosphere here is anything but mournful. In striking contrast with what precedes, people laugh, especially about the times they shared with the deceased, and inquire about each other's lives. Even a mother who just buried her son, and who was screaming in pain several minutes earlier, actively participates in these discussions. The oldest women, who usually come prepared with plastic bags, gather as many sandwiches and cakes as they can to bring home.

Several hours later, the group disperses. Mourners and other family members, however, tend to remain together. People begin drinking heavily and arguments soon break out. Indeed, death is an occasion to rekindle family conflicts, and fights of a more or less serious nature can take place. Questions are raised regarding the supernatural causes of the death or the possibility that foul play was involved.

The ritual entanglement of three types of phenomena

Together, the sorry business camp, the conventional gestures of suffering and compassion, the wounds mourners inflict upon themselves, the weepers' laments, the exposure of the corpse, the clothes worn, the formal succession of the events compose a collective representation of the pain and sorrow brought about by the loss of a family and community member. This shared, public representation is grounded in the fact that those who participate in it undertake complementary actions, in keeping with their respective relationships with the deceased, as relatives, but also for reasons of personal affinity. The participants' performance of these actions gives rise to intimate emotional experiences that they willingly exhibit to others.

These cultural conventions lead those closest to the deceased to externalize their inner emotions. At the same time, those less affected by the death, upon hearing the weepers' laments and witnessing the open expression of suffering associated with bereavement, recall their own dead and experience anew their own feelings of sadness and loss.

Death transforms a person into a cadaver whose weighty, disquieting presence testifies to the end of the relational reciprocity he or she maintained with others. In this type of cultural context, the corpse becomes the centre of attention. Recognition of the radical breach its presence opens up underlies the organization of the funerary performance by grounding it in an ostentatious, emotion-generating exhibition of suffering. The emotions engendered, however, are not oriented in the same direction for the mourners and for the others. The former are incited to outwardly express their inner pain. The latter, on the contrary, are prompted to get in touch with their own inner sensations of sadness and grief linked to previous experiences. This complementarity allows for an ongoing attunement of the intensities whereby different categories of participants express their respective feelings.

One sees here how these three phenomena – the corpse's presence, the emotional reactions of those close to the deceased and collective representations of death – are closely bound up together.

The gisaro of the Kaluli

The corpse's uncanny nature has the paradoxical effect of making people feel at once the irrevocable absence of the deceased and yet his or her atrocious material presence. Among the Kaluli of Papua New Guinea, the absent deceased is once again made present during a *gisaro* ritual[7] performed well after the body has been disposed of. This subsequent ritual can be seen as a further form of collective representation of pain and loss, one that is particularly effective in bringing about shared emotional experiences.

The Kaluli are horticulturalists; married couples work together in their gardens. Men of different localities take turns inviting each other to perform *gisaro*. The visitors are invited to sing songs all night long that describe the local landscape and name particular places. The aim of *gisaro* is to arouse among the hosts memories of the specific places in which they worked together with someone now deceased. Through a particularly strong evocation of such a place, a widower, for example, will be put in touch with the pain he feels at the loss of his wife with whom he used to garden at the place in question. Feeling the sadness and anger associated with the loss that the singing revives – and the best singers provoke the most intense emotions – the widower grabs a burning torch and shoves it against the singer's shoulder. The singer remains perfectly calm and impassible, whereas the widower loudly and ostentatiously expresses his grief, snot and tears running down his face.

Mourners inflict burns on the invited singers throughout the night, and in the morning, those who were burnt offer gifts – subsequently used to make body decorations – to those whose sorrow they caused. At a later date, the singers will invite their hosts to their own local community to sing, such that these shared moments of the experience of grief associated with death partake of the exchange cycles linking different Kaluli groups together. Emotions are reified by wounds inflicted on the singers in exchange for material objects with which the hosts will dress up. These body decorations, like the singers' visible, outside wounds, externalize their hosts' inner, invisible wounds that the singers reopen. As in the Aboriginal case, participants willingly seek to outwardly and conspicuously express their intimate feelings of grief and to be directly affected by the strong emotions of others.

The destiny of the deceased and his or her close ones

In the societies I have referred to, mourners and the deceased, as Van Gennep has suggested, 'constitute a special society, situated between the world of the living and the world of the dead, from which the living leave more or less quickly according to how closely they are related to the deceased'. It is generally the surviving spouse, that is, the person who most shared a physical intimacy with the deceased, who belongs longest to this special, intermediary world from which he or she can only be ritually delivered.

For example, among the Beti of Southern Cameroon,[8] following her husband's death, a widow must dress up in dark blue or black; she must not wash or cut her hair, or wear jewellry. She cannot take part in village festivities; she adopts a reserved demeanour and should not engage in sexual relations. After a year's time, the entire community participates in the lifting of these prohibitions. The widow is led to a riverbank where she is undressed; her hair is shaved off, and she is immersed in the water where her body is rubbed with purifying barks. Upon leaving the river, she is dressed in new cloths and decorated with new jewellry. She can then reintegrate the community of the living and take up the various activities she had interrupted.

Here, as in other cultural contexts, the procedures applied to the corpse and to those close to the deceased are complementary. They help the mourners to separate themselves from the dead person and help the latter to take leave of the living so as to move on to the afterlife. This is also what still took place in France, until not so long ago when most people were born and died at home.

Some French mortuary rites of the very recent past

Yvonne Verdier has described the role of the woman 'who made babies' and 'made the dead' in a small Burgundy town up until the 1960s and 1970s. Called 'the woman-who-helps', Marcelline took on these tasks that the family was loath to perform: 'Indeed, […] handling the newborn or burying the dead inspired a same dread among those who were close to the person concerned. Faced with a newborn child or with a dead person, the same feeling of panic takes hold; one doesn't know what to do and one is afraid' (Verdier 1976: 110). It is worth noting that Marcelline was not paid but thanked in kind with small gifts or services rendered. Here is how she 'made the dead':

> I'm called as soon as someone dies. You have to wash the dead person, shave him if it's a man, [and] properly brush his or her hair […]. Then, I dress him or her in clean cloths […]. When the deceased is ready, well dressed, a man is needed to place him in a chair while I prepare the bed. A sheet is placed on the bed from which everything has been removed, except the sprung bed base […]. Next, one puts the deceased back on his or her bed, close their eyes and shut their mouth. One hides their face with a towel or white handkerchief; one crosses their hands over their stomach and places a set of rosary beads along with a sprig of box tree on top. Then they are covered with another white sheet […]. To place the deceased in the coffin, the top sheet is taken away and the bottom sheet folded over the top of the body.
>
> (ibid. 108–9)

Marcelline then closes the shutters and the windows, and covers the mirrors and the television with a cloth for if not, they would forever reflect the dead person's face. The clocks are stopped until the burial takes place. The night table is covered with a white tablecloth on which is placed a glass of holy water containing a sprig of box tree. A crucifix with a lit candle is placed next to it. Electric lights are turned off; only candlelight is used and no fire is made. A neighbour comes to cook meals, clean the house and milk the cows, for all women's domestic activities are suspended; the deceased's female kin must neither cook, wash nor clean.

The body remains exposed like that for three days. 'Until the burial, there must always be someone with the deceased so that he or she is not alone, but the family doesn't like staying with them' (ibid. 109). During the day, neighbours visit and sprinkle holy water on the dead person; those wishing to see the deceased one last time lift up the handkerchief. At night, the woman-who-helps organizes a vigil for the neighbours who take shifts during the night. At midnight, she makes coffee and serves brandy.

Here, as in many other societies, procedures pertaining to the corpse and to the mourning process are undertaken by intermediaries who are neither payed nor mourners themselves. However, one cannot but be struck by the relational density and the homey, material intimacy these treatments entail.

Managing death in contemporary Western societies

By contrast, at present, in most contemporary Western settings, the handling of bodies, from birth to death, is a medical matter, undertaken by anonymous third parties who are remunerated for the functions they fulfil. It is through the intermediary of health organizations, funeral homes and civil registrars that society manages the deaths of individuals. Their corpse is taken in hand by paid professionals, who, away from the mundane world and the public eye, are responsible for providing the dead with a bearable, sanitized demeanour. Concomitantly, in the public sphere in which mortuary ceremonies occur, ritualization is often reduced to a minimum and is highly constrained in terms of both time and space. On these occasions, expressions of mourners' feelings are dictated more by the demands of decorum and reserve than by those of raucous ostentation. Each person is invited to withdraw deep inside himself or herself to commemorate the deceased. Unlike the Australian Aboriginal ethos described earlier, it is as though propriety requires that one not contaminate one's fellow mourners with one's own feelings, and, indeed, everything is organized so that no one is overly tainted by the emotions of others. Joan Didion's well-known account of her own mourning experience following her husband's death nicely captures this expected lack of emotional demonstration, surely linked to what Norbert Elias (1973) has called the distancing 'civilizing process' underlying contemporary individualism. Quoting Gorer (1965) she speaks of 'the imperative to do nothing which might diminish the enjoyment of others' and the current trend in England and the United States 'to treat mourning as morbid self-indulgence, and to give social admiration to the bereaved who hide their grief so fully that no one would guess that anything had happened' (Didion 2005: 60).

The emotional reactions of those close to the deceased are managed at a distance from the abhorrent, unsettling presence of a loved one's physical decay, notably through counselling dispensed by non-relatives who are paid to provide it. These are psy-whatevers who act as mediating third parties between the living and the dead, and who, precisely because they are not intimate with their patients, can become the custodians of their inner feelings. In consultations with them, those close to the deceased disclose the emotions they stifle in the presence of others because of the anxiety and panic this might cause them. Indeed, the exhortation to undertake one's 'grief work' goes hand in hand with the difficulties people face in sharing with close friends or family members, outside of established venues of mediation, the despair they experience in connection with death and loss.

At the same time, human mortality is the object of very large number of collective representations made available through various media, that is, at a remove from the concrete presence of the corpse as a mass of deteriorating flesh. Death is not concealed by the media; on the contrary, it is made omnipresent. It constantly makes headline news and provides the narrative framework for a large number of books, movies, television shows and autobiographical testimonials. The untimely demise of celebrities like Lady Di or Michael Jackson provides another way of collectively commemorating death. In such cases, precisely because the deceased is not someone one is close to, one can give free rein to one's grief without bothering anybody. On the contrary, such occasions can instill a sense of community founded not on kinship ties but on the expression of shared feelings of loss for distant departed whose death suddenly brings them closer. The role played by the airing of TV series such as *Six Feet Under* is of a somewhat attenuated yet similar nature: through this distanced medium, each individual can experience, for themselves, what the death of a loved one might entail, and even share this feeling, in all security, with preferably distant others.

Death is also exhibited in highly disturbing, often violent images, but which are more likely to concern people living in distant lands or during other historical periods: victims of war or mass murders, natural catastrophes and so on. These images reintroduce, but at a safe remove, the dreadful aspects of putrefying bodies and their aptitude to strongly affect us emotionally, something that has been expunged from actual mortuary proceedings. Similarly, as I have proposed elsewhere (Moisseeff 2013b, 2016b), the proliferation of horror movies can be seen as still another way of providing a mediated, relatively safe experience of the wretchedness of the dead body and the strong reactions it elicits.

Conclusion

I have sought here to highlight certain distinctive features of mortuary practices in contemporary Western societies by contrasting them with funeral rites in other cultural settings. In many cultures, the different phenomena I have identified – the presence of a corpse, the emotional reactions of those close to the deceased and collective representations of death and loss – tend to be treated together. In the contemporary West, they are separated and subject to distinct procedures that are all based on a recourse to distant, third parties who are not relatives but paid professionals. In the former case, an amplified, ostentatious expression of participants' feelings allows for an emotional attunement of the mourners and those less affected by the loss. In the latter case, funerary proceedings are typically governed by the concern to avoid ostentatious emotional expression so that those occupying different positions with respect to the deceased do not contaminate each other with their respective feelings.

This, however, pertains above all to institutionalized ritual procedures undertaken in response to the disruptive effects of individual death. The commemorative practices occasioned by catastrophic social events like Breivik's massacre in Norway or the 2015 terrorist killings in Paris are both different in nature and in some ways the same. On the one hand, these calamities erupt violently and spectacularly into everyday life in a way that makes them difficult to contain by such well-established ceremonial procedures. On the other hand, like the corpse for those close to the deceased and for community members elsewhere, they impose themselves as singular agencies that arouse unresolved feelings of exceptional intensity, thereby encouraging emotional expression in public spaces from which it has otherwise been carefully expunged. In this regard, the as of yet institutionalized initiatives such catastrophic events give rise to are akin to the conventional funerary performances carried out in other, more exotic settings.

Participants' bodily involvement in these collective mourning and memorial practices encourages them to willingly exhibit their feelings to others. In small-scale societies lacking forms of centralized power comparable to nation states, this particular mode of emotional sharing epitomizes what is at stake in democracy as this notion is commonly understood in the contemporary West: as a process that allows for the public expression of disparate perspectives reflecting the heterogeneity of the various parties that make up society as a whole. In communities typically studied by cultural anthropologists, rituals play precisely this role. Their performance is upheld by public displays of emotion that differ in accordance with the places occupied by various categories of participants within shared networks of (kinship and other) relations. In much the same way, the commemorative practices that emerge in reaction to large-scale socially disruptive events in the West often entail ritualized position-taking involving real or imagined confrontations in which individuals and groups – by means of marches, memorial services, mediatized debates and so on – take outspoken stands for ideas and values they feel have come under siege. Such publicly aired differences of opinion, I suggest, are neither a secondary aspect of these practices, nor are they evidence of social disorder. Rather, they are the ritualized expression of a democratically inspired process of reciprocal adjustment. Like mourners' disparate reactions to the corpse in other cultural traditions, the conflicts raised by such commemorations can be seen as allowing persons occupying different positions to participate in an emotional attunement in which physical presence, affective expression and shared representations of loss are made to converge. Like canonical mortuary practices and the reconfiguration of relational networks they mediate in non-Western settings, the spontaneous gatherings in reaction to recent terrorist attacks in the West constitute an essential cultural resource in which the expression of divergent perceptions of emotionally affecting disruptive events can contribute to reassembling a shaken democracy.

11

Reinvented rituals as medicine in contemporary Indigenous films: *Maliglutit*, *Mahana* and *Goldstone*

Ken Derry
University of Toronto

They were nothing more than people, by themselves. Even paired, any pairing, they would have been nothing more than people by themselves. But all together, they have become the heart and muscles and mind of something perilous and new, something strange and growing and great. Together, all together, they are the instruments of change.

Keri Hulme (Māori), *The Bone People* (1986: 4)

Introduction

The horrifying (and wholly un-democratic) violence of European colonialism has included racism, land theft, rape, child abuse, slavery and genocide. This violence in many ways has been made possible by stories. As Métis scholar Jo-Ann Episkenew (2009) points out, the 'story of imagined White superiority'

Thank you to the editors of this volume (Graham, Jone, Michael and Sarah) for their help with an early draft of this chapter. I also want to thank all the organizers of REDO for including me in their 2017 event in Oslo. Many of the participants had been meeting already for a few years and knew each other well. I was very much an outsider and this was a new academic world for me, but everyone was incredibly supportive and welcoming. I found spending a few days listening to a host of smart and thoughtful people discuss the ways in which ritual can literally help improve the world to be a wonderfully profound and moving experience. Being part of that meeting also connected me – as rituals tend to do – to this new community, some members of whom I remain in grateful contact with.

has justified and encouraged hateful colonial attitudes and actions for centuries, and 'continues to have disastrous effects on the health and well-being of Indigenous people' (3). Such stories are so powerful because they both shape and reflect the worlds in which we live, as 'humans in every society construct and articulate their shared reality in the form of narrative' (13). Which is to say: 'We *are* our stories' (13).

Again, colonial myths are predicated on the conviction that European cultures are inherently better and deserve to supplant those in colonized lands:

> Believing that Indigenous epistemologies were merely pagan superstition, the colonizers sought to eradicate those epistemologies by imposing 'modern' education and Christian evangelism. Their goal was to eliminate Indigenous cultures and bring modernity and progress to Indigenous peoples. (5)

At a certain historical point, colonial stories assumed that the elimination of Indigenous cultures had in fact taken place. And so as Tewa/Navajo scholar and film-maker Beverly Singer (2001) points out, these stories either ignore Indigenous people entirely or 'refer to us in the past tense rather than as people who inhabit the present' (2). But Indigenous people of course *do* inhabit the present and continue to suffer the ongoing effects of colonial stories and the acts they support. These effects include the loss of people, land, languages and traditions, as well as what Episkenew has termed 'postcolonial trauma' (2009: 9). This trauma has resulted in depression, poor health, self-loathing, addiction, academic failures, isolation and violence. This violence is directed 'rarely against the settlers but rather against oneself, one's family, or one's community' (8–9).

Episkenew asserts that modern Indigenous stories can challenge colonial myths and in doing so act 'as "medicine" to help cure the colonial contagion by healing the communities that [colonial] policies have injured' (2). These stories highlight flaws in colonial cultures themselves (5–6) while also 'reclaiming the Indigenous knowledges that colonial policies attempted to eradicate' and 'validating Indigenous ideas, values, and beliefs' (16). In such ways, stories can help to overcome the dissolution of Indigenous communities, reconnecting people with their histories, traditions and each other. To describe this effect Episkenew refers to Cherokee scholar Jace Weaver's (1997) notion of 'communitism,' a neologism that mixes 'community' with 'activism' (xii). When Indigenous stories are medicine, in other words, they heal by pushing back against harmful colonial ideas and practices, and by 'reconnecting Indigenous individuals to the larger whole' (Episkenew 2009: 12). Even stories that do not address colonialism directly (or at all) still fundamentally oppose colonial myths. They do this not only by affirming the value of Indigenous people and traditions but also by simply and crucially pointing to their continued existence – Indigenous cultures have *not* in fact been eliminated.

Critically, the *form* in which these stories are told is very often a colonial one. Episkenew, for instance, specifically focuses on Indigenous literature in English. Joy Harjo (Mvskoke) and Gloria Bird (Spokane) (1997) refer to the Indigenous use of colonial media as 'reinventing the enemy's language':

> 'Reinventing' in the colonizer's tongue and turning those images around to mirror an image of the colonized to the colonizers as a process of decolonization indicates that something is happening, something is emerging and coming into focus that will politicize as well as transform literary expression .... It is at this site where 'reinventing' can occur to undo some of the damage that colonization has wrought. (22, 24; see Episkenew 2009: 12)

In reflecting on the similar use of film to tell Indigenous stories, Beverly Singer (2001) explains that this activity 'is part of a social movement that I call "cultural sovereignty," which involves trusting in the older ways and adapting them to our lives in the present' (2). And in line with Weaver's notion of communitism, Singer sees Indigenous films as 'helping to reconnect us with very old relationships and traditions', to 'revive storytelling and restore the old foundation' and to 'threaten traditional practices of Hollywood filmmakers, who often advanced their careers by creating distorted and dishonest images of "Indians"' (2).[1]

In the fall of 2016, I had the tremendous privilege to see three powerful Indigenous movies at the Toronto International Film Festival (TIFF): *Maliglutit*, *Mahana* and *Goldstone*. Each of these films in their own way arguably functions as medicine in Episkenew's sense. In addition, they not only use the colonial medium of film to tell their stories, but all three movies represent a different take on the genre of the American western. They also feature *characters* using colonial tools and practices, together with Indigenous traditions and epistemologies, as part of their own process of overcoming the specific challenges they face. In this chapter, then, I examine the ways in which these three films explore the Indigenous mixtures of traditional and colonial practices – reinvented rituals – that may help Indigenous peoples heal from the varying traumas of (ongoing) colonial violence.

Two quick notes about terms: first, the kind of cultural interconnections I'm looking at are most often referred to as 'hybridity'. The scholar who has arguably had the greatest influence on discussions of hybridity and colonialism is Homi K. Bhabha, particularly in two key essays: 'Of Mimicry and Man: The Ambivalence of Colonial Discourse'; and 'Signs Taken for Wonders: Questions of Ambivalence and Authority under a Tree Outside Delhi, May 1817'. However, I am not discussing 'hybridity' as Bhabha does. In my own readings I find that Indigenous scholars and film-makers rarely if ever use the term 'hybridity', and so I will similarly avoid it here. The word too often implies that there is such a thing as a 'pure' or 'unmixed' culture, that all cultures have not in fact always been in flux for all sorts of reasons. This is a point that Laguna Pueblo author Leslie Marmon Silko makes in her acclaimed novel *Ceremony*:

> The people nowadays have an idea about the ceremonies. They think the ceremonies must be performed exactly as they have always been done .... But long ago when the people were given these ceremonies, the changing began, if only in the aging of the yellow gourd rattle or the shrinking of the skin around the eagle's claw, if only in the different voices from generation to generation, singing the chants. You see, in many ways, the ceremonies have always been changing. (1977: 132)

Another reason for not talking about 'hybridity' in this chapter is that the kinds of inter-cultural practices that I see in the films I am discussing are critically dissimilar from what Bhabha examines. For Bhabha, the colonized engage in 'subversive mimicry', appropriating colonial cultures in order to reveal their inherently problematic nature and to disrupt the colonizers. The three films I am looking at, however, show characters sincerely valuing certain colonial products, acts, media, and so on, using them constructively for their own purposes and not only (and sometimes not at all) to undermine colonialism itself.[2]

The second term to clarify is 'democracy'. Any discussion of democracy in relation to Indigenous people will be somewhat fraught, to put it mildly. Most of the Indigenous communities that existed at the time that Columbus set sail were eventually colonized, killed or enslaved by democratic powers. In addition, one recurring feature of democratic societies has been that they do not in fact regard all citizens equally. In the United States, for instance, voting at one point was specifically restricted to male property owners of European descent. And enfranchisement is not necessarily better, as it can be a tool for assimilation rather than representation. Until 1985, the Indian Act of Canada specified that any person officially designated as First Nation, Métis or Inuit who gained the (colonial) right to vote also *lost* their Indigenous status and rights. In many instances this shift was not a matter of choice – an Indigenous person was automatically enfranchised if they obtained a university degree, for example, or joined the Canadian armed forces.

Another concern regarding democracy is that it does not reflect the traditional governance structures of many Indigenous communities. To say that 'democracy' is the ideal to which these communities should strive is itself a very colonial act. That said, the refusal to allow Indigenous people to fully participate in the larger (colonial) democratic societies of which they are now a part is of course also an act of ongoing violence and colonization. Also, there certainly *have* been democratic Indigenous societies. One of the most well known of these is the Iroquois (Haudenosaunee) Confederacy, which some have argued influenced the development of American democratic theory and practice (Grinde and Johansen 1991). The U.S. Congress in fact passed a resolution in 1988 recognizing the contribution of the Iroquois Confederacy to the American Constitution and Bill of Rights.

For the purposes of this discussion I will be considering how Indigenous films both depict and embody reinvented ritual practices that are 'democratic' in the broad sense of helping to resist tyranny, oppression and the unjust concentration of power in the hands of a few. These reinvented rituals can also empower the Indigenous people who practise them to create healthier, safer, more sustainable communities that involve not only all people but also the larger other-than-human world.

Maliglutit

Inuk film-maker Zacharias Kunuk made history in 2001 with his first non-documentary film, *Atanarjuat: The Fast Runner*, which was based on an Inuk legend and was the first movie written, directed and acted entirely in the Inuktitut language. It won the Camera d'Or at the Cannes Film Festival that year, and in 2015 *Atanarjuat* was voted the best Canadian movie of all time in a TIFF poll of international film-makers and scholars (CBC 2015).

Kunuk's *Maliglutit* (*Searchers*) is also entirely in Inuktitut. This time, however, he turned elsewhere for his story inspiration, deciding to remake John Ford's *The Searchers* (1956). Ford's movie begins in 1868 and famously tells the story of what happens after a Comanche attack on a Texas homestead, during which most of the settler family is killed and the two daughters are kidnapped, one of whom is found dead soon after. John Wayne plays the brother of the home's murdered patriarch, and the movie focuses on the years he spends searching for his remaining niece and for vengeance against the men who took the young women. In the end, both of his searches are successful.

There are similar elements in the plot of Kunuk's film, but key alterations transform its meaning. *Maliglutit* takes place in 1913 in the snow-bound far north, a very different wilderness than the West Texas landscape of the original *Searchers*. The most important change is that this is not a movie about Indigenous-settler conflict; all of the people involved are Inuit. The villains of the piece are four men who are disrupting local communities. These men are shown as selfish and lazy, taking what they want rather than taking responsibility for themselves or working with others for the benefit of the community. The foursome come upon a family while the father Kuanana and his older son Siku are out hunting; they kill the Kuanana's parents and younger son Anguti, and kidnap his wife Ailla and daughter Tagaq as their own new 'wives'.

In contrast to these men, Kuanana and his family share everything and work together for the benefit of the group. They also live in a way that depends on both traditional practices and knowledge, as well as on colonial tools. In order to decide where it is best to hunt, the grandfather performs a ritual to receive guidance from the spirit Apisaaq. Kuanana and his son set out the next morning in search of caribou – armed both with Apisaaq's advice *and* with two pieces of modern technology, a small telescope and a rifle. Kuanana uses these same tools when searching for the men who killed his family and kidnapped his wife and daughter, along with other traditional ones – a spear and his father's spirit helper, the loon Kallulik.

In the end this communal and culturally dynamic approach is as successful with the four murderers as it was with the caribou. Working together with his son, wife and daughter, Kuanana makes use of telescope, rifle, spear and Kallulik to defeat the corrupt men and reunite his family in joy and grief. It is worth

Figure 11.1 Kuanana searches.Benjamin Kunuk as Kuanana. *Maliglutit* (*Searchers*). 2016. Courtesy of Isuma Distribution International.

noting that while all four of the murderers are killed in the end, the film takes care to present these deaths as necessary to free the two women – that is they are not acts of revenge, unlike the killings in Ford's movie. Similarly, the protagonist of Kunuk's early film *Atanarjuat* chooses not to exact revenge on his enemies by killing them – which, again, is unlike what happens in the original (oral) version of the story. As Kunuk explains, 'Revenge is not the subject [of the film], the subject is sharing' (Alexander 2002: 106).

Mahana

Set in the early 1960s on the East Coast of the North Island of New Zealand, *Mahana* adapts the novel *Bulibasha: King of the Gypsies* (1994) by Witi Ihimaera, Māori author of *The Whale Rider* (1987).[3] The project paired Scottish screenwriter John Collee with Māori director Lee Tamahori and was Tamahori's first New Zealand production since the groundbreaking *Once Were Warriors* (1994). That earlier film was set in the 1990s when it was made, and in fact Ihimaera himself sees *Mahana* 'as being a precursor film to *Once Were Warriors* – it shows the generation before *Warriors*' (Wild Bunch 2016: 4).

Mahana includes several direct references to traditional Hollywood westerns, including *3:10 to Yuma* (1957) and *She Wore a Yellow Ribbon* (1949). In a number of interviews, Tamahori has discussed his film's relation to the genre:

> *Mahana* is shot like a western, specifically a 1950s American western. I've always loved the western because it's like a simple morality play, laid out in a way that a child who didn't know the difference between right and wrong could watch it, and see exactly who is right and who is wrong. New Zealand Maori in the 1950s loved US westerns. They loved to go and watch them because they were all farmers, and rode horses, and loved to wear western hats and pretend they were cowboys. I wanted to get a touch of that across in this film. It's not a western but it evokes that feeling. (Johnston 2016)[4]

One way in which the film differs from a western is that in fact it is *not* a simple morality play. Although the apparent villain is Tamihana Mahana, the patriarch who tears his family apart, much of his violence – like that of Jake Heke, the abusive father in *Once Were Warriors* (also played by Temuera Morrison) – is facilitated by colonialism. The old man's desire for colonial status and power manifests most obviously in his bitter feud with Rupeni Poata, the head of another Māori family. Specifically, the two men have for decades competed for the sheep-shearing contract from the settler Collins family. The toxic impact of colonial social and economic structures on the community is evident in the opening scene of the film: both families speed to the funeral of the Collins patriarch to gain an advantage in obtaining the new shearing contract and almost kill each other racing to cross a bridge only wide enough for one car.

Once upon a time, Tamihana and Rupeni were also rivals for the affection of a young woman, Ramona. She had loved Rupeni, which we first discover when her grandson Simeon finds a photo of the two of them from years ago. Eventually we learn that Ramona married Tamihana after he raped and impregnated her. Tamihana's ugliness is also revealed in his battles with the members of his own family, particularly Simeon. In a critical scene, Simeon defies his grandfather's command to stop going to the movies in town; in response, Tamihana drags him out of the house, throws him down the front stairs, kicks him and tries to shear his head like a sheep. He is only stopped when his own son, Simeon's father Joshua, strikes Tamihana – which leads him to banish Joshua and his family from Mahana land.

The healing of this family, the ending of their fighting with each other and the Poatas, involves a blending of settler and Māori practices.[5] These practices are fuelled at first by the deeply communal – and explicitly non-patriarchal – approach that Joshua and his family bring to their new situation. They work together using colonial tools and equipment to build up their own farm and sheep-shearing enterprise, while Ramona sings to the bees to reassure them that her family won't cut down the wildflowers on their new land; in return for this kindness the bees tell Ramona that they will provide the sweetest honey. That Ramona is often the standard-bearer of Māori tradition is not surprising given

Figure 11.2 Ramona sings. Nancy Brunning as Ramona Mahana and Sienna MacKinlay as her granddaughter Gloria. © 2016 The Patriarch Limited. Courtesy of WILD BUNCH SA.

her *moko kauae* (chin tattoo), which links her to her ancestors and stands in clear and pointed contrast to the Christian cross that Tamihana has put above their bed.[6]

The final transformative ritual moments come at Tamihana's funeral, which takes place with everyone in European dress clothes at a *wharenui*, a traditional Māori meeting house. The funeral is disrupted by the arrival of the Poatas performing a *haka*, a group ritual traditionally carried out as a precursor to battle and to mark important events, including funerals. The act in this case suggests both possibilities; to the extent that the *haka* is indeed meant in part as a rebuke against Tamihana, the gesture is completed by Rupeni's statement to his rival that he is glad the old man is finally dead: 'You cast too long a shadow. Take it with you, and leave us in the sun.' At this point Simeon interrupts a brawl that threatens to erupt between the men of the two families, revealing that Tamihana had raped Ramona years before and so she had to marry him despite her love for Rupeni. In English and in Māori his grandmother confirms the story and also affirms that many good things came from their union – including her children and grandchildren.

Another critical act performed at the funeral is the *hongi*, the Māori greeting, between Rupeni and Simeon, and then Rupeni and Ramona, after Ramona's speech. The *hongi* involves two people touching their noses and foreheads to each other and traditionally exchanging *ha* (the breath of life). This ritual demonstrates the ending of the Mahana–Poata feud and starts to (re-)build the bonds between the families. It is also an implicit rebuke to colonialism and the role that settler society has played in the feud. The first time we see the act performed between members of the two families is after Simeon's class visits a New Zealand court. They witness three Māori who do not speak English – including a young Poata boy – tried and convicted in quick succession, with no one present to translate for them. The trials are wholly colonial rituals, in other words, allowing no Indigenous element. Afterwards, Simeon addresses the judge: 'If no one can speak Māori here, how can we Māori possibly defend ourselves?' Afterwards Rupeni finds Simeon and pulls him in for the *hongi*, saying: 'You spoke well today. You spoke on behalf of all of us.'[7]

Mahana does not end with the final *hongi* between Rupeni and Ramona. Instead, once the dust has settled somewhat from the revelation about Tamihana's assault on Ramona, the scene shifts to Simeon sitting on the steps of the *wharenui*. He is approached by the girl he likes, Poppy Poata, who asks if he wants to go see a film with her. She tells him that the movie stars Elvis and is directed by Don Siegel, who Simeon immediately identifies as the director of *Invasion of the Body Snatchers* (1956).[8] This, amazingly, is how Tamahori concludes *Mahana*: by showing us how much two young Māori know about film, how much they *care* about it and how they use it to help bridge inter-Indigenous divides between them, divides created in part by the same colonial culture that produced the films.

Goldstone

Goldstone is Kamilaroi film-maker Ivan Sen's sequel to *Mystery Road* (2013), which once again focuses on Australian Aboriginal police detective Jay Swan. For both films Sen was not only writer and director but also editor, director of photography and composer. *Goldstone* opens with a series of old colonial photographs. These images show European men in front of tents and shacks in the wilderness; Aboriginal people in Victorian clothing; early frontier towns in the process of construction; a line of Chinese labourers; European men digging, looking for something in the earth; five Chinese women in formal Chinese clothing; and a group of European men, with camels, and a few Aboriginal men dressed traditionally. The man in the centre sits on a camel lowered to the ground and has his hand on the head of an Aboriginal man as if he owns him. Showing these photos takes just over a minute and offers an extraordinarily powerful and economical introduction to the film. Sen has not only given us a snapshot (so to speak) of certain aspects of early Australian colonization – aspects directly and specifically relevant to *Goldstone* – but he has literally reframed these images within his own camera. We are looking at an Indigenous view of a colonial view, which is what the film as a whole also gives us. When the last photo is done, the film's title appears.

After the title screen we see Jay arrive in the frontier town of Goldstone, searching for a missing young woman named Mei. He slowly unravels deep-seated capitalist corruption, as the dishonest, murderous mayor (Maureen) has been working with similarly criminal leaders of both the mining company (Johnny) and the local Aboriginal Land Council (Tommy), all of whom hope to profit from a new land deal that would allow the mine to greatly expand its operations. To them, people and land represent only resources to be exploited for personal gain. It is in this context that young women are brought in from China as sex workers for the company's male employees. Jay eventually discovers that Mei was one of these women, dying from exposure when she tried to escape her unbearable circumstances.

Jay begins *Goldstone* as a broken man in many ways, struggling with unknown demons that have come to plague him since the end of the previous film. He is estranged from his ex-wife and mourning his recently deceased daughter. He is depressed and usually drunk and appears almost entirely directionless. His commitment to justice – particularly for the lost and disenfranchised – remains unwavering, however, and seems to be what keeps him moving as he slowly comes to understand what happened to Mei.

As much as Jay finds value in pursuing his case, the key to him more fully regaining his sense of meaning and belonging is local Aboriginal Elder Jimmy. Jay is shocked to learn that Jimmy knew his father who, it seems, was part of Australia's 'Stolen Generations', one of possibly more than 100,000 children who were removed from their families by the government during the first seven decades of the twentieth century.[9] Jimmy also takes Jay in a dugout canoe through a landscape that is filmed to suggest timelessness, a world away from the selfishness and corruption of Goldstone. Water and land fill the screen while Jimmy's song fills the speakers. The landscape includes traditional Aboriginal rock paintings, which often depict creation events connected to that specific place and to the ancestors who lived there. The fact that Jay's father is also from this place means that Jay has, unexpectedly, come home. As Jimmy's daughter Maria tells him: 'This land, you belong to it.'

Ultimately Jay is able to make some progress in fighting both his personal struggles and town corruption by engaging in ritual practices from very different cultures: he follows colonial police procedures while participating in traditional Indigenous acts that link him to the sacredness of the place in which he finds himself, both literally and spiritually. In following these intertwined paths he must similarly rely on both the Aboriginal Elder Jimmy and the very non-Aboriginal local cop, Josh. And just as he learns from Jimmy to watch and protect the birds, he uses his rifle to watch and protect Josh when killers have trapped him.

As with *Maliglutit* and *Mahana*, *Goldstone* plays with the genre of the Hollywood western. The film's press kit indicates that Sen himself refers to the film as a 'Neo Western' (Dark Matter Media 2016: 4) and that he used 'the iconography of a classic Western to flesh out the character of Jay and to bring a particular visual style to the film, as evidenced in wardrobe, location and production design' (7). In an interview with Emmet O'Cuana (2013), Sen also makes it clear that, in his view, Indigenous people inherently disrupt genre norms: 'You could probably make ten genre films in this country [Australia] and if at least one of the lead roles is an Indigenous role, it's going to be unique. That

Indigenous character is going to bring a unique perspective, which the genre hasn't had before. So there's real currency in chasing genre with Indigenous perspective.'[10]

Goldstone represents a play on another genre as Sen also refers to the film as an example of 'Outback Noir' (Dark Matter Media 2016: 4), combining Aboriginal perspectives with film noir. Like traditional noir, *Goldstone* does not end happily in several ways.[11] While Jay and Josh have some success, Maureen and Johnny go unpunished and many good people are hurt or killed, including the Elder, Jimmy. The picture of life that the film paints is bleak in many ways. Despairing of ever being able to overcome the cruelty of her dead-end existence, one character offers a classic noir lament: 'The world is what it is. You cannot change it. You cannot bargain with it.' Initially trying to justify not doing anything about the problems in his town, Josh himself says that all Jay really accomplished in his previous case (from *Mystery Road*) was to kick up a bit of dust that just settled down again. The movie clearly sides with Jay, though, who responds that at least the dust 'is a little bit thinner'.

This is, it seems, one of the Indigenous twists that Sen is putting on film noir. When we think only of ourselves, things will inevitably end badly for everyone. When we think of others, though, when we recognize our true *place*, our actions can have some small, but real, value. We may not be able to do much, but this is more than nothing. Regarding noir's notoriously pessimistic outlook, Foster Hirsch (1981) remarks: 'In all the films where characters are pressed by circumstances, there is no way out as the protagonists stare mutely at lives of absolute dead-ends' (180). While *Goldstone* does not end happily or neatly, Josh and Jay are not at dead ends. Josh puts in a transfer to another town, by the

Figure 11.3 Jay finds his place.Aaron Pedersen as Jay Swan. *Goldstone*. 2016. Courtesy of Arclight Films.

ocean, 'to clean a bit of this dust out of me'. And Jay gets back in the canoe, alone this time, and goes home.

Conclusion

In each of these three very different films, set in different times and places, the Indigenous protagonists learn (or reaffirm) the value of community, of sharing resources, of thinking of others before oneself. At the same time they learn to push back against those who use the power they have to cause suffering. All of these points about community, thoughtfulness, power and violence are also tied to colonialism in some form, implicitly (in *Maliglutit* and *Mahana*) or explicitly (in *Goldstone*). These films highlight the ways in which selfishness is fundamentally violent and anti-democratic, how it disrupts the critical relationships that form communities and how the selfish also suffer in the end.

One way in which this point is made in each film involves sexual violence against women. Many commenters have of course noted the historic links between patriarchy and colonialism (e.g. Jaimes Guerrero 2003; Hanson 2009). But the films also empower the women who are assaulted. Even though all three movies focus on male protagonists – and were written and directed by men – the women are not simply victims of violence but active participants in resolving their circumstances. It may be Kuanana and his son who set out after the murderers of *Maglitutit*, but the women play a pivotal role in reuniting the family – unlike what happens in the original *Searchers*. As Cian Cruise (2017) points out, 'Their escape from the torment of the marauders is only possible with each member's contribution. This isn't the story of one dad saving his womenfolk from other bad men, but a community coming together to heal the rift caused by one violent act.' Similarly, Ramona in *Mahana* may have been forced to marry Tamihana after he rapes her, but when he exiles Joshua and his family she goes with them to her old home on her own land. Her husband forbids this, but she rebukes him: 'Even *your* power', she snaps, 'has its limits'. The corruption in *Goldstone* would never have been exposed, and stopped, if it had not been for Mei's original courageous escape attempt. Her death is what brings Jay to the town. And it's not Jay who convinces local police officer Josh to finally see the corruption himself, but another of the women brought to town from China who defies her captors by telling Josh the truth.

Depicting women with agency in these films is one of the modifications they are making to the Hollywood western. Another is of course the presentation of Indigenous people as complex, fully human beings. In traditional westerns like Ford's *The Searchers*, 'Indigenous people are presented as dehumanized demons and a white man's vengeance is a righteous act' (Cruise 2017). Such films both reflected and provided further support for racist, genocidal views and acts. Offering realistic, affirming and whole portrayals of Indigenous people is one of the simplest and most powerful ways in which *Maliglutit*, *Mahana* and *Goldstone* can function as 'medicine' in Episkenew's sense.

One critical way in which these films show the full humanity of Indigenous people while also emphasizing the importance of community is through inter-Indigenous conflict. In some ways this violence is connected to the self-inflicted harm that Jo-Ann Episknew identifies as resulting from postcolonial trauma. Certainly some of the battles between Indigenous characters in *Mahana*, and all of them in *Goldstone*, result from colonialism. But this is not the case in *Maliglutit*. In fact Zacharias Kunuk has specifically said that the villains in his film are not committing post-contact crimes, as 'wife stealing may be as old as Inuit culture itself' (Kingulliit Productions 2016: 3). This seemingly straightforward narrative idea radically re-figures classic tropes and their underlying meanings:

> Gone is the racial conflict at the core of Ford's film. The marauders in *Maliglutit* are Inuit men who have been exiled from common society. This means the crimes aren't committed against "the Other," but members of one's own community. The simple act of dehumanization is not possible in this context, when one shares custom, creed and code. This choice makes the film more harrowing and thought-provoking. If we could do this to ourselves, then what other dark deeds are we capable of? (Cruise 2017)

These movies do not essentialize Indigenous and non-Indigenous people or behaviours as 'good' or 'bad'. Individuals who belong to either group can and do behave deplorably, while others do what is right. What determines whether one's actions are valued or not is whether they serve the community or instead benefit a few while harming many.

Another way in which Kunuk, Tamahori and Sen appear to be Indigenizing movies is by decentring people in some respects. All three of their narratives are, in important ways, about how certain landscapes at times present challenges for survival. In each film Indigenous people manage by working *with* their environment – asking the loon spirit for help, singing to the bees, paddling through ancient waters in the dessert. These actions are contrasted dramatically with those who try to dominate their world and take what they want, like the four Inuit murderers, or Tamihana Mahana, or the mining company.

Visually, each film reinforces this point by frequently showing how small people are in contrast to their environment. In discussing Ivan Sen's use of drones for filming, Arrernte/Arabana actor Aaron Pedersen (who plays Jay Swan) explains that he is part of a long tradition: 'All the Indigenous paintings throughout history, they were always a bird's eye view … it's the Indigenous way of storytelling' (O'Cuana 2016). In discussing the setting of *Goldstone*, Sen called it 'the most incredible landscape I've ever shot … it was absolutely the most ancient, stunning [landscape] … the drone is there the whole time and you can see the age of this continent and the people moving around on it and the shadows' (Thwaites 2018). When he presented his film at the TIFF in 2016, Sen further said that he intended his overhead drone shots to offer a perspective in which people are simply part of a much, much larger whole.

As exemplified by these three movies, Indigenous film-makers are reinventing traditional storytelling in ways that involve colonial tools and forms while at the same time reinventing those very tools and forms. They have literally taken control of the lenses that frame them and their stories, lenses that have caused (and continue to cause) tremendous harm:

> Indians have been misrepresented in art, history, science, literature, popular films, and by the press in the news, on radio, and on television. The earliest stereotypes associating Indians with being savage, naked, and heathen were established with the founding of America and determined by two factors: religious intolerance for cultural and spiritual differences leading to the destruction of Native cultures, and rejection of Indian cultures as relevant subject matter by traditional historians in the writing of U.S. history. (Singer 2001: 1)[12]

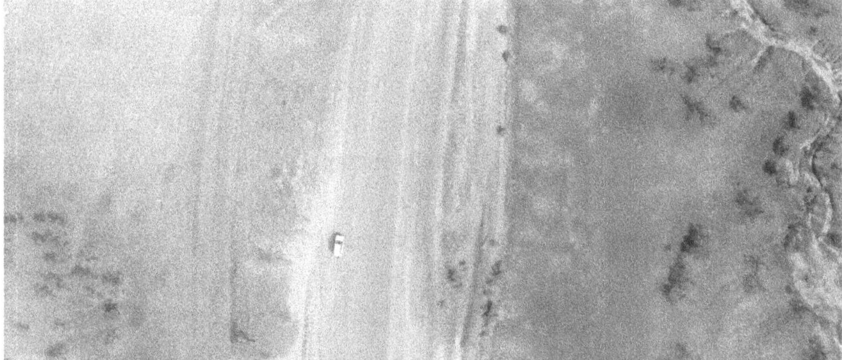

Figure 11.4 Ivan Sen's Indigenous perspective in *Goldstone*. 2016. Courtesy of Arclight Films.

This, again, is the colonial myth that Episkenew critiques, from which all of us need to heal. Significantly, all three movies under discussion take steps in this direction in part by presenting us with Indigenous characters who resolve problems by looking through colonial lenses: Kuanana tracks his enemies with a telescope; Simeon starts to understand his family's pain when he finds the photo of Ramona and Rupeni; and Jay saves Josh's life after watching him through his rifle scope. Reflecting on the use of lenses in *Maliglutit*, Darrell Varga (2019) comments: 'The history of cinema, like the history of colonization, is the expression of control through the gaze, the act of looking. The association of shamanism with vision is not a simple counter-culture trope but here is expressive of the project of decolonization.'[13] *Goldstone* makes this same point with its opening photographs that repeat the well-worn colonial myth of European greatness and Indigenous insignificance; these photos are placed within a very different story the film tells about the colossal harms that continue to result from colonialism and the ways in which Indigenous people, practices and epistemologies matter.

All of this brings us back to the reinvented rituals championed by each film that involve both Indigenous and colonial elements. The point is not that all products of colonial cultures are selfish or violent; they are not all 'bad'. The point instead is that these products are tools that can be used to help *or* to hurt. In this respect, *Mahana* clearly sides with Simeon's argument against his grandfather, Tamihana, that despite their many faults and the damage they have done, Hollywood films can nevertheless be meaningful for Indigenous communities; they can connect people and create relationships. Speaking about *Goldstone*'s protagonist, Ivan Sen remarks: 'The power of film is similar to the power of Detective Jay Swan, to bring cultures together, the world together' (Dark Matter Media 2016: 6). Indigenous films, that is, can both depict and facilitate healing.

As Episkenew (2009) argues, however, this healing is not sufficient if it does not have a material, democratic impact on society – which is to say, 'healing without changing the social and political conditions that first caused the injuries would be ineffectual' (17). Such change can happen through various means related to the notion of story-as-medicine. In their critique of the colonial myth, Indigenous films can 'implicate settler readers by exposing the structures that sustain White privilege and by compelling them to examine their position of privilege and their complicity in the continued oppression of Indigenous people' (17). They can also empower Indigenous people and bring them together through the recognition and affirmation of their vital, whole humanity.

It is not simply the representation of Indigenous people (and settlers) that matters: it is the *process* of representation and particularly the fact that this process is controlled by Indigenous people themselves. This control gives Indigenous film-makers both a literal and a political voice.[14] And this control is key to the power of the reinvented rituals of *Maliglutit*, *Mahana* and *Goldstone*. These acts – like Kuanana firing a rifle or Jay following police protocols or Simeon discussing *Invasion of the Body Snatchers* – are the specific result of the *Indigenization* of colonial artefacts, systems and knowledges. This shift in context and perspective is central to the impact of all these reinvented rituals. This shift is what enables the rituals to function as a resource for democratizing societies, to push back against the harmful effects of personal and systemic violence while working to reaffirm and recreate healthy, reciprocal and just relations among various peoples as well as the other-than-human world.

Notes

Chapter 1

1 Stanley Tambiah (1981: 119) says ritual is 'a culturally constructed system of symbolic communication. It is constituted of patterned and ordered sequences of words and acts, often expressed in multiple media, whose content and arrangement are characterized in varying degree by formality (conventionality), stereotypy (rigidity), condensation (fusion), and redundancy (repetition).'

2 A few weeks before Roy Rappaport died, he said to me on the phone, 'Grimes, just so you know, I added the "more or less" before "invariant" for you.' I am sure he thought the 'more or less' would get me off his back, since we got along well but argued about ritual variation at conferences.

3 This point was made by several interviewees; see (Grimes 2011a, 2011b, 2012b).

4 These actions and the emotions they evoke have a history; see (Høeg 2015).

5 Madson (2005) and Nachmanovitch (1990) are the bibles of improvisation as a way of life.

6 In the video 'Making It Up as We … Go' (Scott-Grimes 2011), the ritual was improvised, made up on the fly in two different locations. However, Cailleah, the film-maker and my daughter, edited the films to give them structure and continuity.

7 For example, collective sermons at St. Lydia's Dinner Church in Brooklyn; see (Grimes 2012f).

8 See Grimes (2017). For crowd estimates, see Pressman and Chenoweth (2017).

9 The project proposed this question, 'Can new rituals create arenas for cross-cultural encounters, democracy and social change for the benefit of all? We are particularly interested in new forms of participatory democracy, where respect for individual differences and the need for community are negotiated in new ways' (REDO 2013).

10 'The circle wampum is a very important belt for the Haudenosaunee. The equal strands of wampum represent the 50 chiefs. Each chief being equal and united. The one longer strand represents the people' (Onondaga Nation 2017).

11 Listen to the CBC podcast 'Tocqueville's America Revisited' (CBC 2017), also to 'American Fascism: It Can't Happen Here?' (CBC 2016).

12 Graham Harvey's (2013) edited collection has reanimated the term 'animistic', which can be of considerable use in discussions of open-system, species-inclusive rituals.

13 The source of this quotation is debated. Maybe Darwin said it, maybe not (Darwin Correspondence Project n.d.).

14 Also see *The Sunflower Forest* (Jordan III 2003), which is about ecological restoration, ritual and the new communion with nature.

15 Philip Deering and others associated with Native Immigrant (http://www.nativeimmigrant.com/) are currently in an email discussion at precisely this convergence point.

16 Michael Houseman (2016) provides some astute observations about the contrived, awkward nature of New Age and Contemporary Pagan rituals.

17 'In general, DNA polymerases are highly accurate, with an intrinsic error rate of less than one mistake for every 107 nucleotides added. In addition, some DNA polymerases also have proofreading ability; they can remove nucleotides from the end of a growing strand in order to correct mismatched bases. Finally, post-replication mismatch repair mechanisms monitor the DNA for errors, being capable of distinguishing mismatches in the newly synthesized DNA strand from the original strand sequence. Together, these three discrimination steps enable replication fidelity of less than one mistake for every 109 nucleotides added' (Wikipedia 2017).

18 One of the most compelling arguments about the creativity of deviations and mistakes is Radiolab's podcast, 'There and Back Again' (2019).

Chapter 2

1 As with most of his other neologisms, *différance*, Derrida suggests, was born of necessity, a response to the inadequacy of the verb *différer* (to differ), which connotes only spatial but not temporal difference. The 'a' in *différance* thus indicates a deferral, 'by means of delay, delegation, reprieve, referral, detour, postponement, reserving', positioning the neologism *différance* at the intersection of the spatial and temporal sense of the verb *différer*, that is, 'to differ' and to 'defer' (Kamuf in Derrida 1985: xii).

Chapter 3

1 The anti-religious communist regime that took power in Mongolia in the 1920s and carried out religious purges in the 1930s, executing numerous high-ranking lamas, secularizing others and destroying a large proportion of Mongolian monasteries (Kaplonski 2014), did not exactly follow a religiously permissive regime either. Actually, one of the reasons the communist regime cared so little about shamans when they undertook their anti-Buddhist policies is because they had already been marginalized by the Buddhist clergy, during the mass (and partly forced) conversion to the Gelugpa school from the sixteenth century onwards.

Some Buddhist missionaries advocated the burning of shamanic artefacts stored in Mongolian households and the fining of those who kept them (Bawden 1989: 31–7). During the eighteenth and nineteenth centuries, shamans mostly retreated to the taiga in the North and would only be found among the Buryat minorities living on both sides of the Mongolian-Russian border.

2 What has been implemented in the 1990s in post-socialist Mongolia is effectively a regime of ethnic discrimination whereby the majority group, the Khalkha, claimed the exclusive possession of a 'pure Mongolian blood' that could only be found in lesser quantity (and quality) among members of the western and northern minority groups or among the 'hybrids' of mixed descent (Shimamura 2014: 22–8). See Uradyn Bulag (1998) for a detailed account of this essentialist regime and its applications in post-socialist Mongolian political life.

3 Although the regime of historicity set up by the People's Republic of Mongolia during the Socialist period was indeed very selective, the idea that it amounted to a complete obliteration or even rewriting of Mongolian 'traditions' and 'history' is a misconception (Aubin 1993). See Christopher Kaplonski (2005) in particular for a convincing case against the claim that Chinggis Khan as an historical figure had been erased from Mongolian history books during the Socialist period.

4 Ariuka's particular arrangement with her mother did not last very long either. In April 2009, she stopped taking part in rituals and went to South Korea to study business and marketing. Her adoptive mother thus took it up from there, finally accomplishing the calling she had her daughter fulfil for both of them in the first place. The reason given for this transition was that Ariuka could not sustain being possessed by a spirit who was not her own biological lineage. Grandfather had to be channelled by Saraa herself. Grandmother, on the other hand, disappeared from the picture, thus depriving the ritual apparatus of one of its halves. In 2012, when I met Saraa again, her mode of ritual operation had changed once more: she had settled at the outskirts of the city, and she had reinstituted a bi-cephalous structure to her shamanic practice. Grandfather was still coming down after nightfall (he was growing more and more irascible though), but now a new spirit from her own genealogy, called 'Queen' (Hatan), would be summoned in the late afternoons. 'Queen' was at the centre of female-only rituals, where women came for more or less the same issues as those taken up to Grandmother before.

5 While Mongolian shamanism, as emphasized previously, would certainly be characterized as 'hierarchical' by Charles Stépanoff (2019) in the dual model he proposed, the disappearance of the medium *behind* the mediation she realizes sounds more typical of what he termed 'heterarchical' apparatuses. As will become clear in the next section of this chapter, some ritual modalities in post-socialist Mongolian shamanism are definitely more 'hierarchical' than others. While Byambadorj's rituals are indeed centred on his mediation and its visibilization through elaborated and highly signifying costumes and stagings

(one could almost say that it is the mediation, in this case, which disappears behind the mediator), several features in Ariuka's story can be likened to what Stépanoff describes as heterarchic shamanism. The prominence of Ariuka as a specialist, as we saw in the previous note, was only temporary, and the proliferation of more or less temporary shamans throughout Mongolia since the 1990s almost looks like the cases he drew on, of some Siberian populations where everybody could become a shaman in turn, for a variable yet always limited period of time. All in all, the presence of heterarchic apparatuses within the otherwise hierarchical Mongolian shamanism might be an incentive to relativize the opposition between these and perhaps take more seriously than Stépanoff did the 'exceptions' he mentions in passing (such as the Selkup) where both ritual modalities can be found simultaneously. What the Mongolian case suggests – more comparative work would be needed to substantiate this intuition – is that heterarchy and hierarchy, in varied dynamic associations, could be seen to form two indissociable components of human-organized attempts to make the invisible manifest in ritual contexts.

Chapter 4

1 The capitalization of terms like 'Indigenous', 'Modern' and 'Western' is deliberate and points to diverse strategic uses and does not indicate an essentialism. Because festivals rarely involve debates about what 'Indigenous' means or whether there is a defining characteristic or taxic indicator of 'Indigeneity', these important topics are not debated here. But see discussions in Hartney and Tower (2016); Johnson and Kraft (2017); and Astor-Aguilera and Harvey (2018). 'Nation States' and other terms are similarly capitalized to draw attention to their strategic deployment (not only or even primarily here) in the project of Modernity.
2 Support from the *Reassembling Democracy: Ritual as Cultural Resource* (REDO) project enabled me to attend the festival four times between 2011 and 2015 and to establish friendships so that I can continue discussing developments.
3 Support from the Open University Faculty of Arts and Social Sciences has enabled me to participate in the festival biennially since 2011 and to collaborate with the festival director and team in various events.
4 That is the homelands of the various Sámi populations now within Norway, Sweden, Finland and Russia.
5 This has already been challenged in Ronald Grimes's contribution to this book.
6 I am grateful to Douglas Davies not only for quoting Árnason (in Davies 2017: 78) but also for a conversation in which we enthused about how thinking about dividuals enriches our work.

Chapter 5

1 The first quotes are from the official Biodanza website (http://www.biodanza.org); the last is one version of an idea often expressed on Biodanza websites and by Biodanza practitioners. Biodanza is well established in South America and Southern Europe; less so in Northern Europe, United States and elsewhere. Official teacher training schools (143 in all, eleven in France) grant diplomas recognized by the worldwide International Biocentric Foundation founded in 2003. There are at present close to 100 active Biodanza teachers in France. Spin-offs of Biodanza include Vital Development or Vitaldanza in the United Kingdom, Dansevita in Germany, Heart in Motion in Norway and Sistema Javier de la Sen and Otra Mirada in Spain.

2 For the social composition and patterns of participation of dance sessions, see Houseman and Mazzella di Bosco (2020).

3 I regularly attended weekly Biodanza sessions run by two different facilitators in Paris, one from 11 September 2014 to 2 July 2015, the other from 15 September 2014 to 13 July 2015 and from 31 August 2015 to 9 May 2016; I also participated in occasional sessions run by other facilitators and in a weekend training workshop. The names of participants have been changed, and all translations from French are mine. I would like to thank the facilitators and participants for their warm and tolerant welcome, as well as Daphna Arbell Kehila, Cath Elderton, Delphine Le Roux, Marika Moisseeff, Sarah Pike, Bambi Schieffelin and Peter Wortsman who kindly commented on previous drafts.

4 Musical selections, while not limited to those of the official repertoire, tend to be 'organic' compositions whose internal coherence is particularly self-evident (Dixieland marches, Latin rhythms and mid-1960 Beatles songs are especially favoured).

5 For the pervasiveness of weak ties in contemporary society, see Blau and Fingerman 2009. The Internet provides further evidence to this effect; as Fine has remarked, 'Chat rooms, discussion boards, networking sites, and email lists enshrine the weak tie as the essential connection of the digital age' (2012: 149).

6 Although not always. Tocqueville, for example, writing in 1886, uses this expression to describe the 'frozen [social] body' (1967: 153) of pre-revolutionary France composed of a multitude of small cohesive interest groups of homogenous persons thinking and acting only for themselves (ibid., 176). More recently, but just as negatively, the CEO of a Danish cooperative bank has castigated a large 'sharing economy' platform like Airbnb or Uber as being 'more like a collective individualism. It organizes a lot of people, but everyone is acting on their own, for themselves' (http://www.we-economy.net/case-stories/merkur-bank.html (accessed 20 April 2017).

7 In a later published paper (Soon and Kluver 2014), she uses the expression 'individualized collectiveness'.

8 https://superbalist.com/thewayofus/2016/12/30/butter-boyz/1065 (accessed 15 April 2017).

Chapter 6

1 I had been visiting Fátima regularly since 2009. In April and May 2016, I spent some weeks in Fátima, as well as on subsequent occasions from August 2016 onwards. In March 2017, I settled in Fátima with my daughter, while I did intensive fieldwork until the end of October 2017. In 2018, I made shorter visits during May and October, as well as staying for two months in July and August to undertake follow-up interviews and observe changes in the ceremonies and devotion of the inhabitants of Fátima after the celebrations of the centenary (2016–2017) were over. I had informal conversations with residents of Fátima and spoke with pilgrims from different countries in Europe, the Americas and Asia. As for my earlier research, the compilation of life stories was particularly useful for understanding the worldview and ritual practices of the pilgrims, as well as their evolution over time and their connection with the cultural and social background. I also stayed in touch with them through WhatsApp and Facebook after their arrival home to see how they described their pilgrimage experiences online, discussed it with fellow pilgrims and/or started preparations for the next pilgrimage.

2 For a more specific focus on embodied ritual experiences, see the special issue 'Ritual Creativity, Emotions and the Body' of the *Journal of Ritual Studies* 28.2 (2014), edited by Anna Fedele and Sabina Magliocco.

3 ('Portugal: High and Rising Emigration in a Context of High, but Decreasing, Unemployment' n.d.). https://www.eurofound.europa.eu/publications/article/2016/portugal-high-and-rising-emigration-in-a-context-of-high-but-decreasing-unemployment (accessed 29 July 2019).

4 The intertwining of Salazarian as well as anti-communist politics and religion in the case of Fátima is particularly evident and has already been analysed by historians and anthropologists (e.g. Zimdars-Swartz 1991; Christian 1996; Scheer 2006). It is not my aim to underplay this dimension, but in the context of my analysis and based on the pilgrims' accounts, this dimension is not of primary importance here.

5 In Portugal, as well as in other Southern European countries, the Scout Movement is strongly related to Catholicism. In Portugal the Scouts are involved in all the most important celebrations in Fátima helping to care for the pilgrims during their walk as well as during the crowded masses.

6 David Soares's research activities were part of the research project funded by FCT (IF/01063/2014/CP1233/CT0001) (2015–2020). Rita and her group knew about his participation in the project I coordinated and the pilgrims David interviewed all gave their written consent.

7 I cannot describe in detail the ritual of the guardian angel, suffice it to say that during the journey every pilgrim was randomly assigned one person she had to protect, care for and even pamper in a concrete but also discrete way, keeping her role as a guardian angel secret. Only at the end of the pilgrimage the pilgrims discovered who their guardian angel was. This ritual helped to strengthen the relationships among the pilgrims, especially among those who did not know each other before the pilgrimage.

Chapter 7

1 Other than on stage, religious symbols are used to advertise Antakya as an interreligious tourist destination. They can be seen on the brochures and posters. In some cases, visual icons of religious symbols indicate and reflect upon the religious diversity in Antakya. The choir has a considerable amount of promotional material that was produced with the support of local Turkish businesses and local television stations and recording studios. The members of the choir even selectively distribute CDs and DVDs that are intended as personal gifts.

Chapter 8

1 In addition to Breivik's own texts and the transcript from his court case in spring 2012, primary data for this chapter are based on participant observation and from regular attendance of his trial. Additional data are drawn from informal conversations with other participants, from footage, film clips and news reports, as well as notes from the multi-workshop in 2014.

2 Hybrid religious imageries á la Breivik are common in the Radical right movements in Europe and North America. Spirituality is not rejected but annexed in the name of 'natural religion'. Yet, what kind of religion is 'natural,' and how does religion support Radical right politics? Editorials in the journal *Telos* regard the joining of the 'spirit' of Christianity with the 'spirit' of Paganism as a specific European, cultural heritage. French New Right philosopher Alain de Benoist disagrees. In *On Being a Pagan* (2004), he argues that a revival of 'high' Paganism must be the sole and supreme organizing social principle for a future European empire of federal (fascist) states. The Russian New Right thinker Aleksandr Dugin (2012) identifies with Russian Orthodox Christianity, which he regards as 'a natural religion' to

Eurasia. Orthodox Christianity is not a foreign religion but claimed to have developed historically in his homeland in conjunction with a specific pre-Christian, Russian local (Pagan) culture. Greg Johnson (2013, 2017), PhD and former adjunct professor of Pacific School of Religion at GTU, Berkeley, now publisher of the Radical right Counter-Currents publishing house, agrees that the religious options available to white nationalists are Christianity and reconstructed Paganism. He believes that both traditions are the true religious heritage to people of European descent.

3 Nevertheless, Breivik named the weapons he used at Utøya after the gods of Norse mythology. He called his pistol *Mjolnir*, after Thor's magic hammer, and his gun *Gugne*, which is Odin's magical spear of eternal return. These names were also carved onto the actual gun and pistol with Rune letters. The same holds for the car he used to Utøya. Breivik named his vehicle *Sleipner*, which is the Old Norse label for Thor's wagon as he roars across the worlds, throws Mjolnir at random and creates thunderstorms and fears of *Ragnarok* – the final cosmic battle and the end of life as we know it. Cf. Gardell (2003) for more on Odinism and gods of the blood.

4 https://www.vg.no/nyheter/innenriks/i/q55qe/breivik-med-ny-hoeyreekstrem-hilsen-eksperter-markerer-at-han-naa-er-nazist.

5 Cf. Griffin (2000). To claim a (religious) worldview is in fact an indication of having a meta-political project.

6 Mouffe (2002: 62). I was first made aware of this fact by Katinka H. Grane when reading her BA thesis in international relations, 'Liberalism, democracy and populist right in Hungary' (University of Oslo, spring 2019).

7 I presented this argument in a paper session at the *Nordic Conference on Violent Extremism*, hosted by C-REX – Center for Research on Extremism, University of Oslo, 29–30 November 2018.

8 Cf. Høeg (2015) and Døving (2017) for more on Ocean of Roses.

9 Different terms were used about these responses in the streets. The gatherings in Oslo were called *Rosehav* (*Ocean of roses*), Blomsterhav (*Ocean of flowers*) and *Rosetog (Rose march).* The Norwegian *Artistic Plan for Memorials after 22 July* (Kunstplan for Minnested er etter 22 juli (KORO)) used *Blomsterhavet* for the experience in Oslo, cf. https://koro.no/content/uploads/2015/12/Minnesteder-Kunstplan.pdf. The Norwegian Language Council found that the most popular term in Norway in 2011 was *Rosetoget,* cf. https://www.sprakradet.no/Vi-og-vart/hva-skjer/Aktuelt-ord/Rosetog-er-arets-ord/. This term was related to the Facebook event 'the torch march', planned to take place all over Norway, Monday 25 July, to protest Breivik's terror in terms of 'counter-acts'. Because of summer heat and fire danger, torches were in most places exchanged with flowers, which thus dominated 'the march' (denoting walking as in demonstrations or rallies). In Oslo there was no 'march' since too many people showed up – it became practically impossible. The flowers and roses, put on the ground, took on a sense of an independent ocean

of flowers and was therefore an expression solely used in Oslo. It referred to the material shape of the ritual objects put on the ground and how 'it moved'. Tellingly, on 28 September 2019, a national memorial named *Iron Roses* was unveiled outside Oslo Cathedral.

10 Seligman (2009: 1077) concludes that generative ritual is not focused on belief and is inherently non-discursive. Ritual does of course create its own world of meaning, but whatever its semantic contents turn out to be, it is still far secondary to its subjunctive creation.

11 Cf. the memorial *Terra Incognita* in Trondheim, which was elected in dialogue with citizen votes. A huge white uneven circle-stone embraces a water pool with seventy-seven lights, one for each of the victims. It was designed by artists Anders Krüger and Marianne Levinsen and inagurated in 2016. The original national plan for a memorial (*Memory Wound,* by Swedish architect Jonas Dahlberg) close to Utøya, as well as near the government building, was in the end cancelled due to massive protests against its 'realist design' of cutting a rock cliff into two as a metonymical sign of the 22 July killing. A temporary memorial was finally unveiled outside the bombed government building 22 July 2017. It consists of a pierced wall of stone and glass with all the victims' names, both the dead and the survivors. Cf. *Kunstplan for Minnested er etter 22 juli.* https://koro.no/content/uploads/2015/12/Minnesteder-Kunstplan.pdf (accessed 29 June 2020).

12 Altogether thirty people participated in this experiment. A majority were female college students. Some of them were recruited through the University of Oslo and also assisted us with practical preparations.

13 Cf. Koro's (2013) QuestBack Survey and the word-cloud figuring the dimensions of peoples' associations with 22 July (p. 47). https://koro.no/content/uploads/2015/12/Minnesteder-Kunstplan.pdf (accessed 29 June 2020).

14 The main results of Anker and Lippe's research in Norwegian schools were already known at this point (published in 2015). See Anker and Lippe (2015) and (2018).

15 3RW Architects, https://www.archdaily.com/770709/the-clearing-memorial-at-utoya-3rw-arkitekter (accessed 29 June 2020).

16 Cf. Amelia Taylor-Hochberg, '"The Clearing", memorial to Norway's July 22 attacks, opens on the tragedy's fourth anniversary', *Archinect News* (22 July 2015), online at https://archinect.com/news/article/132497273 (accessed 29 June 2020).; see also http://www.utoya.no/minnested (accessed 29 June 2020).

17 Thanks to Irene Kiebert for generous help with proofreading the text.

Chapter 9

1 The statistics from 1 January 2018 comprise immigrants (14.1) and Norwegian-born children with immigrant parents (3.2). The statistics from 2011 were slightly lower, with 12.2 per cent immigrants (Statistics Norway).

2 The annual survey on attitudes towards immigrants and immigration, conducted by Statistics Norway, reports that Norwegians have tended to become more positive. In 2014, various indicators showed the highest score since the questions were first posted in 2002. Adults between twenty-five and forty-four years have the most accepting attitudes and young people (16–24) are more tolerant in areas such as acceptance of inter-ethnic marriage and rejection of demands for assimilation (Blom 2014: 30).

3 In 2018, 166,861 Muslims in Norway were affiliated with a Muslim community which received government grants, while in 2011, this figure was 106,735.

4 The number of Muslims at the beginning of 2016 was estimated at between 148,000 and 250,000, between 2.8 and 4.8 per cent of the population. Researchers at Statistics Norway, Lars Østby and Anne Berit Dalgard find that the best but still uncertain estimate of the number of Muslims to be 200,000, or close to 4 per cent of the population (Østby and Dalgard 2017).

5 This means a Muslim undertaker (for Mona and Bano), and Christian (Bano, Rafal) and Muslim faith communities (Mona, Bano, Rafal), the Labour Party (Rafal, Mona, Bano) and the local authority (Rafal).

6 For Bano the memorial assembly was held in the local upper secondary school and for Mona at the local community centre.

7 Rolf Kjøde in the Evangelical Lutheran Mission Society, *Normisjon*, made some critical remarks about the funeral in an editorial printed in the Christian newspaper *Vårt Land,* 5 September 2011. Kjøde asks if the church is of the opinion that it is proper to mix Christian and Muslim funeral rites and beliefs when it comes to death (2011: 20).

Chapter 10

1 See Kaufmann and Gonzalez (2019) for a discussion of the institutionalized and uninstitutionalized nature of emotionally affecting events.

2 See, for example, Gorer (1955, 1965); Kübler-Ross (1969); Vovelle (1974, 1983); Thomas (1975); Aries (1975); Ziegler (1975); Morin (1976); Elias (1998); Dechaux (2001); Memmi (2011).

3 See, for example, Pouchelle (2003, 2008); Godeau (2007); Moisseeff (2013a, 2013b, 2016b).

4 For a paradigmatic example, see Bloch (1982).

5 For an overview of present-day mortuary practices among Aboriginal Australians, see Glaskin et al. (2008).

6 See also Tonkinson (2008). For a similar analysis regarding Amazonian Amerindians, see Allard (2013).

7 See Schieffelin (1976); Feld (1982); Munn (1995).

8 Based on observations made in 1996. For a more detailed description of the end of mourning among the Beti, see Laburthe-Tolra (1985).

Chapter 11

1 The use of film as a non-Indigenous art form to tell Indigenous stories is a common point raised in discussions of Indigenous movies, although these discussions typically do not touch on the ways in which this usage is tied to the films' potential to help heal colonial trauma. See, for example, Columpar (2010); Pearson and Knabe (2015); Schweninger (2013); Wood (2008). In her discussion of self-representation in Indigenous television productions in Canada and Australia, however, Faye D. Ginsburg (2002) does raise points similar to those of Episkenew and Singer. She states, for instance, that 'indigenous people are using screen media not to mask but to recuperate their own collective stories and histories – some of them traumatic – that have been erased in the national narratives of the dominant culture and are in danger of being forgotten within local worlds as well' (40).
For her part, Jane Mills (2018) ventures near the notion of film-as-medicine by considering the outward-facing side of Indigenous Australian cinema. She contends that much of this work employs Hollywood genres and tropes precisely as a way of critiquing the dominant culture in certain respects: 'In discussing some of the ways in which First Nation cinema is in dialogue with American cinema, specifically Hollywood, I argue that cultural hybridization lies at its heart: it questions the norms and knowledges of any culture presented as discrete, whole and separate' (83).

2 For a discussion of an Indigenous film and hybridity that is more in line with Bhabha's conceptions, see Thornley (2015).

3 For an examination of similarities and differences between *Mahana* and *Bulibasha*, see Fox (2017: 203–15).

4 For a further discussion of the links between *Mahana* and Hollywood westerns, see Fox (2017: 208–10). In contrast to my own understanding of the film, Fox does in fact see *Mahana* as a simple morality play – and is critical of the film on this basis. He finds Ihimaera's original novel more satisfyingly complex.

5 In his examination of *Mahana*, Fox (2017) discusses the characters' adoption of colonial behaviours and interests (203–4, 212–13). This discussion does not concern the ways in which the Māori integration of settler culture functions to either help heal Indigenous communities or critique colonialism. Instead, Fox is mainly interested in thinking about 'cultural hybridity' as an indication 'of a culture in the process of change' (203).

6 The press kit for *Mahana* explains that the film-makers took great care not simply to make Ramona's *moko kauae* culturally and historically accurate, but

also acceptable to the community from which it was drawn: 'The *moko* was researched by the film's *kaumatua* (elder) Haare Williams and designed by *tā moko* (tattoo) artist Inia Taylor .... For [Nancy] Brunning [the actress who plays Ramona], the process around creating and wearing the *moko* was important because of conventions prohibiting the wearing of *moko* from another family. "I was a bit worried about where it was coming from but Haare Williams referenced it to an East Coast ancestor and Inia Taylor did a variation, which meant it is connected to the Coast but given to me with permission from some of the *whānau* from that area. And before they put it on me, Haare did a *karakia* (prayer) just to make sure all that transference was OK. Everything seemed to fit really nicely for Ramona, so I was feeling quite safe on set and during the process"' (Wild Bunch 2016: 9).

7 Ihimaera has said that Simeon's experience at the court is autobiographical: 'That scene is exactly as it happened. I was with a school group and at the end of it I was asked to give a speech of thanks to the judge. My life changed in that courtroom. I realised that justice is not always equal and from that point onwards my political path as a Māori writer was forever sealed' (Wild Bunch 2016: 5).

8 As Graham Harvey mentioned in his comments to me on a draft of this chapter, it is perhaps not coincidental that Tamahori concludes *Mahana* with a reference to *Invasion of the Body Snatchers*. This is a film that is commonly seen as referencing American Cold War concerns about being overtaken by communists. In this respect, it reflects a long-standing anxiety of colonial powers about being colonized themselves: 'Like H. G. Wells's *War of the Worlds* (1898), [*Invasion of the Body Snatchers*] is a horror story about colonisation coming home to roost' (Grant 2010: 22). In the context of the final scene in *Mahana*, the allusion to *Body Snatchers* may be Tamahori's tongue-in-cheek way of suggesting that, in some ways, Indigenous people are the new invaders, stealthily taking over and remaking colonial art forms (like film-making) from within. In a recent interview regarding his amazing Indigenous zombie film *Blood Quantum* (2019) – which just had its world premiere at TIFF – Mi'kmaq film-maker Jeff Barnaby makes a similar comment: 'I take tropes from popcorn films and put them in my work to dress up subversive ideas in a way that makes them palatable. My films are Trojan horses for ideas that non-Natives wouldn't normally engage in' (Simonpillai 2019).

9 Between approximately 1905 and 1967, Australian government and church officials took Aboriginal children away from their families in order to raise them in a 'civilized' way. Records were typically not kept, so that when these children grew up they had no way of knowing who their parents were or the location of their true homes. For more information, on the 'Stolen Generations', see Read (2006).

10 For a discussion of how Sen uses genre (including the western) in his films, see Rutherford (2019: 79–83).

11 Film noir is notoriously tricky to define. One helpful, classic attempt is offered by Foster Hirsch (1981). For further considerations of *Goldstone* and 'outback noir', see Dolgopolov (2016); McDonald (2016).

12 Houston Wood (2008) similarly states: 'Some Indigenous people have seen dozens, occasionally even hundreds of films, presenting their culture through the distorting perspectives of outsiders. Many Native film-makers thus make films that explicitly aim at countering the effect that these earlier misrepresentations have had on their own Indigenous, as well as on non-Indigenous, audiences' (73). See also Ginsburg (2002); Columpar (2010: 32); Schweninger (2013: 1–4); and Blackmore (2015: 63–4).

13 Faye D. Ginsburg (2002) makes a similar point regarding Indigenous-controlled television production in Canada and Australia (44, 51).

14 For discussions of the ways in which Indigenous control of various forms of modern/colonial media (including television, internet and newspapers) can have positive social and political effects, see Avison and Meadows (2000); Ginsburg (2002); Baltruschat (2004); Landzelius (2006); and Budka (2009).

References

3:10 to Yuma (1957), [Film] Dir. D. Daves, USA: Columbia Pictures.

Alexander, D. (2002), 'Zacharias Kunuk Q&A', interview with Doug Alexander, *Geographical*, 74 (4): 106.

Albera, D. and M. Couroucli, eds. (2012). *Sharing Sacred Spaces in the Mediterranean: Christians, Muslims, and Jews at Shrines and Sanctuaries*. Bloomington: Indiana University Press.

Allard, O. (2013), 'To Cry One's Distress: Death, Emotion, and Ethics among the Warao of the Orinoco Delta', *Journal of the Royal Anthropological Institute*, 19: 545–61.

Allen, C. (2012), *Trans-Indigenous: Methodologies for Global Native Literary Studies*, Minneapolis: University of Minnesota Press.

Altieri, P. (2000), 'Knowledge, Negotiation and NAGPRA: Reconceptualizing Repatriation Discourse(s)', in P. Edge and G. Harvey (eds), *Law and Religion in Contemporary Society: Communities, Individualism and the State*, 129–49, Aldershot: Ashgate.

Anker, T. and M. von der Lippe (2015), 'Når terror ties i hjel: en diskusjon om 22. juli og demokratisk medborgerskap i skolen', *Norsk pedagogisk tidsskrift*, 99 (2): 85–96.

Anker, T. and M. von der Lippe (2018), 'Controversial Issues in Religious Education: How Teachers Deal with Terrorism in their Teaching' in F. Schweitzer, R. Boschki (eds), *Researching Religious Education: Classroom Processes and Outcomes*, 131–44, Munster: Waxmann Verlag.

Arendt, H. (1998 [1958]), *The Human Condition*, Chicago, IL: University of Chicago Press.

Arieli, Y. (1966), *Individualism and Nationalism in American Ideology*, Baltimore: Penguin Books.

Ariès, P. (1975), *Essais sur l'histoire de la mort en Occident du Moyen âge à nos jours*, Paris: Seuil.

Ariès, P. (1977), *L'homme devant la mort*, Paris: Seuil.

Árnason, A. (2012), 'Individuals and Relationships: On the Possibilities and Impossibilities of Presence', in D. J. Davies and C-W. Park (eds), *Emotion, Identity and Death: Mortality across Disciplines*, 59–70, Farnham: Ashgate.

Astor-Aguilera, M. and G. Harvey, eds, (2018), *Rethinking Personhood: Animism and Materiality*, New York: Routledge.

Atanarjuat: The Fast Runner (2001), [Film] Dir. Z. Kunuk, Canada: Odeon Films.

Atkinson, R. (2007), 'The Ecology of Sound: The Sonic Order of the Urban Space', *Urban Studies*, 44 (10): 1905–17.

Aubin, F. (1993), 'Renouveau gengiskhanide et nationalisme dans la Mongolie post-communiste' , *Cahiers d'Etudes sur la Méditerranée orientale et le monde turco-iranien*, 16: 137–206.

Avison, S. and M. Meadows (2000), 'Speaking and Hearing: Aboriginal Newspapers and the Public Sphere in Canada and Australia', *Canadian Journal of Communication*, 25 (3): 347–66. Available online: https://www.cjc-online.ca/index.php/journal/article/view/1163 (accessed 17 August 2019).

Badone, E. and S. R. Roseman, eds (2004), *Intersecting Journeys: The Anthropology of Pilgrimage and Tourism*, Urbana: University of Illinois Press.

Bailey, D. (1992), *Improvisation: Its Nature and Practice in Music*, Boston: Da Capo.

Baltruschat, D. (2004), 'Television and Canada's Aboriginal Communities: Seeking Opportunities through Traditional Storytelling and Digital Technologies', *Canadian Journal of Communication*, 29 (1): 47–59. Available online: https://cjc-online.ca/index.php/journal/article/view/1403/1495 (accessed 17 August 2019).

Bandak, A. (2014), 'Of Refrains and Rhythms in Contemporary Damascus: Urban Space and Christian-Muslim Coexistence', *Current Anthropology*, 55 (10): 248–61.

Barnett, M. R. (1976), *The Politics of Cultural Nationalism in South India*, Princeton: Princeton University Press.

Barreto, J. (2002), *Religião e Sociedade. Dois Ensaios*, Lisbon: Imprensa de Ciencias Sociais.

Basso, K. (1996), *Wisdom Sits in Places: Landscape and Language among the Western Apache*, Albuquerque: University of New Mexico.

Baumann, M. (2014), *Integration Durch Religion? Geschichtliche Befunde, gesellschaftliche Analysen, rechtliche Perspektiven*, Zürich: Theologischer Verlag Zürich; Auflage: 1 (2 February 2014).

Bawden, C. R. (1989), *The Modern History of Mongolia*, London: Kegan Paul International.

Belgrad, D. (2016), 'Improvisation, Democracy, and Feedback', in G. E. Lewis and B. Piekut (eds), *The Oxford Handbook of Critical Improvisation Studies*, 289–306, New York: Oxford University Press.

Bell, C. (1990), 'The Ritual Body and the Dynamics of Power', *Journal of Ritual Studies*, 4 (2): 299–313.

Bell, C. (1992), *Ritual Theory, Ritual Practice*, New York: Oxford University Press.

Bell, C. (2009), *Ritual: Perspectives and Dimensions*, New York: Oxford University Press.

Bennett, J. S. (2012), *When the Sun Danced: Myth, Miracles, and Modernity in Early Twentieth-Century Portugal*, Charlottesville: University of Virginia Press.

Benoist, A. de (2004), *On Being a Pagan*, Atlanta, GA: Ultra.

Bensaïd, D. (2011), 'Permanent Scandal', in G. Agamben (ed), *Democracy in What State?*, 16–43, New York: Columbia University Press.

Bhabha, H. K. (1984), 'Of Mimicry and Man: The Ambivalence of Colonial Discourse', *October*, 28: 125–33.

Bhabha, H. K. (1985), 'Signs Taken for Wonders: Questions of Ambivalence and Authority under a Tree Outside Delhi, May 1817', *Critical Inquiry*, 12 (1): 144–65.

Bird-David, N. (2018), 'Persons or Relatives? Animistic Scales of Practice and Imagination', in Astor-Aguilera, Miguel and Graham Harvey (eds), *Rethinking Personhood: Animism and Materiality*, 25–34, New York: Routledge.

Blackmore, E. (2015), 'Speakin' Out Blak: New and Emergent Aboriginal Filmmakers Finding Their Voices', in W. G. Pearson and S. Knabe (eds), *Reverse Shots: Indigenous Film and Media in an International Context*, 61–80, Waterloo, ON: Wilfrid Laurier University Press.

Blau, J. (1980), 'When Weak Ties Are Structured', Unpublished manuscript, Department of Sociology, State University of New York.

Blau, J. (1991), 'When Weak Ties Are Structured', in J. Blau and N. Goodman (eds), *Social Roles and Social Institutions: Essays in Honor of Rose Laub Coser*, 133–47, Boulder: Westview Press.

Blau, M. and K. L. Fingerman (2009), *Consequential Strangers*, New York: W. W. Norton.

Blic, D. de (2011), 'Continuités et discontinuités *du* corps chrétien. Une ethnographie *des* reliques *de Thérèse de Lisieux*', *Raisons politiques*, 51–6.

Bloch, M. (1974), 'Symbols, Song, Dance and Features of Articulation. Is Religion an Extreme Form of Traditional Authority?', *European Journal of Sociology*, 15: 55–81.

Bloch, M. (1982), 'Death, Women and Power', in M. Bloch and J. Parry (eds), *Death and the Regeneration of Life*, 211–35, Cambridge: Cambridge University Press.

Blom, S. (2014), *Holdninger til innvandrere og innvandring* [*Attitudes to immigrants and immigration*], Oslo–Kongsvinger: Statistisk sentralbyrå/Statistics Norway. Rapporter 2014/39.

Blood Quantum (2019), [Film] Dir. J. Barnaby, Canada: Prospector Films.

Border Crossings (2019a), 'Origins 2019'. Available online: https://www.bordercrossings.org.uk/programme/origins-2019 (accessed 7 August 2019).

Border Crossings (2019b), ORIGINS 2019 programme. Available online: https://issuu.com/originsfestival/docs/origins-programme_2019-lores (accessed 7 August 2019).

Born, G. (2011), 'Music and the Materialization of Identities', *Journal of Material Culture*, 16 (4): 376–88.

Borradori, G. (2003), *Philosophy in a Time of Terror: Dialogues with Jürgen Habermas and Jacques Derrida*, Chicago: University of Chicago Press.

Borsay, P. (2002), 'Sounding the Town', *Urban History*, 29 (1): 92–102.

Bowman, G. (2012), *Sharing the Sacra: The Politics and Pragmatics of Intercommunal Relations around Holy Places*, New York: Berghahn Books.

Bowman, M., and Ü. Valk, eds (2012), *Vernacular Religion in Everyday Life: Expressions of Belief*, London; Oakville, CT: Equinox Pub.

Breemer, R. van den (2014), 'Graveyards and Secularism in Norway. In Search of a Fitting Category', in R. van den Breemer, J. Casanova and T. Wyller (eds), *Secular and Sacred? The Scandinavian Case of Religion in Human Rights, Law, and Public Space*, 170–96, Göttingen: Vandenhoeck & Ruprecht.

Breivik, A. B. (2016), 'Utterances to Journalists during His Case against the Norwegian State, VG 16, March 2016, Which He Lost'. http://www.vg.no/nyheter/innenriks/anders-behring-breivik-soeksmaalet/breivik-hevder-han-er-gaatt-fra-vold-til-politisk-aktivisme/a/23639646/.

Breivik, A. B. (2011), *2083 – A European Declaration of Independence*, published on internet, 22 July 2011.

Brekke, J-P. (2015), 'Innvandringsskepsis i Norge og Sverige' ['Immigration Scepticism in Norway and Sweden'], *Aftenposten*, 17 March [chronicle].

Budka, P. (2009), 'Indigenous Media Technology Production in Northern Ontario, Canada', in K.-D. Ertler and H. Lutz (eds), *Canada in Grainau/Le Canada à Grainau: A Multidisciplinary Survey of Canadian Studies after 30 Years*, 63–74, Frankfurt am Main: Peter Lang.

Bulag, U. (1998), *Nationalism and Hybridity in Mongolia*, Oxford: Clarendon Press.

Bulley, D. (2006), 'Negotiating Ethics: Campbell, Ontopology and Hospitality', *Review of International Studies*, 32: 645–63.

Butler, J. (2015), *Notes toward a Performative Theory of Assembly*, Cambridge: Harvard University Press.

Buyandelger, M. (2013), *Tragic Spirits. Shamanism, Memory and Gender in Contemporary Mongolia*, Chicago: The University of Chicago Press.

Buyandelgeriyn, M. (1999), 'Who "Makes" the Shaman? The Politics of Shamanic Practices among the Buriats in Mongolia', *Inner Asia*, 1 (2): 221–44.

Cadegan, U. M. (2004), 'The Queen of Peace in the Shadow of War: Fatima and U.S. Catholic Anticommunism', *U.S. Catholic Historian*, 22 (4): 1–15.

Casey, E. S. (2011), 'Strangers at the Edge of Hospitality', in R. Kearney and K. Semonovitch (eds), *Phenomenologies of the Stranger: Between Hostility and Hospitality*, 39–48, New York: Fordham University Press.

Cavallo, G. and A. Fedele (2020) 'The Shrine of Our Lady of Fátima", in: Herigliion: Heritagization of Religion and Sacralization of Heritage in Contemporary Europe, Ebook, 42–45, http://heriligion.eu/ebook/

Christian. 2011. *Divine Presence in Spain and Western Europe, 1500–1960: Visions, Religious Images and Photographs*. Central European University.

Cavanaugh, W. T. (1995), 'A Fire Strong Enough to Consume the House: 'The Wars of Religion' and the Rise of the State', *Modern Theology*, 11 (4): 397–420.

Cavanaugh, W. T. (2009), *The Myth of Religious Violence: Secular Ideology and the Roots of Modern Conflict*, Oxford: Oxford University Press.

CBC (2016), 'American Fascism: It Can't Happen Here?'. Available online: https://www.cbc.ca/radio/ideas/american-fascism-it-can-t-happen-here-1.3826324 (accessed 8 February 2017).

CBC (2017), 'Tocqueville's America Revisited'. Available online: http://www.cbc.ca/radio/ideas/tocqueville-s-america-revisited-part-1-1.3803726; http://www.cbc.ca/radio/ideas/tocqueville-s-america-revisited-part-2-1.3815619 (accessed 12 December 2016).

CBC (2015), 'Atanarjuat Voted No. 1 Canadian Film of All Time', *CBC*, 24 April. Available online: https://www.cbc.ca/news/canada/north/atanarjuat-voted-no-1-canadian-film-of-all-time-1.3047162 (accessed 1 August 2019).

Chabros, K. (1992), *Beckoning Fortune. A Study of the Mongol Dalalya Ritual*, Wiesbaden: Otto Harrassowitz.

Chou, M. (2015), 'From Crisis to Crisis: Democracy, Crisis and the Occupy Movement', *Political Studies Review*, 13: 46–58.

Christian, W. A. (1972), *Person and God in a Spanish Valley. Studies in Social Discontinuity*, New York: Seminar Press.

Christian, W. A. (1996), *Visionaries: The Spanish Republic and the Reign of Christ*, Berkeley: University of California Press.

Christian, W. A. (2011), *Divine Presence in Spain and Western Europe, 1500–1960: Visions, Religious Images and Photographs*, Central European University.

Clark, J. N. (2010), 'Religion and Reconciliation in Bosnia and Herzegovina: Are Religious Actors Doing Enough?' *European-Asian Studies*, 62 (4): 671–94.

Claverie, E. (2003), *Les Guerres de La Vierge: Une Anthropologie Des Apparitions*. NRF Essais, Paris: Gallimard.

Claverie, E. and A. Fedele (2014), 'Incertitudes et Religions Vernaculaires/Uncertainty in Vernacular Religions', *Social Compass*, 61 (4): 487–496.

Clemente, M. et al. (2002), 'Religião e Secularização', in Azevedo, Carlos Moreira, dir. – *História Religiosa de Portugal*, vol. 3, Lisboa: Círculo de Leitores.

Coleman, S. and J. Eade, eds (2018), *Pilgrimage and Political Economy: Translating the Sacred*. Oxford: Berghahn Books.

Columpar, C. (2010), *Unsettling Sights: The Fourth World on Film*, Carbondale: Southern Illinois University Press.

Crouch, C. (2004), *Post-Democracy*, Cambridge: Polity Press.

Cruise, C. (2017), '*Maliglutit* Remakes the Western in Its Own Image', *TIFF*, 13 January. Available online: https://www.tiff.net/the-review/maliglutit-remakes-the-western-in-its-own-image (accessed 1 August 2019).

Csikszentmihalyi, M. (1990), *Flow: The Psychology of Optimal Experience*, New York: Harper and Row.

Czajka, A. (2017), *Democracy and Justice: Reading Derrida in Istanbul*, London: Routledge.

Czajka, A. and B. Isyar (2013), *Europe after Derrida: Crisis and Potentiality*, Edinburgh: Edinburgh University Press.

Dağtaş, S. (2012), 'Tolerated Identities: Secularism, Religious Pluralism and Nationalism in Antakya, Turkey', in S. H. Boyd and M. A. Walter (eds), *Cultural Difference and Social Solidarity: Critical Cases*, 135–48, Cambridge: Cambridge Scholars Publishing.

Dağtaş, S. (2018), 'Nationalism, Displacement, and Ethnoreligious Differentiation in Turkey's Southern Borderlands', *Dialectical Anthropology*, 42: 359–72.

Dark Matter Media (2016), '*Goldstone* Media Kit', Available online: https://www.transmissionfilms.com.au/films/goldstone (accessed 5 August 2019).

Darwin Correspondence Project (n.d.), 'Six Things Darwin Never Said – and One He Did'. Available online: http://www.darwinproject.ac.uk/people/about-darwin/six-things-darwin-never-said#quote3 (accessed 31 December 2019).

Davie, G. (2007), 'Vicarious Religion: A Methodological Challenge', in Nancy T. Ammerman (ed), *Everyday Religion: Observing Modern Religious Lives*, 21–35, Oxford: Oxford University Press.

Davies, D. J. (2017), *Death, Ritual and Belief: The Rhetoric of Funerary Rites*. Third edition, London: Bloomsbury.

Dean, K. (2015a), 'Parallel Universes: Chinese Temple Networks in Singapore, or What Is Missing in the Singapore Model?', in P. van der Veer (ed), *Handbook of Religion and the Asian City: Aspiration and Urbanization in the Twenty-First Century*, 273–96, Oakland, CA: University of California Press.

Dean, K. (2015b), 'Ritual Revolutions: Temple and Trust Networks Linking Putian and Southeast Asia'. *Cultural Diversity in China*. Available online: https://www.degruyter.com/view/j/cdic.2015.1.issue-1/cdc-2015-0002/cdc-2015-0002.xml (accessed 1 January 2020).

Déchaux, J-H. (2001), 'La mort dans les sociétés modernes: la thèse de Norbert Elias à l'épreuve', *Ethnologie française*, 51: 161–83.

Delaplace, G. (2010), 'Marshal Choibalsan's "Second Funeral"', in I. Charleux, G. Delaplace, R. Hamayon and S. Pearce (eds), *Representing Power in Modern Inner Asia*, 97–116, Bellingham: Western Washington University.

Delaplace, G. and C. Humphrey (2013), 'Qu'y a-t-il de nouveau dans le néo-chamanisme? Assemblages et identités flottantes à Ulaanbaatar', *Études Mongoles et Sibériennes, Centre-Asiatiques et Tibétaines*, Hors-série: 87–108.

Delaplace, G. and B. Sambalkhundev (2014), 'Establishing Mutual Misunderstanding. A Buryat Shamanic Ritual in Ulaanbaatar', *Journal of the Royal Anthropological Institute*, 20: 617–34.

Derrida, J. (1985), *The Ear of the Other: Otobiography, Transference, Translation*, trans. Peggy Kamuf, New York: Shocken.

Derrida, J. (1992), *The Other Heading: Reflections on Today's Europe*, trans. P.-A. Brault and M. Naas, Bloomington: Indiana University Press.

Derrida, J. (1994), *Specters of Marx: The State of the Debt, the Work of Mourning, and the New International*, 16, London: Routledge.

Derrida, J. (1997), *The Politics of Friendship*, trans. G. Collins, New York: Verso.

Derrida, J. (1998), 'Hospitality, Justice and Responsibility: A Dialogue with Jacques Derrida', in R. Kerney and M. Dooley (eds), *Questioning Ethics: Contemporary Debates in Philosophy*, 65–83, London: Routledge.

Derrida, J. (2000), 'Hospitality', *Angelaki*, 5 (3): 3–18.

Derrida, J. (2002a), 'Faith and Knowledge: The Two Sources of "Religion" at the Limits of Reason Alone', in *Acts of Religion*, trans. S. Weber, 42–101, New York: Routledge.

Derrida, J. (2002b), 'Taking a Stand for Algeria', in *Acts of Religion*, trans. Boris Belay, 299–308, New York: Routledge.

Derrida, J. (2002c), 'Negotiations', in *Negotiations: Interventions and Interviews, 1971–2001*, trans. E. Rottenberg, 11–40, Stanford, CA: Stanford University Press.

Derrida, J. (2002d), 'Force of Law: The "Mystical Foundations of Authority"', in *Acts of Religion*, trans. M. Quaintance, 228–98, New York: Routledge.

Derrida, J. (2005a), *Rogues: Two Essays on Reason*, trans. P-A. Brault and M. Naas, Stanford, CA: Stanford University Press.

Derrida, J. (2005b), 'The Principle of Hospitality', *parallax*, 11 (1): 6–9.

Didion, J. (2005), *The Year of Magical Thinking*, New York: Alfred Knopf.

Dobernig, K. and S. Stagl (2015), 'Growing a Lifestyle Movement? Exploring Identity-Work and Lifestyle Politics in Urban Food Cultivation', *International Journal of Consumer Studies*, 39 (5): 452–8.

Doğruel, F. (2013), 'An Authentic Experience of Multiculturalism at the Border City of Hatay', *Journal Of Modern Turkish History Studies* 13 (26): 273–295.

Dolgopolov, G. (2016), 'Balancing Acts: Ivan Sen's *Goldstone* and Outback Noir', *Metro Magazine*, 190 (Winter).

Døving, C.A. (2009), 'Ritualer og sosial endring. Norsk-pakistanske eksempler', *Norsk tidsskrift for migrasjonsforskning*, 1: 51–66 [Norwegian Journal of Migration Research].

Døving, C. A. and S. E. Kraft (2013), *Religion i pressen* [*Religion in the press*], Oslo: Universitetsforlaget.

Døving, C. A. (2017), 'Homeland Ritualised: An Analysis of Written Messages Placed at Temporary Memorials after the Terrorist Attacks on 22 July 2011 in Norway', *Mortality, 23*:, 231–46. https://www.tandfonline.com/doi/full/10.1080/13576275.2017.1346597

Dugin, A. (2012), 'Interview with Alexander Dugin', Posted by A. Dugin on The North American New Right, 27 July 2012. http://www.counter-currents.com/2012/07/interview-with-alexander-dugin/print/

Duque, J. (2017), *Fátima uma aproximação*, Poéticas do viver crente, Prior Velho: Paulinas.

Durkheim, E. (1995 [1912]), *The Elementary Forms of Religious Life*, New York: The Free Press.

Eade, J. and M. Katić (2017), *Military Pilgrimage and Battlefield Tourism: Commemorating the Dead*, London; New York: Routledge.

Eade, J. and M. Sallnow (1991), *Contesting the Sacred: The Anthropology of Christian Pilgrimage*, London; New York: Routledge.

Eliade, M. (1964), *Shamanism: Archaic Techniques of Ecstasy*, Princeton: Princeton University Press.

Elias, N. ([1969] 1973), *La civilisation des moeurs*, Paris: Calmann-Lévy.

Elias, N. ([1982] 1998), *La solitude des mourants*, Paris: C. Bourgois.

Elias, N. (1991), *The Society of Individuals*, London: Blackwell.

Emery, M. ed (1993), *Participative Design for Participative Democracy*, Canberra: Australian National University, Center for Continuing Education.

Empson, R. (2011), *Harnessing Fortune: Personhood, Memory and Place in Mongolia*, Oxford: Oxford University Press.

Episkenew, J-A. (2009), *Taking Back Our Spirits: Indigenous Literature, Public Policy, and Healing*, Winnipeg, MB: University of Manitoba Press.

Ercan, S. A. and J. P. Gagnon (2014), 'The Crisis of Democracy: Which Crisis? Which Democracy?', *Democratic Theory*, 1 (2): 1–10.

Faudree, P. (2012), 'Music, Language, and Texts: Sound and Semiotic Ethnography', *Annual Review of Anthropology*, 41: 519–36.

Fedele, A. (2013), *Looking for Mary Magdalene: Alternative Pilgrimage and Ritual Creativity at Catholic Shrines in France*, Oxford Ritual Studies, New York: Oxford University Press.

Fedele, A. (2014a), 'Créativité et Incertitude Dans Les Nouveaux Rituels Contemporains', *Social Compass*, 61 (4): 497–510.

Fedele, A. (2014b), 'Energy and Transformation in Alternative Pilgrimages to Catholic Shrines: Deconstructing the Tourist/Pilgrim Divide', *Journal of Tourism and Cultural Change*, 12 (2): 150–65.

Fedele, A. (2017), 'Pellegrinaggio, topografia sacra e religione vissuta a Fátima', *Annali di Studi Religiosi*, 18: 83–95, https://books.fbk.eu/media/uploads/files/Fedele.pdf.

Fedele, A. (2020), '"God Wants Spiritual Fruits Not Religious Nuts": Spirituality as a Middle Way between Religion and Secularism at the Marian Shrine of Fátima', in A. Fedele and K. Knibbe (eds), *Secular Societies, Spiritual Selves?*, London and New York: Routledge. pp. 166–183.

Feld, S. (1982), *Sound and Sentiment*, Philadelphia: University of Pennsylvania Press.

Fernandes, A. T. (1999), *O confronto de ideologias na segunda década do século XX: à volta de Fátima*. Biblioteca das ciências do homem 28, Porto: Afrontamento.

Fey, T. (2011), *Bossypants*, New York: Reagan Arthur Books.

Fine, G. A. (2012), *Tiny Publics. A Theory of Group Action and Culture*, New York: Russell Sage Foundation.

Fingerman, K. L. (2009), 'Consequential Strangers and Peripheral Partners: The Importance of Unimportant Relationships', *Journal of Family Theory and Review*, 1: 69–86.

Fox, A. (2017), *Coming-of-Age Cinema in New Zealand: Genre, Gender and Adaptation*, Edinburgh: Edinburgh University Press.

Franco, J. E. and B. C. Reis. (2017), *Fátima: lugar sagrado global*, Lisboa: Circulo de Leitores.

Frey, N. L. (1998), *Pilgrim Stories: On and Off the Road to Santiago, Journeys along an Ancient Way in Modern Spain*. First Printing edition, Berkeley: University of California Press.

Fritsch, M. (2002), 'Derrida's Democracy to Come', *Constellations*, 4 (9): 574–97.

Fritsch, M. (2011), 'Deconstructive Aporias: Quasi-transcendental and Normative', *Continental Philosophy Review*, 44: 439–68.

Gardell, M. (2003), *Gods of the Blood: The Pagan Revival and White Separatism*, Durham, NC: Duke University Press.

Geertz, C. (1998), 'Deep Hanging Out', *The New York Review of Books*, 22 October 1998. Available online: http://www.nybooks.com/articles/archives/1998/oct/22/deep-hanging-out/ (accessed 1 August 2019].

Gemzöe, L. (2000), *Feminine Matters: Women's Religious Practices in a Portuguese Town*, Stockholm, Sweden: Dept. of Social Anthropology, Stockholm University.

Gennep, A. van ([1909] 1981), *Les Rites de passage*, Paris: Picard.

Giddens, A. (1991), *Modernity and Self-Identity. Self and Society in the Late Modern Age*, Cambridge: Blackwell.

Ginsburg, F. D. (2002), 'Screen Memories: Resignifying the Traditional in Indigenous Media', in F. D. Ginsburg, L. Abu-Lughod and B. Larkin (eds), *Media Worlds: Anthropology on New Terrain*, 39–57, Berkeley, CA: University of California Press.

Glaskin, K., M. Tonkinson, Y. Musharbach and V. Burbank (2008), *Mortality, Mourning and Mortuary Practices in Indigenous Australia*, Farnham & Burlington: Ashgate.

Godeau, E. (2007), *L'esprit de corps. Sexe et mort dans la formation des internes en médecine*, Paris: Éditions MSH.

Goldstone (2016), [Film] Dir. Ivan Sen, Australia: Bunya Productions.

Gorer, G. (1955), 'Pornography of Death', *Encounter*, 5: 49–52.

Gorer, G. (1965), *Death, Grief and Mourning in Contemporary Britain*, London: Cresset Press.

Granovetter, M. S. (1973), 'The Strength of Weak Ties', *American Journal of Sociology*, 78 (6): 1360–80.

Granovetter, M. S. (1983), 'The Strength of Weak Ties: A Network Theory Revisited', *Sociological Theory*, 1: 201–33.

Grant, B. K. (2010), *Invasion of the Body Snatchers*, New York: Palgrave Macmillan.

Griffin, R. (1992), *The Nature of Fascism*, London & New York: Routledge.

Griffin, R. (2000), 'Between Metapolitics and Apoliteia: The Nouvelle Droite's Strategy for Conserving the Fascist Vision in the "Interregnum"', *Modern & Contemporary France*, 8 (1): 35–53.

Grimes, R. L. (1990), *Ritual Criticism: Case Studies in Its Practice, Essays on Its Theory*. First edition. Studies in Comparative Religion, Columbia, S.C: University of South Carolina Press.

Grimes, R. L. (2000), *Deeply into the Bone: Re-Inventing Rites of Passage*. Life Passages, Berkeley: University of California Press.

Grimes, R. L. (2000), 'Ritual', in W. Braun and R. T. McCutcheon eds), *Guide to the Study of Religion*, 259–70, London: Continuum.

Grimes, R. L. (2006), *Rite Out of Place: Ritual, Media, and the Arts*, Oxford, New York: Oxford University Press.

Grimes, R. L. (2011a), 'Juggling Musically'. Available online: https://vimeo.com/ronaldlgrimes/juggling (accessed 7 November 2017).

Grimes, R. L. (2011b), 'Musical Improvisation: An Interview with Casey Sokol'. Available online: https://vimeo.com/ronaldlgrimes/sokolinterview (accessed 17 November 2017).

Grimes, R. L. (2011c), 'Restraint and Exuberance in Christian Worship: An Interview with Don Saliers'. Available online: https://vimeo.com/ronaldlgrimes/exuberance-and-restraint (accessed 7 November 2017).

Grimes, R. L. (2012a), 'A Footwashing Ritual for Maundy Thursday'. Available online: https://vimeo.com/40054208 (accessed 3 March 2017).

Grimes, R. L. (2012b), 'Improvisation, Imagination, and Christian Worship: An Interview with Janet Walton'. Available online: http://vimeo.com/ronaldlgrimes/improv-imag-worship (accessed 3 March 2014).

Grimes, R. L. (2012c), 'Organ Improvisation: An Interview with Jeffrey Brillhart'. Available online: http://vimeo.com/ronaldlgrimes/organimprov (accessed 8 February 2017).

Grimes, R.L. (2012d), 'Rite to Play: Ritual Creativity, Improvisation, and the Arts'. Available online: https://vimeo.com/55104563 (accessed 13 March 2017).

Grimes, R.L. (2012e), 'Ritual Creativity, Improvisation, and the Arts'. Available online: https://vimeo.com/album/1524902 (accessed 24 January 2017).

Grimes, R. L. (2012f), 'St. Lydia's'. Available online: http://vimeo.com/ronaldlgrimes/st-lydias (accessed 8 February 2017).

Grimes, R. L. (2013), 'Performance Is Currency in the Deep World's Gift Economy', in G. Harvey (ed), *Handbook of Contemporary Animism*, 501–12, New York: Routledge.

Grimes, R. L. (2014a), *The Craft of Ritual Studies*, New York: Oxford University Press.

Grimes, R. L. (2014b), 'A Mohawk Condolence Ceremony for Myriam'. Available online: https://vimeo.com/111301903 (accessed 3 March 2017).

Grimes, R. L. (2015), 'The Day the Clock Stopped'. Available online: https://vimeo.com/142457602 (accessed 16 March 2017).

Grimes, R. L. (2017), 'Women's March: Democracy'. Available online: https://vimeo.com/201452781 (accessed 16 March 2017).

Grinde, D. A. Jr. and B. E. Johansen (1991), *Exemplar of Liberty: Native America and the Evolution of Democracy*, Los Angeles, CA: American Indian Studies Center, UCLA.

Groen, B. (2016), Personal communication to Ronald L. Grimes.

Haddad, S. (2013), *Derrida and the Inheritance of Democracy*, Bloomington: Indiana University Press.

Hamayon, R. N. (1995), 'Pour en finir avec la 'transe' et 'l'extase' dans l'étude du chamanisme', *Études Mongoles et Sibériennes*, 26: 155–90.

Handelman, D. (2004), 'Re-Framing Ritual', in J. Kreinath, C. Hartung and A. Deschner (eds), *The Dynamics of Changing Rituals: The Transformation of Religious Rituals within Their Social and Cultural Context*, 9–20, New York: Peter Lang.

Handelman, D. (2005), Epilogue. Toing and Froing the Social, *Ritual in Its Own Right: Exploring the Dynamics of Transformation*, D. Handelman and G. Lindquist (eds), 213–22, Oxford: Berghahn Books.

Hann, C. M. (2003), 'Creeds, Cultures, and the "Witchery of Music"', *Journal of the Royal Anthropological Institute*, 9: 223–39.

Hanson, E. (2009), 'Marginalization of Aboriginal Women', *Indigenous Foundations, The University of British Columbia*. Available online: https://indigenousfoundations.arts.ubc.ca/marginalization_of_aboriginal_women (accessed 13 August 2019).

Harjo, J. and G. Bird (1997), 'Introduction', in J. Harjo and G. Bird (eds), *Reinventing the Enemy's Language: Contemporary Women's Writings of North America*, 19–31, New York: W.W. Norton.

Hartney, C. (2016), 'Indigenous or Non-Indigenous: Who Benefits from Narrow Definitions of Religion?', in C. Hartney and D. J. Tower (eds), *Religious Categories and the Construction of the Indigenous*, 203–27, Leiden: E.J. Brill.

Hartney, C. and D. J. Tower, eds (2016), *Religious Categories and the Construction of the Indigenous*, Leiden: E.J. Brill.

Harvey, G., ed (2013), *The Handbook of Contemporary Animism*, Durham, UK: Acumen.

Harvey, G. (2005), *Ritual and Religious Belief: A Reader*. London: Routledge.

Harvey, G. (2013), *Food, Sex and Strangers: Understanding Religion as Everyday Life*, New York: Routledge.

Harvey, G. (2016), 'Art Works: A Relational Rather Than Representational Understanding of Art and Buildings', in T. Hutchings and J. McKenzie (eds), *Materiality and the Study of Religion: The Stuff of the Sacred*, 103–18, London: Routledge.

Harvey, G. (2017), *Animism: Respecting the Living World*, London: Hurst.

Harvey, G. (2018), 'Indigenous Rituals'/ORIGINS Festival 2017 Opening Ceremony Film, https://www.open.edu/openlearn/history-the-arts/religious-studies/indigenous-rituals (accessed 7 August 2019).

Heaney, S., ed. (1980), 'The Sense of Place', in *Preoccupations: Selected Prose 1968–1978*, 131–49, London: Faber & Faber.

Hilder, T. (2014), *Sámi Musical Performance and the Politics of Indigeneity in Northern Europe*, New York: Rowman & Littlefield.

Hill, L. (2007), *The Cambridge Introduction to Jacques Derrida*, Cambridge: Cambridge University Press.

Hirsch, F. (1981), *The Dark Side of the Screen: Film Noir*, San Diego, CA: A.S. Barnes

Høeg, I. M. (2013), 'Folkekirken som sorgfellesskap. Den norske kirkes svar på 22 juli. [The National Church as a Mourning Community]', in O. Aagedal, P. K. Botvar, I. M. Høeg (eds), *Den offentlige sorgen. Markeringer, ritualer og religion etter 22. juli*, 63–85, Oslo: Universitetsforlaget.

Høeg, I. M. and I. Pajari (2013), 'Introduction to the Nordic Issue of Mortality', *Mortality*, 2 (18): 109–15.

Høeg, I. M. (2015), 'Silent Actions – Emotion and Mass Mourning Rituals after the Terrorist Attacks in Norway on 22 July 2011', *Mortality, Promoting the Interdisciplinary Study of Death and Dying*, 20 (3): 197–214. https://www.tandfonline.com/doi/abs/10.1080/13576275.2015.1012488

Hoffman, L. A. (2016), Personal communication to Ronald L. Grimes.

Højer, L. (2019), *The Anti-Social Contract. Injurious Talk and Dangerous Exchanges in Northern Mongolia*, New York: Berghahn Books International.

Houseman, M. (2006), 'Relationality', in J. Kreinath, J. Snoek and M. Stausberg (eds), *Theorizing Rituals. Issues, Topics, Approaches, Concepts*, 413–28, Leiden: Brill.

Houseman, M. (2007), 'Menstrual Slaps and First Blood Celebrations. Inference, Simulation and the Learning of Ritual', in D. Berliner and R. Sarró (eds), *Learning Religion: Anthropological Approaches*, 31–48, Oxford and New York: Berghahn Books.

Houseman, M. (2010), 'Des rituels contemporains de permière menstruation', *Ethnologie Française*, 40: 57–66.

Houseman, M. (2016), 'Comment comprendre l'esthétique affectée des cérémonies New Age et néopaïennes?', *Archives de Sciences Sociales des Religions*, 174: 213–37.

Houseman, M. and C. Severi (1998), *Naven, or, The Other Self: A Relational Approach to Ritual Action*. Studies in the History of Religions, vol. 79, Leiden: Brill.

Houseman, M., M. Mazzella di Bosco and E. Thibault (2016), 'Renaître à soi-même. Pratiques de danses rituelles en Occident contemporain', *Terrain*, 66: 62–85.

Houseman, M. and M. Mazzella di Bosco (2020), 'Dances of Self-development as a Resource for Participatory Democracy', in S. M. Pike, J. Salomonsen, and P-F. Tremlett (eds.), *Ritual and Democracy: Protests, Publics, and Performances*, 115–38, Sheffield: Equinox Publishing.

Howe, L. (2013), *Chocktalking on Other Realities*, San Francisco: Aunt Lute.

Hugh-Jones, S. (1994), 'Shamans, Prophets, Priests, and Pastors', in C. Humphrey and N. Thomas (eds), *Shamanism, History and the State*, 32–75, Ann Arbor: The University of Michigan Press.

Hulme, K. (1986), *The Bone People*, London: Picador.

Humphrey, C. (1992), 'The Moral Authority of the Past in Post-Socialist Mongolia', *Religion, State and Society*, 20 (3–4): 375–89.

Humphrey, C. (1994), 'Shamanic Practices and the State in Northern Asia: Views from the Center and the Periphery', in C. Humphrey and N. Thomas (eds), *Shamanism, History and the State*, 191–228, Ann Arbor: The University of Michigan Press.

Humphrey, C. and J. Laidlaw (1994), *The Archetypal Actions of Ritual. A Theory of Ritual Illustrated by the Jain Rite of Worship*, Oxford: Clarendon Press.

Humphrey, C. and N. Thomas, eds (1994), *Shamanism, History and the State*, Ann Arbor: The University of Michigan Press.

Hüsken, U. (2016), Personal communication to Ronald L. Grimes.

Ingold, T. (2007), 'Against Soundscape', in A. Carlyle (ed), *Autumn Leaves: Sound and the Environment in Artistic Practice*, 10–13, Paris: Double Entendre.

International Migration 2013–2014. *IMO Report for Norway* (2014), Oslo: Norwegian Ministry of Education and Research, Norwegian Ministry of Children, Equality and Social Inclusion, Norwegian Ministry of Justice and Public Security, Norwegian Ministry of Labour and Social Affairs.

Invasion of the Body Snatchers (1956), [Film] Dir. D. Siegel, USA: Allied Artists.

Irvine, R.D.G. (2018), 'Seeing Environmental Violence in Deep Time', *Environmental Humanities*, 10 (1): 257–72.

Isnart, C. (2012), 'The Mayor, the Ancestors and the Chapel: Clientelism, Emotion and Heritagisation in Southern France', *International Journal of Heritage Studies*, 18 (5): 479–94.

Isnart C. and A. Leblon, eds (2012), 'Au-delà du consensus patrimonial. Résistances et usages contestataires du patrimoine', *Civilisations*, 61 (1): 9–22.

Jahnke, R. (2006), 'Māori Art towards the Millennium', in M. Mulholland (ed), *State of the Māori Nation: Twenty-first Century Issues in Aotearoa*, 41–51, Auckland: Reed.

Jaimes Guerrero, M. A. (2003), '"Patriarchal Colonialism" and Indigenism: Implications for Native Feminist Spirituality and Native Womanism', *Hypatia: A Journal of Feminist Philosophy*, 18 (2): 58–69.

Johnson, G. (2013), *New Right vs Old Right & Other Essays*, San Francisco, CA: Counter Currents.

Johnson, G. (2017), 'The Christian Question in White Nationalism, North American New Right'(988 words), posted Counter Currents 31 December 2017. https://www.counter-currents.com/2017/12/the-christian-question-in-white-nationalism-2/

Johnson, G. and S. E. Kraft (2017), *Handbook on Indigenous Religion(s)*, Leiden: Brill.

Johnson, P. C. (2005), 'Migrating Bodies, Circulating Signs: Brazilian Candomblé and the Garifuna of the Caribbean and the Category of Indigenous Religions', in G. Harvey and C. D. Thomson (eds), *Indigenous Diasporas and Dislocations*, 37–51, Aldershot: Ashgate.

Johnston, O. (2016), 'Mahana (The Patriarch): An Interview with Lee Tamahori and His Cast', *The Upcoming*, 16 February. Available online: https://www.theupcoming.co.uk/2016/02/16/berlin-film-festival-2016-mahana-the-patriarch-an-interview-with-lee-tamahori-and-his-cast (accessed 11 August 2019).

Jordan III, W. R. (2003), *The Sunflower Forest: Ecological Restoration and the New Communion with Nature*, Berkeley: University of California Press.

Justice, D. H. (2008), *Why Indigenous Literatures Matter*, Waterloo: Wilfred Laurier Press.

Kaplonski, C. (2005), 'The Case of the Disappearing Chinggis Khaan: Dismembering the Remembering', *Ab Imperio*, 4: 147–73.

Kaplonski, C. (2014), *The Lama Question. Violence, Sovereignty, and Exception in Early Socialist Mongolia*, Honolulu: University of Hawai'i Press.

Kaufmann, L. and P. Gonzalez (2019), 'Ces événements qui nous affectent', in L. Amiotte-Suchet and M. Salzbrunn (eds), *L'événement en religion: ruptures historiques, constructions biographiques et mobilisations collectives*, 204–91, Rennes: Presses Universitaires de Rennes.

Kellogg, S. B. (2015), 'Ritual Sounds, Political Echoes: Vocal Agency and the Sensory Cultures of Secularism in the Dutch Syriac Diaspora', *American Ethnologist*, 42 (3): 431–45.

Kelman, A. Y. (2010), 'Rethinking the Soundscape: A Critical Genealogy of a Key Term in Sound Studies', *The Senses and Society*, 5 (2): 212–34.

King, R. R. and S. L. Tan., eds (2014), *(un)Common Sounds: Songs of Peace and Reconciliation among Muslims and Christians*, Eugene: Cascade.

Kingulliit Productions (2016), '*Maliglutit* Press Notes'. Available online: http://s3.amazonaws.com/isuma.attachments/maliglutitsearchers-notes-final_160825.pdf (accessed 1 August 2019).

Kjøde, Rolf (2011), 'Mellom trusformidling' ['Between beliefs'], *Vårt Land*, 10 September: 20 [chronicle].

Kraft, S. E. (2009), 'Sami Indigenous Spirituality: Religion and Nation-building in Norwegian Sápmi', *Temenos*, 45 (2): 179–206.

Kreinath, J. (2014), 'Virtual Encounters with Hızır and Other Muslim Saints: Dreaming and Healing at Local Pilgrimage Sites in Hatay, Turkey', *Anthropology of the Contemporary Middle East and Central Eurasia*, 2 (1): 25–66.

Kreinath, J. (2016), 'Intertextualität und Interritualität als Mimesis: Zur Ästhetik interreligiöser Beziehungen unter Juden, Christen und Muslimen in Hatay', *Zeitschrift für Religionswissenschaft*, 24 (2): 153–85.

Kreinath, Jens (2019a), 'Aesthetic Sensations of Mary: The Miraculous Icon of Meryem Ana and the Dynamics of Interreligious Relations in Antakya', in B. Meyer and T. Stordalen (eds), *Figurations and Sensations of the Unseen in Judaism, Christianity and Islam: Contested Desires*, 155–71, London: Bloomsbury Academic.

Kreinath, J. (2019b), 'Playing with Frames of Reference in Veneration Rituals: Fractal Dynamics in Encounters with a Muslim Saint', *Anthropological Theory*, 1–30. DOI: 10.1177/1463499619841212.

Kreinath, J. and R. Sarıönder (2018), 'Dynamics of Ritual Reflexivity in the Alevi Cem, Istanbul', *Society and Religion*, 9 (1): 145–59.

Kübler-Ross, E. (1969), *On Death and Dying*, New York: Macmillan.

Kulturutredningen (2014), https://www.regjeringen.no/contentassets/1e88e03c840742329b9c46e18159b49c/no/pdfs/nou201320130004000dddpdfs.pdf.

Kunstplan for Minnested er etter 22 juli (KORO) (2015), https://koro.no/content/uploads/2015/12/Minnesteder-Kunstplan.pdf

Laack, I. (2015), 'Music', in Kocku von Stuckrad and Robert Segal (eds), *Vocabulary for the Study of Religion*, 486–93, Leiden: Brill.

Laburthe-Tolra, P. (1985), *Initiations et sociétés secrètes au Cameroun. Essai sur la religion beti*, Paris: Karthala.

Landzelius, Ky., ed (2006), *Native on the Net: Indigenous and Diasporic Peoples in the Virtual Age*, London: Routledge.

Latour, B. (1993), *We Have Never Been Modern*, Cambridge, MA: Harvard University Press.

Latour, B. (2005), *Reassembling the Social. An Introduction to Actor-Network-Theory*, Oxford: Oxford University Press.

Latour, B. (2009), 'A Collection of Humans and Non-Humans: Following Daedalus's Labyrinth', in D.M. Kaplan (ed), *Readings in the Philosophy of Technology*, 156–67, Plymouth: Rowman and Littlefield.

Latour, B. (2013), *An Inquiry into Modes of Existence. An Anthropology of the Moderns*, Cambridge: Harvard University Press.

Law, J. (1999), 'After ANT. Complexity, Naming and Topology', in J. Law and J. Hassard (eds), *Actor Network Theory and After*, Oxford: Blackwell.

Laws, D. and J. Forester (2015), *Conflict, Improvisation, Governance: Street Level Practices for Urban Democracy*, New York: Routledge.

Le Bart, C. (2008), *L'individualisation*, Paris: Presses de la Fondation Nationale de Sciences Politiques.

Lehmann, A. C. and R. Kopiez (n.d.), 'Revisiting Composition and Improvisation with a Historical Perspective'. Available online: www.escom.org/proceedings/ESCOM2002/sources/Pdf/symposium/Lehmann.pdf (accessed 24 March 2017).

Lévi-Strauss, C. (1969), *Totemism*, Harmondsworth: Penguin.

Lewis, G. E. (2011), 'University Lecture with Professor George E. Lewis'. Available online: https://www.youtube.com/watch?v=3cswYCMQnl4&t=3340s (accessed 14 January 2017).

Lewis, G. E. and B. Piekut, eds. (2016), *The Oxford Handbook of Critical Improvisation Studies*, New York: Oxford University Press.

Long, Norman (2013), 'The Power of Music: Issues of Agency and Social Practice', *Social Analysis*, 57 (2): 21–42.

Lopes, P. (1992), *Signification de Fatima dans une situation d'émigration*, Albufeira: Edições Poseidon.

Lourenço, I. and R. Cachado (2018), 'Hindu Diaspora in Portugal: The Case of Our Lady of Fatima Devotion', in P. Jain, R. D. Pankaj, M. Khanna (eds), *Hinduism and Tribal Religions*: Encyclopedia of Indian Religions, 1–18, Leiden: Springer Netherlands.

Madson, P. (2005), *Improv Wisdom: Don't Prepare, Just Show Up*, New York: Harmony.

Mahana (*The Patriarch*) (2016), [Film] Dir. L. Tamahori, New Zealand: Jump Film.

Maliglutit (*Searchers*) (2016), [Film] Dir. Z. Kunuk, Canada: Kinguliit Productions.

Mapril, J., and R. L. Blanes, eds (2013), *Sites and Politics of Religious Diversity in Southern Europe: The Best of All Gods*, Leiden: Brill.

Marriott, M. (1976), 'Hindu Transactions: Diversity without Dualism', in B. Kapferer (ed), *Transaction and Meaning: Directions in the Anthropology of Exchange and Symbolic Behavior*, 109–42, Philadelphia: ISHI.

Maslow, A. H. (1968), *Toward a Psychology of Being*, New York: Van Nostrand Reinhold.

Mauss, M. (1921), 'L'expression obligatoire des sentiments (rituels oraux funéraires australiens)', *Journal de psychologie*, 18: 425–34.

Mazzella di Bosco, M. (forthcoming), 'Danser la relation. Interactions en mouvement dans les danses libres en conscience', *Ateliers d'anthropologie*, 47.

McDonald, J. (2016), 'Goldstone Takes Film Noir into Outback Noir', *Australian Financial Review*, 6 July. Available online: https://www.afr.com/lifestyle/arts-and-entertainment/film-and-tv/goldstone-takes-film-noir-into-outback-noir-20160706-gpzhs6 (accessed 30 July 2018).

Memmi, D. (2011), *La seconde vie des bébés mort*, Paris: Éditions de l'EHESS.

Merli, L. (2010), *De l'ombre à la lumière, de l'individu à la nation. Ethnographie du renouveau chamanique en Mongolie post-communiste*, Paris: EMSCAT (Nord-Asie 2).

Michaud-Nérard, F. (2007), *La révolution de la mort*, Paris: Vuibert.

Miller, J. H. (2008), 'Derrida's Politics of Autoimmunity', *Discourse*, 30 (1&2): 208–25.

Mills, J. (2018), 'Representations and Hybridizations in First Nation Cinema: Change and Newness by Fusion', in A. Danks et al. (eds), *American-Australian Cinema: Transnational Connections*, 67–90, Cham, Switzerland: Palgrave Macmillan.

Moisseeff, M. (1999), *An Aboriginal Village in South Australia. A Snapshot of Davenport*, Canberra: AIATSIS.

Moisseeff, M. (2004), 'Sociétés à tiers payant/sociétés à tiers familial: deux conceptions de la médiation', 9th symposium of the French Society of Family Therapy (SFTF), Paris 08/10/04.

Moisseeff, M. (2012), 'L'Objet de la transmission: un choix culturel entre sexe et reproduction', in K-L. Schwering (ed), *Se construire comme sujet entre filiation et sexuation*, 47–76, Toulouse: ERES.

Moisseeff, M. (2013a), 'La chair, le sacré et le culte de l'homme dans les sociétés occidentales contemporaines', *Revue du MAUSS*, 41: 173–92.

Moisseeff, M. (2013b), 'Requiem pour une morte: Aftermath (Cerdà 1994), Ou l'art paradoxal de réhumaniser le cadavre', *Techniques & culture*, 60: 160–79.

Moisseeff, M. (2016a), 'Extraterrestrial Pregnancies and Nasal Implants: A Mythologization of Biopower?', in V. Marinescu and B. Mitu (eds), *Health and the Media: Essays on the Effect of Mass Communication*, 138–51, Jefferson: McFarland.

Moisseeff, M. (2016b), 'Cadavres et Churinga: des objets cultuels exemplaires?', *Archives de Sciences Sociales des Religions*, 174: 255–78.

Moisseeff, M. (2016c), 'Le mort, ses proches et les autres: ici et ailleurs', in A. Caiozzo (ed), *Mythes, rites et émotions, les funérailles le long de la Route de la soie*, 29–48, Paris: Honoré Champion.

Moisseeff, M. (2017), 'Setting Free the Son, Setting Free the Widow: Relational Transformation in Arrernte Life-Cycle Rituals (Central Australia)', *Anthropological Forum*, 27 (1): 34–48.

Moisseeff, M. and M. Houseman (forthcoming), 'L'orchestration rituelle du partage des émotions et ses ressorts interactionnels', in L. Quéré and L. Kaufmann (eds), *Émotions collectives*, Paris: Éditions de l'École des Hautes Études en Sciences Sociales.

Moll, A. (2002), *The Body Multiple: Ontology in Medical Practice*, Durham: Duke University Press.

Morin, E. ([1951] 1976), *L'homme et la mort*, Paris: Seuil.

Mouffe, C. (2002), 'Which Public Sphere for a Democratic Society?' *Theoria: A Journal of Social and Political Theory*, (1), June 2002: 55–65.

Mouffe, C. (2015), *Om det politiske*, Oslo: Cappelen Damm Akademisk.

Munn, N. (1995), 'An Essay on the Symbolic Construction of Memory in the Kaluli *Gisalo*', in D. de Coppet and A. Iteanu (eds), *Cosmos and Society in Oceania*, 83–104, Oxford: Berg Publishers.

Mystery Road (2013), [Film] Dir. I. Sen, Australia: Bunya Productions.

Naas, M. (2006),'"One Nation … Indivisible': Jacques Derrida on the Autoimmunity of Democracy and the Sovereignty of God', *Research in Phenomenology*, 36: 15–44.

Nachmanovitch, S. (1990), *Free Play: Improvisation in Life and Art*, New York: Tarcher/ Putnam.

NRK National Norwegian Broadcasting (2017), 'Documenting Breivik's Case for the Court of Appeal', 10 January 2017. https://www.nrk.no/norge/breivik-krenket-retten-igjen-1.13312661.

O'Cuana, E. (2013), '*Mystery Road* – An Interview with Ivan Sen and Aaron Pedersen', *Crosslight*, 3 November. Available online: https://crosslight.org.au/2013/11/03/ mystery-road-an-interview-with-ivan-sen-and-aaron-pedersen (accessed 11 August 2019).

O'Cuana, E. (2016), 'Interview with Ivan Sen/Aaron Pedersen on *Mystery Road*', *Medium*, 10 June. Available online: https://medium.com/0040EmmetOC_/ interview-with-ivan-sen-aaron-pedersen-on-mystery-road-b32de2782a2c (accessed 11 August 2019).

Once Were Warriors (1994), [Film] Dir. L. Tamahori, New Zealand: Fine Line Features.

Onondaga Nation (2017), 'Circle Wampum'. Available online: http://www. onondaganation.org/culture/wampum/circle-wampum/ (accessed 8 February 2017).

Open University (2016), *Indigenous in London*. Film published on YouTube at https:// www.youtube.com/watch?v=4gBNgXHRAQc (accessed 6 August 2019).

Orsi, R. A. (2010), *The Madonna of 115th Street: Faith and Community in Italian* Harlem, *1880-1950*. Third edition, New Haven, CT: Yale University Press.

Ortiz, A. (1977), On Becoming a Pueblo Sacred Clown, unpublished manuscript.

Østby, L. and A. B. Dalgard (2017), 'Det religiøse mangfoldet. 4 % muslimer i Norge?' ['The religious diversity. 4% Muslims in Norway?']. Samfunnsspeilet, April 2017. https://www.ssb.no/befolkning/artikler-og-publikasjoner/4-prosent-muslimer-i-norge–351303 (accessed 6 November 2018).

Pearson, W. G. and S. Knabe, eds (2015), *Reverse Shots: Indigenous Film and Media in an International Context*, Waterloo, ON: Wilfrid Laurier University Press.

Pereira, P. (2003), *Peregrinos: um estudo antropológico das peregrinações a pé a Fátima*. Crença e razão 42, Lisboa: Instituto Piaget.

Perry, N., and L. Echeverria (1988), *Under the Heel of Mary*. First edition, London; New York: Routledge.

Perry, R. B. (1949), *Characteristically American*, New York: Alfred A. Knopf.

Pike, S. M. (2017), 'The Dance Floor as Urban Altar. How Ecstatic Dancers Transform the Lived Experience of Cities', in V. Hegner and P. J. Margry (eds), *Spiritualizing the City. Agency and Resilience of the Urban and Urbanesque Habitat*, 51–68, New York: Routledge.

Pike, S. M. (2017), *For the Wild: Ritual and Commitment in Radical Eco-Activism*. First edition, Oakland, California: University of California Press.

Poljarevic, E. (2012), 'In Pursuit of Authenticity: Becoming a Salafi', *Comparative Islamic Studies*, 8 (1–2): 139–64.

'Portugal: High and Rising Emigration in a Context of High, but Decreasing, Unemployment'. Eurofound. https://www.eurofound.europa.eu/publications/article/2016/portugal-high-and-rising-emigration-in-a-context-of-high-but-decreasing-unemployment (accessed 29 July 2019).

Post, P. et al., eds (2003), *Disaster Ritual: Explorations of an Emerging Ritual Repertoire*, Leuven, Belgium: Peeters.

Pouchelle, M-C. (2003), *L'hôpital corps et âme. Essais d'anthropologie hospitalière*, Paris: Seli Arslan.

Pouchelle, M-C. (2008), *L'hôpital ou le théâtre des opérations*, Paris: Seli Arslan.

Prager, L. (2013), 'Alawi Ziyāra Tradition and Its Interreligious Dimensions: Sacred Places and Their Contested Meanings among Christians, Alawi and Sunni Muslims in Contemporary Hatay (Turkey)', *The Muslim World*, 103 (13): 41–61.

Pressman, J. and E. Chenoweth (2017), 'Crowd Estimates'. Available online: https://docs.google.com/spreadsheets/d/1xa0iLqYKz8x9Yc_rfhtmSOJQ2EGgeUVjvV4A8LsIaxY/edit#gid=0 (accessed 10 February 2017).

Radiolab (2019), 'There and Back Again'. Available online: https://www.wnycstudios.org/podcasts/radiolab/articles/there-and-back-again (accessed 23 December 2019).

Rappaport, R. A. (1979), *Ecology, Meaning and Religion*, Berkeley: North Atlantic Books.

Rappaport, R. A. (1999), *Ritual and Religion in the Making of Humanity*, Cambridge: Cambridge University Press.

Ratzinger, J. (2000), *The Spirit of the Liturgy*, San Francisco: Ignatius.

Read, P. (2006), *The Stolen Generations: The Removal of Aboriginal Children in New South Wales 1883 to 1969*, Surry Hills, NSW: New South Wales Department of Aboriginal Affairs.

Reader, I. (2014), *Pilgrimage in the Marketplace*, New York: Routledge.

REDO (2013), 'Reassembling Democracy: Ritual as Cultural Resource'. Available online: http://www.tf.uio.no/english/research/projects/redo/ (accessed 8 February 2017).

Riddu Riđđu (2019), https://riddu.no/en/about-riddu-riddu (accessed 26 July 2019).

Robertson, C. (2010), 'Music and Conflict Transformation in Bosnia: Constructing and Reconstructing the Normal', *Music and Arts in Action*, 2 (2): 38–55.

Rose, D. B. (1992), *Dingo Makes Us Human: Life and Land in an Australian Aboriginal Culture*, Cambridge: Cambridge University Press.

Rose, D. B. (1997), 'Common Property Regimes in Aboriginal Australia: Totemism Revisited', in P. Larmour (ed.), *The Governance of Common Property in the Pacific Region*, 127–43, Canberra: NCDS.

Rose, D. B. (2004), *Reports from a Wild Country: Ethics for Decolonisation*, Sydney: University of New South Wales Press.

Rutherford, A. (2019), 'Ivan Sen's Cinematic Imaginary: Restraint, Complexity, and a Politics of Place', in F. Collins et al. (eds), *A Companion to Australian Cinema*, 68–88, Hoboken, NJ: Wiley Blackwell.

Rygnestad, K. (1955), *Dissentarspørsmålet i Noreg frå 1845 til 1891. Lovgjeving og administrativ praksis* [*Dissenter question in Norway from 1845 to 1891. Legislation and administrative practices*], Oslo: Lutherstiftelsen Forlag.

Salomonsen, J. (2002), *Enchanted Feminism: Ritual, Gender and Divinity among the Reclaiming Witches of San Francisco*, London: Routledge.

Salomonsen, J. (2003), 'The Ethno-Methodology of Ritual Invention in Contemporary Culture – Two Pagan and Christian Cases', *Journal of Ritual Studies*, 17 (2): 15–24.

Salomonsen, J. (2013), 'Kristendom, paganisme og kvinnefiendskap', in A. R. Jupskås (ed), *Akademiske perspektiv på 22 juli*, 103–14, Oslo: Akademika Forlag.

Salomonsen, J. (2015), 'Graced Life After All? Terrorism and Theology on July 22, 2011', *Dialog*, 54 (3), September 2015: 249–59. https://onlinelibrary.wiley.com/doi/abs/10.1111/dial.12186.

Salomonsen, J. (2017), 'Det som Gud skapte mest likt sitt bilde', in. Holte, R. Jensen and M. T. Mjaaland (eds), *Totalitær livstolkning og teologisk respons, Skapelsesnåde. Festskrift til Svein Aage Christoffersen*, 185–212, Oslo: Novus Forlag.

Samuels, D. W., L. Meintjes, A. M. Ochoa and T. Porcello (2010), 'Soundscapes: Toward a Sounded Anthropology', *Annual Review of Anthropology*, 39: 329–45.

Schafer, R. M. (1993), *The Soundscape: Our Sonic Environment and the Tuning of the World*, Rochester: Destiny Books.

Scheer, M. (2006), *Rosenkranz und Kriegsvisionen: Marienerscheinungskulte im 20. Jahrhundert*, Tübinger Vereinigung für Volkskunde e.V.

Schieffelin, E. (1976), *The Sorrow of the Lonely and the Burning of the Dancers*, New York: Saint Martin's Press.

Schweninger, L. (2013), *Imagic Moments: Indigenous North American Film*, Athens, GA: University of Georgia Press.

Scott-Grimes, C. (2011), 'Making It Up as We … Go'. Available online: http://www.vimeo.com/22743987 (accessed 8 February 2017).

The Searchers (1956), [Film] Dir. J. Ford, USA: Warner Brothers.

Seligman, A. B. (2009), 'Ritual, the Self, and Sincerity', *Social Research*, 76 (4), The Religious-Secular Divide: The U.S. Case (Winter 2009): 1073–96.

Severi, C. (2015), *The Chimera Principle. An Anthropology of Memory and Imagination*, trans. Janet Lloyd, Chicago: Hau Books.

Shannon, H. (2004), 'The Aesthetics of Spiritual Practice and Creation of Moral and Musical Subjectivities in Aleppo, Syria', *Ethnology*, 43 (4): 381–91.

She Wore a Yellow Ribbon (1949), [Film] Dir. J. Ford, USA: Argosy Pictures.

Shimamura, I. (2014), *The Roots Seekers: Shamanism and Ethnicity among the Mongol Buryats*, Yokohama: Shumpusha Publishing.

Silko, L. M. (1977), *Ceremony*, New York: Penguin.

Simonpillai, R. (2019), 'TIFF 2019: Indigenous Artists Are Using Horror to Unpack Colonial Trauma', *NOW Magazine*, 4 September. Available online: https://nowtoronto.com/movies/features/Indigenous-horror-blood-quantum-tiff–2019.

Singer, B. R. (2001), *Wiping the War Paint off the Lens: Native American Film and Video*, Minneapolis, MN: University of Minnesota Press.

Small, C. (1987), *Music of the Common Tongue: Survival and Celebration in Afro-American Music*, New York: Riverrun.

Small, C. (1998), *Musicking: The Meanings of Performing and Listening*, Hanover, NH: Wesleyan University Press.

Smith, J. Z. (1980), 'The Bare Facts of Ritual', *History of Religion*, 20 (1–2): 112–27.

Smith, J. Z. (1982), *Imagining Religion: From Babylon to Jonestown*, Chicago: Chicago University Press.

Soon, C. (2010), 'Activist Bloggers and Collective Action: Collective Individualism as a Force to Contend With', Paper presented at the annual meeting of the International Communication Association (Singapore), abstract downloaded from citation.allacademic.com/meta/p404063_index.html.

Soon, C. and R. Kluver (2014), 'Uniting Political Bloggers in Diversity: Collective Identity and Web Activism', *Journal of Computer-Mediated Communication*, 19: 500–15.

Statistics Norway, https://www.ssb.no/innvbef and https://www.ssb.no/kultur-og-fritid/statistikker/trosamf/aar/2014-11-18 (accessed 11 April 2015).

Stépanoff, C. (2019), *Voyager dans l'invisible. Techniques chamaniques de l'imagination*, Paris: La Découverte.

Stokes, M. (1998), 'Imagining "The South": Hybridity, Heterotropies and Arabesk on the Turkish Syrian Border', in T. M. Wilson and H. Donnan (eds), *Border Identities: Nation and State at International Frontiers*, 263–88, Cambridge and New York: Cambridge University Press.

Strathern, M. (1988), *The Gender of the Gift: Problems with Women and Problems with Society in Melanesia*, Berkeley: University of California Press.

Stroud, J. T. et al. (2015), 'Is a Community Still a Community? Reviewing Definitions of Key Terms in Community Ecology', *Ecology and Evolution*. Available online: https://www.ncbi.nlm.nih.gov/pmc/articles/PMC4662321/ (accessed 13 February 2017).

Sullivan, M. (2002), *Questions and Answers on Vatican II*, New York: Paulist.

Swancutt, K. (2008), 'The Undead Genealogy: Omnipresence, Spirit Perspectives, and a Case of Mongolian Vampirism', *Journal of the Royal Anthropological Institute*, 14 (4): 843–64.

Tambiah, S. J. (1981), 'A Performative Approach to Ritual', *Proceedings of the British Academy*, 65 (1979): 113–69.

Taylor, C. (2007), *A Secular Age*, Cambridge: The Belknap Press of Harvard University Press.

Thomas, L-V. (1975), *Anthropologie de la mort*, Paris: Payot.

Thompson, E. A. (2002), *The Soundscape of Modernity: Architectural Acoustics and the Culture of Listening in America, 1900–1933*, Cambridge, MA: MIT Press.

Thornley, D. (2015), 'Playing with Land Issues: Subversive Hybridity in *The Price of Milk*', in W. G. Pearson and S. Knabe (eds), *Reverse Shots: Indigenous Film and Media in an International Context*, 301–13, Waterloo, ON: Wilfrid Laurier University Press.

Thwaites, S. (2018), 'In Conversation with Ivan Sen', *Axon* 8 (2). Available online: http://axonjournal.com.au/issue-15/conversation-ivan-sen (accessed 1 August 2019).

Tocqueville, A. de ([1856] 1967), *L'ancien régime et la Révolution*, Paris: Gallimard.

Tocqueville, A. de ([1835] 2000), *Democracy in America*, Chicago: University of Chicago Press.

Tonkinson, M. (2008), 'Solidarity in Shared Loss: Death-related Observances among the Martu of the Western Desert', in K. Glaskin, M. Tonkinson, Y. Musharbach and V. Burbank (eds), *Mortality, Mourning and Mortuary Practices in Indigenous Australia*, 37–53, Farnham & Burlington: Ashgate.

Treanor, B. (2011), 'Putting Hospitality in Its Place', in R. Kearney and K. Semonovitch (eds), *Phenomenologies of the Stranger: Between Hostility and Hospitality*, 49–66, New York: Fordham University Press.

Tronvik, A. M. (2011a), 'En vond dag – som gir håp' ['A difficult day – that gives hope'], *Luthersk kirketidende*, 16 September 2011, 146.

Tronvik, A. M. (2011b), 'Ingen blanding av religioner' ['No mix of religions'], *Vårt Land*, 10 September: 41 [chronicle].

Turner, V. (1979), 'Frame, Flow and Reflection: Ritual and Drama as Public Liminality', *Japanese Journal of Religious Studies*, 6 (4) (December 1979): 465–99.

Turner, V. (1989 [1967]), *The Ritual Process. Structure and Anti-Structure*, Ithaca, NY: Cornell University Press.

Turner, V. and E. Turner (1978), *Image and Pilgrimage in Christian Culture: Anthropological Perspectives*, Oxford: Blackwell.

Tweed, T. A. (1997), *Our Lady of the Exile: Diasporic Religion at a Cuban Catholic Shrine in Miami*, New York: Oxford University Press.

Varga, D. (2019), 'Indigenous Resistance and Popular Cinema: *Rhymes for Young Ghouls* and *Maliglutit*', presented at the International Conference on Religion & Film, Halifax, Nova Scotia, 14 June.

Verdier, Y. (1976), 'La-femme-qui-aide et la laveuse', *L'Homme*, 16 (2–3): 103–28.

Vilaça, H. (2006), *Da Torre de Babel às Terras Prometidas Pluralismo Religioso em Portugal*, Porto: Edições Afrontamento.

Vizenor, G. (1999), *Manifest Manners: Narratives on Postindian Survivance*, Lincoln: University of Nebraska Press.

Vizenor, G. (2009), *Native Liberty: Natural Reason and Cultural Survivance*, Lincoln: University of Nebraska Press.

Vizenor, G. (2019), *Native Provenance: The Betrayal of Cultural Creativity*, Lincoln: University of Nebraska Press.

Vovelle, M. (1974), *Mourir autrefois. Attitudes collectives devant la mort aux XVIIe et XVIIIe siècles*, Paris: Gallimard.

Vovelle, M. (1983), *La mort et l'Occident, de 1300 à nos jours*, Paris: Gallimard.

Warner, M. (1983), *Alone of All Her Sex: The Myth and the Cult of the Virgin Mary*. First Vintage Books edition, New York: Vintage.

Weaver, J. (1997), *That the People Might Live: Native American Literatures and Native American Community*, New York: Oxford University Press.

Weiner, I. (2014), *Music Out Loud: Religious Sound, Public Sphere, and American Pluralism*, London: Routledge.

Whitehead, A. (2013), *Religious Statues and Personhood: Testing the Role of Materiality*, London: Bloomsbury.

Wikipedia (2017), 'DNA Replication'. Available online: https://en.wikipedia.org/wiki/DNA_replication (accessed 8 February 2017).

Wild Bunch (2016), '*The Patriarch* aka *Mahana* Press Kit'. Available online: http://distribution.paradisbio.dk/log/film/Patriarken%20_290_/press%20kit%20-%20the%20patriarch%20.pdf (accessed 7 December 2016).

Wilke, A. (2019), 'Sonality', in A. Koch and K. Wilkens (eds), *The Bloomsbury Handbook of Cultural and Cognitive Aesthetics of Religion*, 107–16, London: Bloomsbury.

Winnicott, D. W. (1965), 'The Capacity to Be Alone', *International Journal of Psycho-Analysis*, 39: 416–20.

Wood, H. (2008), *Native Features: Indigenous Films from around the World*, New York: Continuum.

Ziegler, J. (1975), *Les vivants et la mort*, Paris: Seuil.

Zimdars-Swartz, S. L. (1991), *Encountering Mary: From La Salette to Medjugorje*, Princeton, NJ: Princeton University Press.

Index